S0-EHD-558

EARLY ENGLISH LYRICS

No mon this book he take away,
  Ni kutt owte noo leef; I say for why,
For hit is sacrelege, sirus, I yow say,
  Beth acursed in the dede, truly!
  Yef ye wil have any copy,
Askus leeve and ye shul have.

John Awdlay.

Early English Lyrics

AMOROUS, DIVINE, MORAL AND TRIVIAL

chosen by

E. K. CHAMBERS & F. SIDGWICK

OCTOBER HOUSE INC.
NEW YORK

This edition published 1967 by
October House Inc.
134 East 22nd Street
New York, N.Y. 10010

Library of Congress catalogue card no. 67-10783
Printed in Great Britain

TO

A. H. BULLEN

CONTENTS

PREFACE

THE purpose of this book is to provide an anthology of English lyrical poetry earlier than the advent of the sonnet with Wyatt and Surrey during the sixteenth century. The choice of poems has therefore been made in most cases on the ground of their literary qualities alone, and we have adopted a division under the four heads of Amorous, Divine, Moral, and Trivial. The first three groups are arranged roughly in chronological order; the fourth is further subdivided according to subject-matter.

Three or four poems are here printed for the first time; the others have been taken from the best texts available, and many of them have been freshly collated with the manuscripts.

The ground covered is so wide as to render three different modes of treating the orthography desirable. Poems written before 1400 are left practically in the spelling of the scribes; those of the fifteenth century are slightly normalised, in the way explained at the beginning of the Notes; those still later are altogether modernised. Following the practice of the Globe *Chaucer*, we have attempted to indicate the fully sounded e by a single dot (ė); but the task is not an easy one with the lawless language of the fifteenth century, and we do not feel that, even if our philological inexperience had been less, the results would have been altogether satisfactory.

Our gratitude is due to Lord Howard de Walden and to Lord Harlech for the use of material; and to Professors J. A. H. Murray, W. P. Ker, and L. M. Brandin, Dr. H. F. Heath and Mr. A. W. Pollard for various and ready help.

E. K. C.

March, 1907. F. S.

EARLY ENGLISH LYRICS

AMOROUS LYRICS

Gardein ways, cumfort of flowres,
So hight my leman ; what hight yowres ?
That is, Alisson.

MS. Balliol 354

EARLY ENGLISH LYRICS

AMOROUS

I

MIRIE it is while sumer ilast
  With fugheles song;
Oc nu necheth windes blast
  And weder strong.
Ei, ei, what this nicht is long!
And ich with wel michel wrong
Soregh and murne and fast.

2. *fugheles*, fowls.
3. *oc*, but : *necheth*=nigheth, approacheth.

II

Sing cuccu nu ! Sing cuccu !
Sing cuccu ! Sing cuccu nu !

SUMER is icumen in,
Lhudė sing cuccu ;
Groweth sed and bloweth med
And springth the wdė nu.
Sing cuccu !
Awė bleteth after lomb,
Lhouth after calvė cu ;
Bulluc sterteth, buckė verteth ;
Murie sing cuccu.
Cuccu, cuccu,
Wel singės thu, cuccu,
Ne swik thu naver nu.

9. *lhouth*, loweth. 10. *verteth*, harbours in the green.
14. *swik*, cease.

III

FOWELĖS in the frith,
The fisses in the flod.
And I mon waxė wod ;
Mulch sorwe I walkė with
For best of bon and blod.

3. *wod*, mad.

IV

BYTUENĖ Mersh ant Averil,
When spray biginneth to springe,
The lutel foul hath hire wyl
On hyre lud to synge.
Ich libbe in love-longinge
For semlokest of allė thinge;
He may me blissė bringe;
Icham in hire baundoun.
An hendy hap ichabbe yhent;
Ichot from hevene it is me sent;
From allė wymmen mi love is lent
Ant lyht on Alysoun.

On heu hire her is fayr ynoh,
Hire browė broune, hire eyė blake;
With lossum chere he on me loh,
With middel smal ant wel ymake.
Bote he me wollė to hire take,
Fortė buen hire owen make,
Longe to lyven ichulle forsake,
Ant feye fallen adoun.

4. *lud*, voice.
5. *libbe*, live.
6. *semlokest*, seemliest.
7. *he*, she.
8. *baundoun*, lordship.
9. *hendy*, fair : *yhent*, gained.
11. *lent*, turned.
13. *her*, hair.
15. *lossum*, lovesome : *loh*, laughed.
17. *bote*, unless.
18. *fortė buen*, for to be.
20. *feye*, lifeless.

Nihtės when I wende ant wake,
  Forthi myn wongės waxeth won.
Levedi, al for thinė sake
  Longinge is ylent me on.
  In world nis non so wytermon,
  That al hire bountė tellė con.
  Hire swyre is whittore then the swon
Ant feyrest may in toune.

Icham for wowing al forwake,
  Wery so water in wore.
Lest eny revė me my make,
  Ichabbe y-yernėd yore.
  Betere is tholien whylė sore,
  Then mournen evermore.
  Geynest under gore,
Herknė to my roun.
    An hendy hap ichabbe yhent;
    Ichot from hevene it is me sent;
    From allė wymmen mi love is lent
  Ant lyht on Alysoun.

21. *wende*, turn.
22. *forthi*, therefore : *wongės*, cheeks.
23. *levedi*, lady.
25. *nis*, is not : *wytermon*, wise man.
27. *swyre*, neck.
29. *forwake*, spent with vigils.
30. *wore*, weir.
31. *make*, mate.
32. *yore*, long.
33. *tholien*, to endure.
35. *geyn*, graceful : *gore*, skirt.
36. *roun*, song.

V

LENTEN is come with love to toune,
With blosmen and with briddės roune,
That al this blissė bryngeth,
Dayės-eyės in this dales,
Notės suete of nyhtėgales;
Uch foul song singeth.
The threstelcoc him threteth oo;
Away is huere wynter woo,
When woderovė springeth.
This foulės singeth ferly fele
Ant wlyteth on huere wynter wele,
That al the wodė ryngeth.

The rosė rayleth hire rode;
The levės on the lyhtė wode
Waxen al with wille.
The monė mandeth hire bleo;
The lilie is lossom to seo,
The fenyl ant the fille.
Wowės thisė wildė drakes;
Milės murgeth huere makes,
Ase strem that striketh stille.
Mody meneth, so doht mo.
Ichot ycham on of tho
For love that likės ille.

2. *roune*, song.
7. *threteth oo*, always chides.
8. *huere*, their.
10. *ferly fele*, wondrous many.
11. *wlyteth*, look.
13. *rayleth*, prepares, arranges.
15. *wille*, desire.
16. *mandeth*, sends forth.
20. *Milės murgeth*, wild creatures make merry.
21. *striketh*, flows.
22. The passionate man complains, as do more.

The monė mandeth hire lyht;
So doth the semly sonnė bryht,
When briddės singeth breme.
Deawės donketh the dounes,
Deorės with huere dernė rounes,
Domės fortė deme.
Wormės woweth under cloude;
Wymmen waxeth wounder proude,
So wel hit wol hem seme.
Yef me shal wontė wille of on,
This wunnė weole I wole forgon,
Ant wyht in wodc be fleme.

27. *breme*, valiantly.
28. *donketh*, moisten.
29. *dernė*, secret.
31. *cloude*, rock.
35. *wunnė weole*, wealth of delight.
36. *fleme*, fugitive.

VI

WHEN the nyhtėgalė singes,
The wodės waxen grene,
Lef ant gras ant blosmė springes
In Averyl, I wene;
Ant love is to myn hertė gon
With onė spere so kene,
Nyht ant day my blod hit drynkes,
Myn hertė deth to tene.

Ich have lovėd al this yer
That I may love namore;
Ich have sikėd moni syk,
Lemmon, for thin ore.
Me nis love never the ner,
Ant that me reweth sore.
Suetė lemmon, thench on me,
Ich have lovėd thee yore.

Suetė lemmon, I preyė thee
Of love onė speche.
Whil I lyve in world so wyde
Other nulle I seche.
With thy love, my suetė leof,
My blis thou mihtės eche;
A suetė cos of thy mouth
Mihtė be my leche.

8. *tene*, vex. 12. *lemmon*, leman, mistress: *ore*, favour.

Suetė lemmon, I preyė thee
  Of a lovė bene.
Yef thou me lovest, ase men says,
  Lemmon, as I wene,
Ant yef hit thy willė be,
  Thou loke that hit be sene;
So muchel I thenke upon the
  That al I waxė grene.

Bituenė Lyncolne ant Lyndeseye,
  Norhamptoun ant Lounde,
Ne wot I non so fayr a may,
  As I go fore ybounde.
Suetė lemmon, I preyė the,
  Thou lovie me a stounde!
I wolė mone my song
On wham that hit is on ylong.

38. *stounde*, while, moment. 40. *hit is on ylong*, it refers to, depends on.

VII

'MY deth I love, my lyf ich hate,
For a levedy shene;
Heo is briht so daiės liht,
That is on me wel sene.
Al I falewe so doth the lef
In somer when hit is grene;
Yef mi thoht helpeth me noht,
To wham shal I me mene?

'Sorewe and syke and drery mod
Byndeth me so faste,
That I wenė to walkė wod,
Yef hit me lengore laste.
My sorewe, my care, al with a word
He myhte awey caste.
Whet helpeth thee, my suete lemmon,
My lyf thus fortė gaste?'

'Do wey, thou clerc, thou art a fol,
With thee bydde I noht chyde.
Shalt thou never lyve that day
Mi love that thou shalt byde.
Yef thou in my boure art take,
Shame thee may bityde.
Thee is bettere on fotė gon
Then wycked hors to ryde.'

5. *falewe*, turn yellow, fade.
8. *mene*, moan.
11. *wod*, mad.
15. *lemmon*, leman, mistress.
16. *gaste*, spoil.

'Weylawei! whi seist thou so?
  Thou rewe on me, thy man!
Thou art ever in my thoht
  In londė wher ich am.
Yef I deyė for thi love,
  Hit is thee mykel sham.
Thou lete me lyve, and be thi luef,
  And thou my suete lemman!'

'Be stille, thou fol, I calle thee riht!
  Const thou never blynne?
Thou art wayted day and nyht
  With fader and al my kynne.
Be thou in mi bour ytake,
  Letė they for no synne
Me to holde, and thee to slou,
  The deth so thou maht wynne.'

'Suetė lady, thou wend thi mod,
  Sorewe thou wolt me kythe.
Ich am al so sory mon,
  So ich was whylen blythe.
In a wyndou, ther we stod,
  We custe us fyfty sythe.'
'Feir biheste maketh mony mon
  Al is sorewes mythe.'

34. *blynne*, cease.
41. *wend*, change.
42. *kythe*, show.
46. *custe*, kissed.
48. *mythe*, conceal.

'Weylawey! why seist thou so?
My sorewe thou makest newe.'
'I lovede a clerk al *par amours*;
Of love he wes ful trewe.
He nes nout blythe never a day,
Bote he me sonė seye.
Ich lovede him betere then my lyf;
Whet bote is hit to leye?'

'Whil I wes a clerc in scole,
Wel muchel I couthe of lore.
Ich have tholėd for thy love
Woundės felė sore,
Fer from hom and eke from men
Under the wodė gore.
Suetė ledy, thou rewe of me!
Nou may I no more.'

'Thou semest wel to ben a clerc,
For thou spekest so stille.
Shalt thou never for mi love
Woundės tholė grylle.
Fader, moder, and al my kun
Ne shal me holde so stille,
That I nam thyn, and thou art myn,
To don al thi wille.'

54. *seye*, saw.
58. *couthe*, knew.
60. *felė*, many.
62. *gore*, strip.
68. *grylle*, fierce, keen.

VIII

DE AMICO AD AMICAM

A CELUY que pluys eyme en mounde,
Of allė tho that I have found,
Carissima,
Saluz od treyé amour,
With grace and joye and alle honour,
Dulcissima.

Sachez bien, pleysant et beele,
That I am right in good heele,
Laus Christo!
Et moun amour doné vous ay,
And also thine owene night and day
In cisto.

Ma tresduce et tresamé,
Night and day for love of thee
Suspiro.
Soyez permenant et leal;
Love me so that I it fele,
Requiro.

Jeo suy pour toy dolant et tryst;
Thou me peinist bothe day and night
Amore.
Mort ha! tret tost sun espeye.
Lovė me wel er I deye
Dolore.

Saches bien par verité
Yif I deye I clepe to thee
Causantem;
Et par ceo jeo vous treser
Love me well withouten daunger
Amantem.

Et de vous enpense tut dyz;
Of al the world thou berist the pris
Decora.
Vous aves moy enpresoné;
Allas, thine lovė wele me sle
Cum mora.

Cest est ma volunté,
That I mightė be with thee
Ludendo.
Vostre amour en moun qoer
Brenneth hote as doth the fyr
Cressendo.

Douce, bele, plesaunt et chere,
In all this lond ne is thine pere
Inventa.
Claunchant ou la cler note
Thou art in myn hertė rote
Retenta.

Tost serroy joyous et seyn,
Yif thou woldist me sertein
Amare;
Et tost serroy joious et lé;
There nis no thing that schal me
Gravare.

Ma tresbele et tresamé,
Yif thou wist I letė be
Langorem.
De cestis portes entendement,
And in youre herte taketh entent
Honorem.

A vous jeo suy tut doné ;
Mine herte is full of love to thee
Presento ;
Et pur ceo jeo vous pry,
Sweting, for thin curtesy,
Memento.

Jeo vous pry par charité,
The wordės that here wreten be
Tenete ;
And turne thy hertė me toward.
O à Dieu que vous gard !
Valete.

IX

RESPONCIO

A SOUN treschere et special,
Fer and ner and overal
In mundo,
Que soy ou saltz et gré,
With mouth, word and hertė free
Jocundo.

Jeo vous pry sanz debat
That ye wolde of mine stat
Audire.
Sertefyés a vous jeo fay,
I wil in timė whan I may
Venire.

Quant a vous venu serray,
I you swerė be this day
Pro certo.
Mes jeo fuyss en maladye,
Yif ye me lovė sikerlie
Converto.

Lamour de vous moy fayt dolent;
But ye me lovė I am schent
Dolendo.
Sy suyre estoy de vostre amour,
I were as light as the flour
Florendo.

De moy, jeo pry, aves pyté ;
I falle so doth the lef on the tree
Tristando.
Tot le mounde longe et lé
I woldė leve and takė thee
Zelando.

Pur vostre amour, allas, allas,
I am wersė than I was
Per multa.
Jeo suy dolorouse en tut manere ;
Wolde God in youre armės I were
Sepulta!

Jeo a vous pleyne grevousement
That thine lovė hath me schent
Amando.
De moy, jeo pry, avez peté ;
Turneth your herte and loveth me
Letando.

A cestys ay maunde de vous ore.
What bote ist to strivė more
Amore?
Remaundé vostre volunté
Yif I schal trewely trostė thee
Dulcore.

Vous estes ma morte et ma vye.
I preye you for youre curteisie
Amate.
Cestes maundes jeo vous pry
In youre hertė stedefastly
Notate.

X

NOW welcom somer, with thy sonnė softe,
That hast this wintrės weders over-shake,
And driven awey the longė nightės blake !

Seynt Valentyn, that art ful hy on lofte,
Thus singen smalė foulės for thy sake
'Now welcom somer, with thy sonnė softe,
That hast this wintrės weders over-shake.'

Wel han they causė for to gladen ofte,
Sith ech of hem recoverėd hath his make ;
Ful blisful may they singen whan they wake
'Now welcom somer, with thy sonnė softe,
That hast this wintrės weders over-shake,
And driven awey the longė nightės blake.'

GEOFFREY CHAUCER.

XI

HYDE, Absolon, thy giltė tresses clere;
Ester, ley thou thy meknesse al adoun;
Hyde, Jonathas, al thy frendly manere;
Penalopee, and Marcia Catoun,
Make of your wyfhod no comparisoun;
Hyde ye your beautės, Isoude and Eleyne.
My lady cometh, that al this may disteyne.

Thy fairė body, lat hit nat appere,
Lavyne; and thou, Lucresse of Romė toun,
And Polixene, that boghten love so dere,
And Cleopatre, with al thy passioun,
Hyde ye your trouthe of love and your renoun;
And thou, Tisbe, that hast of love swich peyne.
My lady cometh, that al this may disteyne.

Hero, Dido, Laudomia, alle yfere,
And Phyllis, hanging for thy Demophoun,
And Canace, espyėd by thy chere,
Ysiphile, betraysėd with Jasoun,
Maketh of your trouthė neyther boost ne soun;
Nor Ypermistre or Adriane, ye tweyne.
My lady cometh, that al this may disteyne.

GEOFFREY CHAUCER.

7. *disteyne*, discolour, bedim. 19. *soun*, vaunt.

XII

MADAMĖ, ye ben of al beautė shryne
As fer as cerclėd is the mappėmounde;
For as the cristal glorious ye shyne,
And lykė ruby ben your chekės rounde.
Therwith ye ben so mery and so jocounde,
That at a revel whan that I see you daunce,
It is an oynėment unto my wounde,
Thogh ye to me ne do no daliaunce.

For thogh I wepe of terės ful a tyne,
Yet may that wo myn hertė nat confounde.
Your seemly voys that ye so smal out-twyne
Maketh my thoght in joye and blis habounde.
So curteisly I go, with lovė bounde,
That to myself I sey, in my penaunce,
Suffyseth me to love you, Rosėmounde,
Thogh ye to me ne do no daliaunce.

Nas never pyk walwėd in galauntyne
As I in love am walwėd and ywounde;
For which ful ofte I of myself divyne
That I am trewė Tristam the secounde.
My love may not refreyd be nor afounde.
I brenne ay in an amorous plesaunce.
Do what you list, I wil your thral be founde,
Thogh ye to me ne do no daliaunce.

TREGENTIL. GEOFFREY CHAUCER.

2. *mappėmounde*, map of the world. 9. *tyne*, barrel.
17. *walwed in galauntyne*, rolled in sauce, soused.
21. *refreyd*, cooled; *afounde*, perish.

XIII

I

YOUR yėn two wol slee me sodenly;
I may the beautė of hem not sustene,
So woundeth hit throughout my hertė kene.

And but your word wol helen hastily
My hertės woundė, whyl that hit is grene,
Your yėn two wol slee me sodenly;
I may the beautė of hem not sustene.

Upon my trouthe I sey yow feithfully,
That ye ben of my lyf and deeth the quene;
For with my deeth the trouthė shal be sene.
Your yėn two wol slee me sodenly;
I may the beautė of hem not sustene,
So woundeth hit throughout my hertė kene.

1. *yėn*, eyes.

II

So hath your beautė fro your hertė chaced
Pitee, that me ne availeth not to pleyne;
For Daunger halt your mercy in his cheyne.

Giltles my deeth thus han ye me purchaced;
I sey you sooth, me nedeth not to feyne.
  So hath your beautė fro your hertė chaced
  Pitee, that me ne availeth not to pleyne.

Allas! that nature hath in you compassed
So greet beautė, that no man may atteyne
To mercy, though he stervė for the peyne.
  So hath your beautė fro your hertė chaced
  Pitee, that me ne availeth not to pleyne;
  For Daunger halt your mercy in his cheyne.

16. *halt*, holds.

III

Sin I fro Love escapėd am so fat,
I never thenk to ben in his prison lene ;
Sin I am free, I counte him not a bene.

He may answere, and seyė this or that ;
I do no fors, I speke right as I mene.
Sin I fro Love escapėd am so fat,
I never thenk to ben in his prison lene.

Love hath my name ystrike out of his sclat,
And he is strike out of my bokės clene
For evermo ; ther is non other mene.
Sin I fro Love escapėd am so fat,
I never thenk to ben in his prison lene.
Sin I am free, I counte him not a bene.

GEOFFREY CHAUCER.

31. *fors*, care. 34. *sclat*, slate.

XIV

MADAMĖ, for your newė-fangelnesse,
Many a servaunt have ye put out of grace.
I take my leve of your unstedfastnesse,
For wel I wot, whyl ye have lyvės space,
Ye can not love ful half yeer in a place.
To newė thing your lust is ever kene;
In stede of blew, thus may ye were al grene.

Right as a mirour nothing may enpresse,
But, lightly as it cometh, so mot it pace,
So fareth your love, your workės bereth witnesse.
Ther is no feith that may your herte embrace;
But, as a wedercok, that turneth his face
With every wind, ye fare, and that is sene;
In stede of blew, thus may ye were al grene.

Ye might be shrynėd, for your brotelnesse,
Bet than Dalyda, Creseide or Candace,
For ever in chaunging stant your sikernesse;
That tache may no wight fro your herte arace.
If ye lese oon, ye can wel tweyn purchace.
Al light for somer, ye woot wel what I mene,
In stede of blew, thus may ye were al grene.

GEOFFREY CHAUCER.

1. *newė-fangelnesse*, desire for novelty.
9. *pace*, depart.
15. *brotelnesse*, fickleness.
17. *sikernesse*, safety.
18. *tache*, defect.

XV

ALONE walking,
In thought pleyning,
And sore sighing,
All desolate,
Me remembring
Of my living,
My deth wishing,
Bothe erly and late,

Infortunate
Is so my fate,
That—wote ye what?—
Out of mesure
My lyf I hate.
Thus desperate
In pore estate
Do I endure.

Of other cure
Am I nat sure;
Thus to endure
Is hard, certain.
Such is my ure,
I yow ensure.
What creature
May have more pain?

21. *ure*, destiny.

My trouth so pleyn
Is take in veyn,
And gret disdeyn
In remembraunce;
Yet I ful feyn
Wold me compleyn,
Me to absteyn
From this penaunce.

But in substaunce
Noon allegeaunce
Of my grevaunce
Can I nat finde.
Right so my chaunce
With displesaunce
Doth me avaunce.
And thus an ende.

34. *allegeaunce*, alleviation.

XVI

I HAVE the obit of my lady dere
Made in the chirche of love full solempnely,
And for her soule the service and prayere
In thought wailing have songe hit hevily.
The torch is sett of sighės pitously
Which was with sorow sett aflame.
The toumbe is made als to the same
Of karefull cry depainted all with teeris,
The which richely is write about,
That here lo lith withouten dout
The hool tresoure of all worldly bliss.

Of gold on her there lith an image clere
With safyr blew isett so inrichely,
For hit is write and seide how the safere
Doth token trouthe, and gold to ben happy,
The which that welbisetteth her hardily,
Forwhy hit was an eurous trewe madame,
And of goodnes ay flowren may hir name;
For God, the which that made her, lo iwis,
To make such oon me thinke a might ben prout,
For lo, she was, as right well be she mout,
The hool tresoure of all worldly bliss.

17. *eurous*, happy (Fr. *heureux*).

O pese ! no more ! min hert astoneth here
  To here me praise her vertu so trewly,
Of her that had no faut withouten were,
  As all the world hit saith as well as I,
The whiche that knew her deedes inthorowly.
  God hath her tane, I trowe, for her good fame,
  His hevene the more to joy with sport and game,
The more to plese and comfort his seintis ;
  For certės well may she comfort a rout.
  Noon is she saint, she was here so devout,
The hool tresoure of all worldly bliss.

Not vaileth now, though I complainė this ;
  Al most we deye, thereto so lete us lout,
  For ay to kepe there is no wight so stout
The hool tresoure of all worldly bliss.

Charles of Orleans (?)

25. *were*, doubt.

XVII

MY gostly fader, I me confesse,
First to God and then to you,

That at a window—wot ye how?—
I stale a cosse of grete sweteness,
Which don was out avisėness;
But hit is doon not undoon now.
My gostly fader, I me confesse,
First to God and then to you.

But I restore it shall doutless
Agein, if so be that I mow;
And that to God I make a vow
And elles I axė foryefness.
My gostly fader, I me confesse,
First to God and then to you.

CHARLES OF ORLEANS (?)

4. *cosse*, kiss.

XVIII

NOW wolde I faine some merthės make,
All only for my lady's sake,
When her I see;
But now I am so far fro her
It will not be.

Thogh I be far out of her sight,
I am her man bothe day and night,
And so wol be.
Therefore wolde as I love her
She lovėd me.

Whan she is mery, than am I glad;
Whan she is sory, than am I sad;
And causė why,
For he liveth not that loveth her
As well as I.

She saith that she hath seen hit wreten
That seldin seen is soon forgeten;
It is not so,
For in good feith, save only her,
I love no mo.

Wherefore I pray bothe nighte and day
That she may cast alle care away,
And leve in rest,
And evermore wherever she be
To love me best.

And I to her for to be trew,
And never chaunge her for no new
Unto mine end,
And that I may in her servise
For ever amend.

A. Godwhen.

XIX

THE NUTBROWN MAID.

Squire.

BE it right, or wrong, these men among
  On women do complaine,
Afferming this, how that it is
  A labour spent in vaine,
To love them wele, for never a dele
  They love a man againe;
For lete a man do what he can,
  Ther favour to attaine,
Yet if a newe to them pursue,
  Ther furst trew lover than
Laboureth for nought, and from her thought
  He is a banisshed man.

Puella.

I say not nay, but that all day
  It is bothe writ and saide,
That woman's faith is as who saithe
  All utterly decayed;
But nevertheles, right good witnes
  In this case might be laide,
That they love trewe, and continew.
  Record the Nutbrowne maide,
Which from her love, whan, her to prove,
  He cam to make his mone,
Wolde not departe, for in her herte
  She loved but him allone.

5. *dele*, bit.

Squire.

Than betwene us lete us discusse,
What was all the maner
Betwene them too ; we will also
Telle all the paine in fere,
That she was in. Now I beginne,
So that ye me answere.
Wherefore all ye that present be
I pray you geve an eare.
I am the knight ; I cum be night,
As secret as I can,
Saing 'Alas ! thus stondeth the cas,
I am a banissched man.'

Puella.

And I your wille for to fulfille
In this will not refuse,
Trusting to shewe, in wordės fewe,
That men have an ille use
To ther owne shame wimen to blame,
And causeles them accuse.
Therefore to you I answere now,
Alle wimen to excuse,
'Mine owne hert dere, with you what chiere ?
I prey you, telle anoon,
For in my minde of all mankinde
I love but you allon.'

Squire.

'It stondeth so ; a dede is do ;
  Wherefore moche harme shall growe.
My desteny is for to dey
  A shameful dethe, I trowe,
Or elles to flee ; the ton must be.
  None other wey I knowe,
But to withdrawe as an outlaw,
  And take me to my bowe.
Wherefore adew, my owne hert trewe !
  None other rede I can,
For I muste to the grene wode go
  Alone a banisshed man.'

Puella.

'O Lorde, what is this worldės blisse,
  That chaungeth as the mone ?
My somer's day in lusty May
  Is derked before the none.
I here you saye farwel. Nay, nay,
  We departe not so sone.
Why say ye so ? wheder will ye go ?
  Alas ! what have ye done ?
Alle my welfare to sorow and care
  Shulde chaunge, if ye were gon,
For in my minde of all mankinde
  I love but you alone.'

53. *ton*, one.   58. *rede*, counsel.

Squire.

'I can beleve, it shall you greve,
And somwhat you distraine;
But afterwarde your painės harde
Within a day or tweine
Shall sone aslake, and ye shall take
Comfort to you againe.
Why shuld ye nought? for, to take thought,
Your labur were in vaine.
And thus I do; and pray you to,
As hertely as I can,
For I must to the grene wode go
Alone a banisshed man.'

Puella.

'Now sith that ye have shewed to me
The secret of your minde,
I shall be plaine to you againe,
Like as ye shall me finde.
Sith it is so, that ye will go,
I wol not leve behinde;
Shall never be said the Nutbrowne maid
Was to her love unkind.
Make you redy, for so am I,
All though it were anoon,
For in my minde of all mankinde
I love but you alone.'

74. *distraine*, affect.

Squire.

'Yet I you rede to take good hede
  Whan men will thinke and sey;
Of yonge and olde it shall be tolde
  That ye be gone away
Your wanton wille for to fulfille,
  In grene wood you to play,
And that ye might from your delite
  No lenger make delay.
Rather than ye shuld thus for me
  Be called an ille woman,
Yet wolde I to the grene wodde go
  Alone a banisshed man.'

Puella.

'Though it be songe of olde and yonge
  That I shuld be to blame,
Theirs be the charge, that speke so large
  In hurting of my name;
For I will prove that feithful love
  It is devoid of shame,
In your distresse and hevinesse
  To parte with you the same.
And sure all tho that do not so
  Trewe lovers are they noon;
But in my minde of all mankinde
  I love but you alone.'

117. *tho*, those.

Squire.

‘I councel you, remembre how
It is no maiden’s lawe,
Nothing to dought, but to renne out
To wode with an outlawe;
For ye must there in your hande bere
A bowe, redy to drawe,
And as a theef thus must ye live,
Ever in drede and awe,
By whiche to you grete harme might grow.
Yet had I lever than,
That I had to the grene wode go
Alone a banisshed man.’

Puella.

‘I thinke not nay, but as ye saye,
It is no maiden’s lore;
But love may make me for your sake,
As I have said before,
To com on fote, to hunte and shote,
To gete us mete and store,
For so that I your company
May have, I aske no more;
From whiche to parte it maketh mine herte
As colde as ony stone,
For in my minde of all mankinde
I love but you alone.’

123. *renne*, run.

Squire.

'For an outlawe, this is the lawe,
That men him take and binde,
Without pitee hangèd to be,
And waver with the winde.
If I had neede, as God forbede!
What rescous coude ye finde?
Forsothe I trowe you and your bowe
Shuld drawe for fere behinde;
And no merveile, for litel availe
Were in your councel than.
Wherefore I to the woode will go
Alone a banisshed man.'

Puella.

'Full well knowe ye that wimen be
Full febil for to fight;
No womanhede is it in deede
To be bolde as a knight.
Yet in such fere if that ye were,
With enemys day and night,
I wolde withstonde, with bowe in hande,
To greve them as I might,
And you to save, as wimen have
From deth many one;
For in my minde of all mankinde
I love but you alone.'

150. *rescous*, rescue. 161. *fere*, company.

Squire.

'Yet take good hede, for ever I drede
  That ye coude not sustein
The thorney wayes, the depe valeis,
  The snowe, the frost, the rein,
The colde, the hete, for, drie or wete,
  We must lodge on the plain,
And, us above, noon other rove
  But a brake bussh or twaine;
Which sone shuld greve you, I beleve,
  And ye wolde gladly than
That I had to the grenewode go
  Alone a banisshed man.'

Puella.

'Sith I have here ben partinere
  With you of joy and blisse,
I muste also parte of your wo
  Endure, as reason is.
Yet am I sure of oon plesure;
  And, shortly, it is this,
That where ye be, me semeth, perdė,
  I coude not fare amisse.
Without more speche, I you beseche
  That we were soon agone,
For in my minde of all mankinde
  I love but you alone.'

Squire.

'Yef ye go theder, ye must consider,
Whan ye have lust to dine,
There shall no mete be for to gete,
Nor drinke, bere, ale, ne wine;
Ne shetės clene to lie betwene,
Made of thred and twine;
Noon other house but leves and bowes
To kever your hed and mine.
Lo, mine herte swete, this ille diet
Shuld make you pale and wan;
Wherefore I to the wood will go
Alone a banisshed man.'

Puella.

'Amonge the wilde dere, suche an archier,
As men say that ye be,
Ne may not faile of good vitaile,
Where is so grete plentė;
And watir clere of the rivere
Shall be full swete to me,
With whiche in hele I shall right wele
Endure, as ye shall see.
And ere we go, a bed or two
I can provide anoon,
For in my minde of all mankinde
I love but you alone.'

211. *hele*, health.

Squire.

'Lo, yet before ye must do more,
If ye will go with me,
As cutte your here up by your ere,
Your kirtel by the knee,
With bowe in hande, for to withstonde
Your enmys, if nede be;
And this same night before daylight,
To woodward will I flee.
If that ye wille all this fulfille,
Do it shortely as ye can;
Elles will I to the grenewode go
Alone a banisshed man.'

Puella.

'I shall as now do more for you
Than longeth to womanhed,
To short my here, a bowe to bere,
To shote in time of nede.
O my swete moder, before all other
For you I have most drede;
But now, adiew! I must ensue
Where fortune doth me leede.
All this make ye. Now lete us flee,
The day commeth fast upon;
For in my minde of all mankinde
I love but you alone.'

Squire.

'Nay, nay, not so! ye shall not go,
  And I shall telle you why.
Your appetite is to be light
  Of love, I wele aspie;
For, right as ye have said to me,
  In like wise hardėly
You wolde answere who so ever it were
  In way of company.
It is said of olde, sone hote, sone colde;
  And so is a woman.
Wherefore I to the woode will go
  Alone a banisshed man.'

Puella.

'Yef ye take hede, yet is no nede
  Suche wordes to say by me;
For ofte ye preyd, and longe assayed,
  Or I you loved, parde.
And though that I of auncestry
  A baron's doughter be,
Yet have you proved how I you loved,
  A squier of lowe degree;
And ever shall, what so befalle,
  To dey therefore anoon,
For in my minde of all mankinde
  I love but you alone.'

Squire.

'A baron's childe to be begiled,
 It were a cursséd dede;
To be felow with an outlawe,
 Almighty God forbede!
Yet better were the power squier
 Alone to forest yede,
Than ye shall saye another day
 That by my wiked dede
Ye were betrayed. Wherefore, good maide,
 The best rede that I can,
Is that I to the grenewode go
 Alone a banissched man.'

Puella.

'Whatsoever befalle, I never shall
 Of this thing you upbraid;
But if ye go, and leve me so,
 Than have ye me betrayed.
Remembre you wele how that ye dele;
 For if ye, as ye saide,
Be so unkinde to leve behinde
 Your love, the Notbrowne maide,
Trust me truly, that I shall dey
 Sone after ye be gone,
For in my minde of all mankinde
 I love but you alone.'

270. *yede*, go.

Squire.

'Yef that ye went, ye shulde repent;
For in the forest now
I have purveyd me of a maide,
Whom I love more than you.
Another more faire than ever ye were,
I dare it well avowe;
And of you bothe eche shuld be wrothe
With other, as I trowe.
It were mine ease to live in pease,
So will I, if I can;
Wherefore I to the wode will go
Alone a banisshed man.'

Puella.

'Though in the wood I understode
Ye had a paramour,
All this may nought remeve my thought,
But that I will be your;
And she shall finde me softe and kinde
And curteis every hour,
Glad to fulfille all that she wille
Commaunde me to my power.
For had ye, lo, an hondred mo,
Yet wolde I be that one,
For in my minde of all mankinde
I love but you alone.'

Squire.

'Mine owne dere love, I see thee prove
  That ye be kinde and trewe,
Of maide and wif, in all my lif,
  The best that ever I knewe.
Be mery and glad, be no more sad!
  The case is chaungėd newe,
For it were ruthe that for your trouth
  You shuld have cause to rewe.
Be not dismayed! Whatsoever I said
  To you, whan I began,
I will not to the grene wode go;
  I am no banisshed man.'

Puella.

'Theis tidinges be more glad to me
  Than to be made a quene,
If I were sure they shuld endure;
  But it is often seen,
When men will breke promise, they speke
  The wordės on the splene.
Ye shape some wile me to begile
  And stele fro me, I wene.
Then were the case wurs than it was,
  And I more wo begone;
For in my minde of all mankinde
  I love but you alone.'

Squire.

'Ye shall not nede further to drede.
  I will not disparage
You, God defende! sith you descende
  Of so grete a linage.
Now understonde! To Westmerlande,
  Whiche is my heritage,
I will you bringe, and with a ringe
  By wey of mariage
I will you take, and lady make
  As shortly as I can.
Thus have ye wone an erlės son,
  And not a banisshed man.'

Ambo.

Here may ye see that wimen be
  In love, meke, kinde, and stable.
Late never man repreve them than,
  Or calle them variable;
But rather prey God that we may
  To them be comfortable,
Whiche sometime proveth suche as he loveth,
  If they be charitable.
For sith men wolde that wimen sholde
  Be meke to them each one,
Moche more ought they to God obey,
  And serve but Him alone.

XX

TO MISTRESS MARGERY WENTWORTH.

WITH margerain gentle,
The flower of goodlihead,
Embroidered the mantle
Is of your maidenhead.

Plainly I cannot glose,
Ye be as I divine
The pretty primrose,
The goodly columbine.

With margerain gentle,
The flower of goodlihead,
Embroidered the mantle
Is of your maidenhead.

Benign, courteous, and meek,
With words well devised,
In you who list to seek
Be virtues well comprised.

With margerain gentle,
The flower of goodlihead,
Embroidered the mantle
Is of your maidenhead.

JOHN SKELTON.

1. *margerain*, marjoram.

XXI

TO MISTRESS ISABEL PENNELL.

BY Saint Mary, my lady,
Your mammy and your daddy
Brought forth a goodly baby.

My maiden Isabel,
Reflaring rosabel,
The flagrant camomel,

The ruddy rosary,
The sovereign rosemary,
The pretty strawberry,

The columbine, the nepte,
The gilliflower well set,
The proper violet,

Ennewėd your colour
Is like the daisy flower
After the April shower.

Star of the morrow gray,
The blossom on the spray,
The freshest flower of May,

10. *nepte*, mint. 13. *Ennewėd*, freshly tinted.

Maidenly demure,
Of womanhood the lure;
Wherefore I make you sure

It were an heavenly health,
It were an endless wealth,
A life for God himself,

To hear this nightingale
Among the birdės small
Warbling in the vale,

'Dug, dug, jug, jug!
Good year and good luck!'
With 'Chuck, chuck, chuck, chuck!'

JOHN SKELTON.

XXII

TO MISTRESS MARGARET HUSSEY.

MERRY Margaret,
As midsummer flower,
Gentle as falcon
Or hawk of the tower,
With solace and gladness,
Much mirth and no madness;
All good and no badness,
So joyously,
So maidenly,
So womanly,
Her demeaning
In every thing
Far far passing
That I can endite
Or suffice to write
Of merry Margaret,
As midsummer flower,
Gentle as falcon
Or hawk of the tower.

As patient and as still,
And as full of good will,
As fair Isaphill,
Coliander,
Sweet pomander,
Good Cassander,

Steadfast of thought,
Well made, well wrought.
Far may be sought
Erst that ye can find
So courteous, so kind,
As merry Margaret,
  This midsummer flower,
Gentle as falcon
  Or hawk of the tower.

JOHN SKELTON.

XXIII

Green groweth the holly; so doth the ivy.
Though winter blastės blow never so high,
Green groweth the holly.

As the holly groweth green,
And never changeth hue,
So I am, ever hath been
Unto my lady true;

As the holly groweth green
With ivy all alone,
When flowerės can not be seen
And green wood leaves be gone.

Now unto my lady
Promise to her I make,
From all other only
To her I me betake.

Adieu, mine own lady,
Adieu, my special,
Who hath my heart truly,
Be sure, and ever shall!

Henry the Eighth.

15. *betake*, give.

XXIV

WHERETO should I express
  My inward heaviness?
No mirth can make me fain,
  Till that we meet again.

Do way, dear heart, not so!
  Let no thought you dismay.
Though ye now part me fro,
  We shall meet when we may.

When I remember me
  Of your most gentle mind,
It may in no wise agree
  That I should be unkind.

The daisy delectable,
  The violet wan and blo,
Ye are not variable.
  I love you and no moe.

I make you fast and sure.
  It is to me great pain
Thus long to endure
  Till that we meet again.

HENRY THE EIGHTH.

14. *blo*, pale.

XXV

You and I and Amyas,
Amyas and you and I,
To the green wood must we go, alas !
You and I, my life, and Amyas.

THE knight knocked at the castle gate ;
The lady marvelled who was thereat.

To call the porter he would not blin ;
The lady said he should not come in.

The portress was a lady bright ;
Strangėness that lady hight.

She askėd him what was his name ;
He said 'Desire, your man, madame.'

She said 'Desire, what do ye here ?'
He said 'Madame, as your prisoner.'

He was counselled to brief a bill,
And show my lady his own will.

'Kindness,' said she, 'would it bear,'
'And Pity,' said she, 'would be there.'

Thus how they did we can not say ;
We left them there and went our way.

WILLIAM CORNISH.

7. *blin*, stay.

XXVI

IF I had wit for to endite
  Of my lady both fair and free,
Of her goodness then would I write.
  Shall no man know her name for me,
  Shall no man know her name for me.

I love her well with heart and mind;
  She is right true, I do it see;
My heart to have she doth me bind.
  Shall no man know her name for me.

She doth not waver as the wind;
  Nor for no new me change doth she;
But alway true I do her find.
  Shall no man know her name for me.

If I to her then were unkind,
  Pity it were, that I should thee;
For she to me is alway kind.
  Shall no man know her name for me.

Learning it were for women all
  Unto their lovers true to be.
Promise I make that know none shall,
  Whiles that I live, her name for me.

15. *thee*, thrive.

My heart she hath, and ever shall,
  Till by death departed we be.
Hap what will hap, fall what shall fall,
  Shall no man know her name for me.

XXVII

THIS other day
I heard a may
Right piteously complain.
She said alway,
Without denay,
Her heart was full of pain.

She said, alas!
Without trespass,
Her dear heart was untrue.
'In every place
I wot he has
Forsake me for a new.

'Sith he, untrue,
Hath chosen a new,
And thinks with her to rest,
And will not rue,
And I so trew;
Wherefore my heart will brest.

'And now I may,
In no manner way,
Obtain that I do sue;
So ever and aye,
Without denay,
Mine own sweet heart, adieu!

'Adieu, darling,
Adieu, sweeting,
Adieu, all my welfare!
Adieu, all thing
To God pertaining!
Christ keep you for my care!

'Adieu, full sweet,
Adieu, right meet
To be a lady's heir!'
With tearės wet
And eyes replete,
She said, 'Adieu, my dear!

'Adieu, farewell,
Adieu, *le bel*,
Adieu, both friend and foe!
I cannot tell,
Where I shall dwell;
My heart it grieveth me so.'

She had not said,
But at a braid
Her dear heart was full near;
And said, 'Good maid,
Be not dismayed,
My love, my darling dear!'

44. *braid*, instant.

In arms he hent
That lady gent.
In voiding care and moan,
That day they spent
To their intent
In wilderness alone.

49. *hent*, seized.

XXVIII

'Hey, troly loly lo, maid, whither go you?'
'I go to the meadow to milk my cow.'
'Then at the meadow I will you meet,
To gather the flowers both fair and sweet.'
'Nay, God forbid, that may not be!
I wis my mother then shall us see.'

'Now in this meadow fair and green
We may us sport and not be seen;
And if ye will, I shall consent.
How say ye, maid? be ye content?'
'Nay, in good faith, I'll not mell with you!
I pray you, sir, let me go milk my cow.'

'Why will ye not give me no comfort,
That now in these fields we may us sport?'
'Nay, God forbid, that may not be!
I wis my mother then shall us see.'

'Ye be so nice and so meet of age,
That ye greatly move my courage.
Sith I love you, love me again;
Let us make one, though we be twain.'
'I pray you, sir, let me go milk my cow.'

11. *mell*, meddle.

'Ye have my heart, say what ye will;
Wherefore ye must my mind fulfill,
And grant me here your maidenhead,
Or ellės I shall for you be dead.'
'I pray you, sir, let me go milk my cow.'

'Then for this once I shall you spare;
But the next time ye must beware,
How in the meadow ye milk your cow.
Adieu, farewell, and kiss me now!'
'I pray you, sir, let me go milk my cow.'

XXIX

'COME over the woodės fair and green,
  Thou goodly maid, thou lusty wench,
To shadow you from the sunnė sheen.
  Under the wood there is a bench.'
  'Sir, I pray you, do none offence
To me, a maid, this I make my moan,
  But as I came let me go hence,
For I am here myself alone.

I would for no worldly good
  Be found with you in this place
All alone under this wood;
  Therefore I put me now in your grace.'
  'Thou goodly maiden fair of face,
Sit down under this greenwood tree
  And talk with me a little space,
For comfort is none alone to be.

The custom and the manner here
  Of maidens is and ever was,
That gather the flowers without a fere,
  To pay a trepitt, or they pass.'
  'Then of my mouth come take a bass;
For other goodės have I none
  But flowers fair among the grass
Which I have gatherėd all alone.

20. *trepitt*, fine. 21. *bass* = buss, kiss.

My mother can the hourės tell
  While I am here ; so doth my sire.
Long with you I may not dwell ;
  Let me depart, I you require.'
  'Against all right is all your desire
Sȯ suddenly to go from me.
  Abide till ye have paid your hire,
For comfort is none alone to be.

I must observe the courtė-law
  By courteous manner or by might ;
Custom may I none withdraw
  That hath be usėd here by right.'
  'Now for this time let me go quite.
You to withstand strength have I none.
  And nevermore I will you plight
To gather the flowers all alone.

But if there be none other way,
  But I must pay at your request,
What ye will then must ye say
  That of all flowers ye love best.'
  'Than all the flowers both east and west,
Your company is more leve to me ;
  For to depart ye be too prest,
Sith comfort is none alone to be.

47. *prest*, ready.

My heart beginneth to rejoice
  Sith ye have made me boldly to crave
And hath put fully in my choice
  The fairest flower now that ye have.'
  'I mean your custom for to save.
Of all my flowers take ye one.
  Choose the best of all that I have
In my arm gatherėd all alone.

Behold these flowers bright and sheen,
  Cowslips, daisies, and the primrose
And basil, that herb both gentle and green,
  And else the lusty ruddy rose.'
  'Another flower is better for my purpose,
And none of these to take in gree.
  To dwell with me yourself dispose,
For comfort is none alone to be.

Sweet mistress mine, ye shall have no wrong,
  But as ye grant me, sith we be met,
That fair flower that ye have kept so long
  I call it mine own as my very debt.'
  'I trow ye be not of that set
To spill my flowers every one.
  I will no more gather the violet
Under this wood myself alone.

62. *in gree*, with goodwill.

But shall I gather the flowers here?
  Nay, nevermore, I make a vow;
And if I do withouten a fere
  Do to me then as ye did now.'
  'O ye fair maiden, sweet lady now,
Come gather the flowers again with me,
  And ye shall find it for your prow
For comfort is none alone to be.'

79. *prow*, advantage.

XXX

LET not us that youngmen be
From Venus' ways banished to be.
Though that age with great disdain
Would have youth love to refrain,
In their minds consider you must
How they did in their most lust.

For if they were in like case,
And would then have gotten grace,
They may not now then gainsay
That which then was most their joy.
Wherefore indeed, the truth to say,
It is for youth the meetest play.

XXXI

WESTERN wind, when will thou blow,
The small rain down can rain ?
Christ, if my love were in my arms
And I in my bed again !

XXXII

THE little pretty nightingale
  Among the leavės green,
I would I were with her all night.
  But yet ye wot not whom I mean.

The nightingale sat on a brere
  Among the thornės sharp and keen,
And comfort me with merry cheer.
  But yet ye wot not whom I mean.

She did appear all on her kind
  A lady right well to be seen;
With words of love told me her mind.
  But yet ye wot not whom I mean.

It did me good upon her to look;
  Her corse was closėd all in green;
Away fro me her heart she took.
  But yet ye wot not whom I mean.

'Lady,' I cried with rueful moan,
  'Have mind of me that true hath been;
For I love none but you alone.'
  But yet ye wot not whom I mean.

XXXIII

BY a bank as I lay,
Musing myself alone, hey ho!
A birdės voice
Did me rejoice,
Singing before the day;
And me thought in her lay
She said, winter was past, hey ho!
Then dyry come dawn, dyry come dyry, come dyry!
Come dyry, come dyry, come dawn, hey ho!

The master of music,
The lusty nightingale, hey ho!
Full merrily
And secretly
She singeth in the thick;
And under her breast a prick,
To keep her fro sleep, hey ho!
Then dyry come dawn, dyry come dyry, come dyry!
Come dyry, come dyry, come dawn, hey ho!

Awake therefore, young men,
All ye that lovers be, hey ho!
This month of May,
So fresh, so gay,
So fair be fields on fen;
Hath flourish ilk again.
Great joy it is to see, hey ho!
Then dyry come dawn, dyry come dyry, come dyry!
Come dyry, come dyry, come dawn, hey ho!

XXXIV

'I love, I love, and whom love ye?'
'I love a flower of fresh beauty.'
'I love another as well as ye.'
'That shall be provèd here anon,
'If we three can agree in one.'

'I LOVE a flower of sweet odour.'
'Marjoram gentle, or lavender?'
'Columbine golds of sweet flavour?'
'Nay, nay, let be!
Is none of them
That liketh me.'
'I love, I love, and whom love ye?' etc.

'There is a flower, where so he be,'
'And shall not yet be named for me.'
'Primrose, violet, or fresh daisy?'
'He pass them all
In his degree,
That best liketh me.'
'I love, I love, and whom love ye?' etc.

'One that I love most entirely.'
'Gilliflower gentle, or rosemary?'
'Camomile, borage, or savory?'
'Nay, certainly
Here is not he
That pleaseth me.'
'I love, I love, and whom love ye?' etc.

'I choose a flower freshest of face.'
'What is his name that thou chosen has?'
'The rose, I suppose; thine heart unbrace!'
  'That same is he,
  In heart so free,
  That best liketh me.'
'I love, I love, and whom love ye?' etc.

'The rose, it is a royal flower.'
'The red or the white? shew his colour!'
'Both be full sweet and of like savour.'
  'All one they be,
  That day to see,
  It liketh well me.
Now have I loved, and whom love ye?' etc.

'I love the rose both red and white.'
'Is that your pure perfit appetite?'
'To hear talk of them is my delight.'
  'Joyed may we be
  Our prince to see,
  And roses three.
Now have I loved, and whom love ye?' etc.

SIR THOMAS PHILIPPS.

42. *perfit*, perfect.

XXXV

BENEDICITE, what dreamėd I this night ?
Methought the world was turnėd up so down ;
The sun, the moon, had lost their force and light ;
The sea also drownėd both tower and town.
Yet more marvel how that I heard the sound
Of onės voice saying 'Bear in thy mind,
Thy lady hath forgotten to be kind.'

To complain me, alas, why should I so,
For my complaint it did me never good ?
But by constraint now must I shew my woe
To her only which is mine eyės food,
Trusting sometime that she will change her mood,
And let me not alway be guerdonless,
Sith for my truth she needeth no witness.

XXXVI

WHO shall have my fair lady ?
Who shall have my fair lady ?
Who but I, who but I, who but I ?
Under the leavės green !

The fairest man
That best love can,
Dandirly, dandirly, dandirly dan,
Under the leavės green !

XXXVII

O MISTRESS, why
Outcast am I
All utterly
From your pleasance;
Sith ye and I
Or this truly
Familiarly
Have had pastance,

And lovingly
Ye would apply
My company
To my comfort?
But now truly
Unlovingly
Ye do deny
Me to resort;

And me to see
As strange ye be
As though that ye
Should now deny,
Or else possess
That nobleness
To be duchess
Of great Savoy.

8. *pastance*, pastime.

But sith that ye
So strange will be
As towards me
  And will not mell,
I trust percase
To find some grace,
To have free chase
  And speed as well.

28. *mell*, meddle. 29. *percase*, perhaps.

XXXVIII

'MOURNING, mourning,
Thus may I sing,
Adieu, my dear, adieu!
By God alone,
My love is gone;
Now may I go seek a new.'

'Nay, nay, no, no!
Iwis not so;
Leave off and do no more,
For verily
Some women there be,
The which be brittle store.'

'I lovèd one
Not long agone,
On whom my heart was set;
So did she me;
Why should I lie?
I can it not forget.

'Her letters will prove
She was my love,
And so I will her complain.
Though my sweet heart
Be fro me start,
She is the more to blame.

'Though my sweet heart
Be fro me start,
  And changed me for a new,
I am content
And will assent
  With him that hath her now.

'For by Saint Gile
And Mary mild,
  He is a minion man ;
Much proper and good,
Come of gentle blood,
  And much good pastime he can.

'He is worthy
Much better than I
  To have the love of her.
Therefore, sweet heart,
Farewell my part,
  Adieu, sometime my dear !'

XXXIX

As I lay sleeping,
  In dreamės fleeting,
Ever my sweeting
  Is in my mind.
She is so goodly,
With locks so lovely
. . . .
  Such one can find.

Her beauty so pure,
It doth under lure
My poor heart full sure,
  In governance;
Therefore now will I
Unto her apply,
And ever will cry
  For remembrance.

Her fair eye piercing
My poor heart bleeding,
And I abiding
  In hope of meed;
But thus have I long
Entwinėd this song,
With painės full strong,
  And cannot speed.

Alas, will not she
Now shew her pity,
But thus will take me
  In such disdain?
Methinketh iwis
Unkind that she is,
That bindeth me thus
  In such hard pain.

Though she me bind,
Yet shall she not find
My poor heart unkind,
  Do what she can;
For I will her pray,
Whiles I live a day,
Me to take for aye,
  For her own man.

XL

THE maidens came
  When I was in my mother's bower;
I had all that I would.
  The bailey beareth the bell away;
  The lily, the rose, the rose I lay.
The silver is white, red is the gold;
The robes they lay in fold.
  The bailey beareth the bell away;
  The lily, the rose, the rose I lay.
And through the glass window shines the sun.
How should I love, and I so young?
  The bailey beareth the bell away;
  The lily, the lily, the rose I lay.

XLI

My lady is a pretty one,
A pretty pretty pretty one ;
My lady is a pretty one
As ever I saw.

SHE is gentle and also wise ;
Of all other she beareth the prize,
That ever I saw.

To hear her sing, to see her dance !
She will the best herself advance,
That ever I saw.

To see her fingers that be so small !
In my conceit she passeth all
That ever I saw.

Nature in her hath wonderly wrought.
Christ never such another bought,
That ever I saw.

I have seen many that have beauty,
Yet is there none like to my lady
That ever I saw.

Therefore I dare this boldly say,
I shall have the best and fairest may
That ever I saw.

XLII

Ah, my sweet sweeting,
My little pretty sweeting,
My sweeting will I love wherever I go.

SHE is so proper and so pure,
Full steadfast, stable and demure,
There is none such, ye may be sure,
As my sweet sweeting.

In all this world, as thinketh me,
Is none so pleasant to my eye,
That I am glad so oft to see,
As my sweet sweeting.

When I behold my sweeting sweet,
Her face, her hands, her minion feet,
They seem to me there is none so meet
As my sweet sweeting.

Above all other praise must I
And love my pretty piggésnie,
For none I find so womanly
As my sweet sweeting.

17. *piggésnie* (lit. pig's eye), a term of endearment.

XLIII

IS it not sure a deadly pain,
To you I say that lovers be,
When faithful hearts must needs refrain
The one the other for to see?
I you assure ye may trust me,
Of all the pains that ever I knew,
It is a pain that most I rue.

XLIV

WHAT meanest thou, my fortune,
  From me so fast to fly ?
Alas, thou art importune
  To work thus cruelly.

Thy waste continually
  Shall cause me call and cry ;
Woe worth the time that I
  To love did first apply !

DIVINE LYRICS

'Alas, that ever that speche was spoken
    That the fals aungel seid onto me!
Alas! oure maker's bidding is broken,
    For I have touchèd his owen dere tree.
Oure flescly eyn bin all unloken;
    Naked for sinne oureself we see;
That sory appel that we han soken
    To dethe hathe brouth my spouse and me.'

Ludus Coventriae, ii. 118

DIVINE

XLV

SEINTĖ Mari moder milde,
Mater salutaris;
Feirest flour of eni felde
Vere nuncuparis.
Thorou ihesu crist thou were wid childe;
Thou bring me of my thouhtės wilde
Potente,
That maket me to dethė tee
Repente.

Mi thounc is wilde as is the ro
Luto gratulante.
Ho werchet me ful muchel wo
Illaque favente.
Bote yef he wolė wende me fro,
Ic wene myn herte breket a two
Fervore.
Ic am ifaiht bo day ant naiht
Dolore.

8. *tee*, go. 17. *ifaiht*, tamed.

Jhesu, thorou thi muchele miht
Omnia fecisti;
The holi gost in Marie liht
Sicut voluisti.
Forthi he is icleped ur driht,
Ihesu, bring my thouht to Crist
Constanter,
That it be stable ant nout chaungable
Fraudanter.

Jhesu Crist, thou art on loft
Digno tu scandente;
Hevene ant erthe thou havest iwrouht
Victore triumphante;
Monkun wid thi bodi abouht,
Thou noldest lesen hym for nouht,
Nec dare
Ant yeve the blod that was so god
Tam gnare.

Suetė levedi, flour of alle,
Vere consolatrix,
Thou be myn help that I ne fall,
Cunctis reparatrix!
Mildest quene ant best icorn,
Niht ant day thou be me forn
Precantis!
Yef me grace to see thi face
Infantis!

23. *driht*, lord. 41. *icorn*, chosen.

That I thorou thi suetė bene,
Tutrix orphanorum,
Mot leven al this worldės tene,
Solamen miserorum;
Ant to the levedi mot I take,
And myn sunnės al fursake
Volente,
That I ne misse of thinė blisse
Poscente.

46. *bene*, prayer.

XLVI

OF on that is so fayr and bright
    Velud maris stella,
Brighter than the day is light,
    Parens et puella;
Ic crie to the, thou se to me,
Levedy, preyė thi sone for me,
    Tam pia,
That ic motė comė to the,
    Maria!

Of karė conseil thou ert best,
    Felix fecundata;
Of allė wery thou ert rest,
    Mater honorata.
Bisek him wiz mildė mod,
That for ous allė sad is blod
    In cruce,
That we moten comen til him
    In luce.

Al this world was forlore,
    Eva peccatrice,
Tyl our lord was ibore
    De te genetrice.
With *Ave* it went away
Thuster nyth and comet the day
    Salutis;
The wellė springet hut of the
    Virtutis.

10. *conseil*, consolation.
14. *Bisek*, beseech.
24. *Thuster*, dark.

Levedi, flour of allė thing,
Rosa sine spina,
Thu bere Jhesu, hevenė king,
Gratia divina;
Of allė thu berst the pris,
Levedi, quene of Parays
Electa,
Maydė mildė, moder *es*
Effecta.

Wel he wot he is thi sone,
Ventre quem portasti;
He wyl nout wernė the thi bone,
Parvum quem lactasti.
So hendė and so god he his,
He havet brout ous to blis
Superni,
That havez hidut the foulė put
Inferni.

39. *wernė*, refuse.
41. *hendė*, kindly, courteous.
44. *hidut*, closed : *put*, pit.

XLVII

ON hire is al mi lif ylong
Of wham ic willė singen,
And herien him ther among
That gon us botė bringen
Of hellė pinė that is strong,
Ant brut us blisse that is so long,
Al thurut hire childinke.
We biddit hire in urė song
He yef us god hendinke,
Thau we don wrong.

Al this world hid sal agon
Wid serue and wid sore ;
And al this blisse ic mot for gon,
Lof thingit me so sore.
This world nis bute urė fon
Thar for ic wille hennė gon
And lernin Godis lore.
This worldis blisse nis wrd a flo.
I biddė, God, thin hore,
Nu and hever mo.

3. *herien*, praise. 8. *biddit*, ask.
7. *childinke*, child-bearing. 19. *hore*, mercy.

To longe ic abbė sot iben,
Ful sorre I me adrede.
Ylovid ic abbe gomin and gle,
And hevir fayrė wedin.
Al that nis nout ful wel ic seo;
Ther fore we sulin ur sunnis flen
And urė sothede.
We biddit hire us to seo,
That con wissin and redin,
That is so freo.

Heo is helė and lef and licte
And helpit al moncunne;
Ho us havet ful wel idiit;
Ho yaf us wele and wunne.
Thu brutis us day and Evė nit;
Heo brout wou, thu brought rid,
Thu almesse, and heo sunne.
Thu do us merci, lavedi brit,
Wenė we sulin henne;
Ful wel thu mit.

21. *sot*, foolish.
28. *seo*, protect.
29. *wissin*, guide : *redin*, advise.
33. *idiit*=idight, prepared.
34. *wunne*, joy.

Agult ic havė, weylawey !
  Sunful ic am a wreche.
Thu do me merci, lavedi brit,
  Ar det me hennė fecche.
Yif me thi love, ic am redi ;
Let me live and amendi,
  That fendės me ne letten.
Of mine sunnin ic am sori,
  Of mi lif ic ne recche.
    Lavedi, merci !

41. *Agult*, sinned. 44. *Ar det*, ere death.

XLVIII

NOU skrinketh rose and lylie flour,
That whilen ber that suete savour
In somer, that suete tyde;
Ne is no quene so stark ne stour,
Ne no levedy so bryht in bour,
That ded ne shal by glyde.
Whosė wol fleyshlust forgon,
And hevenė blis abyde,
On Jesu be is thoht anon,
That therlėd was ys side.

From Petresbourh in o morewenyng,
As I me wende omy pleyghyng,
On mi folie I thohte.
Menen I gon my mournyng
To hire that ber the hevenė kyng;
Of merci hire bysohte,
'Ledy, preye thi sone for ous,
That us duerė bohte,
Ant shild us from the lothė hous
That to the fend is wrohte!'

1. *skrinketh*, shrink.
6. *ded*, death.
7. *Whosė* = whoso.
10. *therlėd*, pierced.
12. *omy*, on my.
14. *menen*, to lament.

Myn herte of dedės wes fordred,
Of synne that I have my fleish fed,
Ant folewėd al my tyme,
That I not whider I shal be led,
When I lygge on dethės bed,
In ioie ore in to pyne.
On a ledy myn hope is,
Moder and virgyne ;
We shulen in to hevenė blis
Thurh hire medicine.

Betere is hire medycyn
Then eny mede or eny wyn ;
Hire erbės smulleth suete.
From Catenas in to Dyvelyn
Nis ther no lechė so fyn
Oure serewės to bete.
Mon that feleth eni sor,
Ant his folie wol lete,
Withoute gold other eny tresor,
He may be sound ant sete.

26. *pyne*, torture.
34. From Caithness to Dublin.
36. *bete*, remedy.
40. *sete*, proper, whole.

Of penaunce is hire plastre al,
Ant ever serven hire I shal,
  Nou ant al my lyve.
Nou is fre that er wes thral,
Al thourh that levedy gent ant smal.
  Heried be hyre ioiės fyve!
Wher so eny sek ys,
  Thider hyė blyve;
Thurh hire beoth ybroht to blis
  Bo maiden ant wyve.

For he that dude his body on tre,
Of oure sunnės have piete,
  That weldės heouenė boures!
Wymmon, with thi iolyfte,
  Thou thench on Godės shoures;
Thah thou be whyt and bryht on ble,
  Falewen shule thy floures.
Jesu, have merci of me,
  That al this world honoures.
      Amen.

46. *heried*, honoured.
48. Thither hasten quickly.
53. *weldės*, rules.
55. *shoures*, fear, terror.
57. *faleewn*, fade.

XLIX

MAIDEN moder milde,
Oiez cel oreysoun!
From shamė thou me shilde,
E de ly malfeloun!
For love of thinė childe
Me menez de tresoun!
Ich wes wod ant wilde,
Ore su en prisoun.

Thou art feyr ant fre,
E plein de doucour;
Of thee sprong the ble,
Ly soverein creatour.
Maydė, byseche I thee
Vostre seint socour,
Meoke ant mylde, be with me
Per la sue amour!

Tho Judas Jesum founde,
Donque ly beysa.
He wes bete ant bounde,
Que nus tous fourma.
Wydė were is wounde
Que le Gyw ly dona;
He tholede hardė stounde,
Me poi le greva.

7. *wod*, mad.
11. *ble*, appearance, form.
17. *Tho*, when.
23. *tholede*, endured.

On ston ase thou stode,
Pucele, tot pensaunt,
Thou restest the under rode,
Ton fitz veites pendant;
Thou seye is sides of blode,
Lalme de ly partaunt.
He ferede uch an fode
En mound que fust vivaunt.

Ys siden werė sore;
Le sang de ly cora.
That lond wes forlore,
Mes il le rechata.
Uch bern that wes ybore
En enfern descenda.
He tholede deth ther fore;
En ciel puis mounta.

Tho Pilat herde the tydynge,
Molt fu joyous baroun;
He lette byfore him brynge
Jesu Nazaroun.
He was ycrounėd kynge
Per nostre redempcioun.
Whosė wol me synge,
Auera grant pardoun.

31. *fode*, child. 47. *Whosė*, whoso.

L

ADAM lay ibounden,
 Bounden in a bond;
Four thousand winter
 Thoght he not too long;
And all was for an appil,
 An appil that he tok,
As clerkės finden
 Wreten in here book.
Ne hadde the appil takė ben,
 The appil taken ben,
Ne haddė never our lady
 A ben hevenė quene.
Blessėd be the time
 That appil takė was.
Therefore we moun singen
 '*Deo gracias.*'

8. *here*, their. 15. *moun*, may.

LI

Of a rose, a lovely rose,
Of a rose is all mine song.

LESTENETH, lordinges, bothe elde and yinge,
How this rosė began to springe;
Swich a rosė to mine likinge
In all this world ne knowe I none.

The aungil cam fro hevenė tour,
To grete Mary with gret honour,
And seidė sche schuld bere the flour,
That schuldė breke the fendės bond.

The flour sprong in heye Bedlem,
That is bothė bright and schene.
The rose is Mary, hevenė quene;
Out of her bosum the blosmė sprong.

The ferstė braunche is full of might,
That sprong on Cirstemessė night;
The sterre schon over Bedlem bright,
That is bothė brod and long.

The secunde braunchė sprong to helle,
The fendės power down to felle;
Therein might none sowlė dwelle.
Blessed be the time the rosė sprong!

12. *schene*, fair.

The threddė braunche is good and swote,
It sprang to hevenė crop and rote,
Therein to dwellen and ben our bote;
 Every day it scheweth in prestės hond.

Prey we to her with gret honour,
Sche that bare the blessėd flour,
Sche be our helpe and our socour
 And schild us fro the fendės bond!

25. *bote*, profit.

LII

THERE is no rose of swich vertu
  As is the rose that bare Jhesu.
    Alleluia.

For in this rose conteinėd was
Hevene and erthe in litel space,
    Res miranda.

Be that rosė we may weel see
There be o God in persones three,
    Pares forma.

The aungeles sungen the schepherdes to
Gloria in excelsis Deo.
    Gaudeamus.

Leve we all this werdly merthe,
And folwė we this joyful berthe.
    Transeamus.

8. *o*, one. 13. *werdly*, worldly.

LIII

Alma redemptoris mater.

AS I lay up on a night
My thought was on a berd so bright
That men clepen Marye full of might,
Redemptoris mater.

To here cam Gabriel with light,
And seid 'Heil be thou, blissful wight,
To ben clepėd now art thou dight
Redemptoris mater.'

At that wurd that lady bright
Anon conseived God full of might.
Than men wist weel that sche hight
Redemptoris mater.

Whan Jhesu on the rode was pight,
Mary was doolful of that sight,
Til sche sey him rise up right,
Redemptoris mater.

Jhesu, that sittest in hevenė light,
Graunt us to comen beforn thy sight,
With that berd that is so bright,
Redemptoris mater.

3. *berd*, maiden. 14. *pight*, fastened.

LIV

I SING of a maiden
  That is makėles,
King of all kinges
  To her sone sche ches.
He cam also stille
  There his moder was,
As dew in Aprille
  That falleth on the grass.
He cam also stille
  To his moderės bour,
As dew in Aprille
  That falleth on the flour.
He cam also stille
  There his moder lay,
As dew in Aprille
  That falleth on the spray.
Moder and maiden
  Was never non but sche;
Well may swich a lady
  Godės moder be.

2. *makėles*, without a mate. 4. *ches*, chose.

LV

A, a, a, a,
Nunc gaudet Maria.

MARY is a lady bright;
Sche hath a sone of mechė might;
Over all this word sche is light.
Bona natalicia.

Mary is so fair and sote,
And her sone so full of pote;
Over all this word he is bote.
Bona voluntaria.

Mary is so fair of face,
And her sone so full of grace;
In hevene he make us a place,
Cum sua potencia.

Mary is bothė good and kinde;
Evere on us sche hath mende,
That the fend schall us not schende,
Cum sua malicia.

Mary is quene of allė thinge,
And her sone a lovely kinge.
God graunt us allė good endinge!
Regnat dei gracia.

7. *sote*, sweet.
8. *pote*, power.
9. *bote*, profit.
16. *mende*, mind.
17. *shende*, ruin.

LVI

AVE maris stella,
The sterre on the see,
Dei mater alma,
Blessėd mot sche be!
Atque semper virgo,
Pray thy sone for me,
Felix celi porta,
That I may come to thee.
Gabriel, that archangel,
He was massanger;
So faire he gret our Lady,
With an *Ave* so clere.
Heil be thou, Mary,
Be thou, Mary,
Full of Godės grace,
And quene of mercy!
Alle that arn to grete
Withouten dedly sinne,
Forty dayės of pardoun
God graunteth him.

LVII

There is a floure sprung of a tree,
The rote thereof is called Jesse;
A floure of price,
There is none seche in Paradise!

THIS flour is faire and fresche of heue;
Hit fadès never, bot ever is new;
The blissful branche this flour on grew
Was Mary mild that bare Jesu.
A flour of grace,
Ayains all sorow hit is solas!

The sede hereof was Godès sond,
That God him selve sew with his hond
In Bedlem in that holy londe;
Amedis here herbere there he hir fond.
This blissful floure
Sprang never bot in Marys boure.

When Gabrael this maid met,
With '*Ave Maria*' he here gret;
Betwene hem two this flour was set,
And kept was, no mon schul wit;
But on a day
In Bedlem hit con spred and spray.

11. *sond*, sending. 14. *Amedis*, amidst.

When that floure began to spred,
And his blosum to brede,
Riche and pore of every lede
Thay marvelt hou this flour might sprede ;
And kingės three
That blessful floure come to see.

Angeles there cam out of here toure
To loke apon this freschele floure,
Houe faire he was in his coloure,
And hou sote in his savoure,
And to behold
How soche a flour might spring in golde.

Of lilly, of rose of rise,
Of primrol, and of flour-de-lyse,
Of all the flours at my devise,
That floure of Jesse yet bers the pris,
As most of hele
To slake oure sorows every dele.

I pray youe flours of this cuntrė,
Where evere ye go, where ever ye be,
Hold hup the flour of good Jesse
Fore your frescheness and youre beutė,
As fairest of all,
And ever was, and ever schall.

25. *lede*, speech. 32. *sote*, sweet.
35. *rise*, twig, branch. 39. *hele*, health.

LVIII

'ECCE *ancilla domini!*'
  Seid tho virgin withouten vice;
When Gabriell hur gret graciously,
  That holy pinakell preved of price,
  'Of thee schall springe a full swete spice.'
Then seide the meydon full mildėly,
  'And sithen I ame so litill of price,
Ecce ancilla domini!'

'Heill be thou, gracious withouten gilte,
  Meydon borne alderbest!
Within thy body schall be fulfilled
  That all these prophetes han preched so preste;
  God will be borne within thy brest.'
Then seide tho meydon full mildėly,
  'To me he schall be a welcome geste;
Ecce ancilla domini!'

Bot when sche sawe an angell bright,
  Sche was aferde in all her thoght,
And of his speche elles wondur sche might.
  Then seide tho angell, 'Drede thee noght!
  A blestful tithinge I have thee broght.'
Then seide tho meydon full mildėly,
  'As God will, so be it wroght;
Ecce ancilla domini!'

10. *alderbest*, best of all.
12. *preste*, readily.
21. *tithinge*, tiding.

That angell seide, 'Conceive thou schalt
  Within thy body bright
A childe that Jesu schall be called,
  That is grate Goddės son of might.
  Thou art his tabernakull idight.'
Then seide tho meydon full mildėly,
  'Sethen he seide never ayeyns right,
Ecce ancilla domini!'

'Call him Jesu of Nazareth,
  God and mon in on degree.
Right as mon schall suffur dethe
  And regne in David dignite.
  A blestfull worde he sende to thee.'
Then seide tho meydon full mildėly,
  'He schall be dere welcum to me;
Ecce ancilla domini!'

'Bot with mannės modė never I mette;
  Now, lorde, how schall I go with childe?'
Then seide tho angell that her grett,
  'With nonė suche thou schalt be filede,
Tho holy goste will in thee bildon.'
  Then seide tho meydon full mildėly,
'As God will, so be it done;
  Ecce ancilla domini!'

44. *filede*, defiled.

When tho angell was vanesched awey,
  Sche stode al in hur thoght,
And to herselfė sche can sey,
  'All Goddės willė schall be wroght;
For he is well of all witte,
  As witnesses welle his story.'
At that wordė knot was knitte;
  '*Ecce ancilla domini!*'

LIX

Nowel, nowel, nowel, nowel, nowel, nowel !

OUT of youre slepe arise and wake,
For God mankind now hathe itake
All of a maide without any make ;
Of all women she berethe the belle.

And throwe a maidė faire and wis
Now man is made of full grete pris ;
Now angeles knelen to manes servis ;
And at this time all this bifel.

Now man is brighter than the sonne ;
Now man in heven an hie shall wonne ;
Blessėd be God this game is begonne
And his moder emperesse of helle.

That ever was thralle, now is he free ;
That ever was smalle, now grete is she ;
Now shall God deme bothe thee and me
Unto his blisse, if we do well.

Now man may to heven wende ;
Now heven and erthe to him they bende ;
He that was fo now is oure frende.
This is no nay that I you telle.

Now blessėd brother, graunte us grace,
A domės day to see thy face,
And in thy court to have a place,
That we mow there singė nowel.

16. *deme*, judge.

LX

Now sing we right as it is,
Quod puer natus est nobis.

THIS babė to us now is born,
Wonderfull werkės he hath wrought,
He wold not lesse that was forlorn,
But again he hath us bought.
And thus it is,
For soth iwis,
He asketh no thing but that is his.

A dulefull deth to him was mente,
Whan on the rode his body was spred,
And as a theff he was there hente,
And on a spere his liff was lede.
And thus it is, etc.

'Man, why art thou unkind to me?
What woldest thou I did for thee more?
Geve me thy trew harte, I pray thee.
If thou be dampned, it ruthe me sore.'
And thus it is, etc.

'Man, I love thee; whom loveste thou?
I pray thee torne to me again,
And thou shalt be as welcom nowe
As he that never in sin was seyn.'
And thus it is, etc.

12. *hent*, taken. 23. *seyn*, seen.

LXI

All that leve in Cristen lay,
Worshup every Cristmes day.

A MAN was the first gilt,
And therefor he was spilt.
The profecy was never fulfilt,
Till on the Cristmes day.

The first day that lely sprong,
Jhesu Crist be us among;
Ever we thowte it was too long,
Till on the Cristmes day.

It was derk, it was dim,
For men that levėd in gret sin;
Lucifer was us all within,
Till on the Cristmes day.

There was weping, there was wo,
For every man to hell gan go.
It was litel mery tho,
Till on the Cristmes day.

1. *lay*, creed, belief. 17. *tho*, then.

LXII

Puer nobis natus est
De virgine Maria.

BE glad, lordinges, bethe more and lesse,
I bring you tidinges of gladnesse,
As Gabriel me bereth wetnesse.
Dicam vobis quia.

I bring you tidinges that ben gode.
Mary hath borne a blissful fode
That boght us all upon the rode
Sua morte pia.

For the trespas of Adam,
Fro the fader of heven he cam.
Hereto mirthė us bigan
Teste prophecia.

Mary, modur and leve virgin,
That bare a child withouten sin,
Kepe us all fro hellė pin !
De virgine Maria.

8. *fode*, child.
15. *leve*, dear.
17. *pin*, torment.

LXIII

Lullay, my child, and wepe no more,
Slepe and be now still.
The king of bliss thy fader is
As it was his will.

THIS endris night I saw a sight,
A maid a cradell kepe,
And ever she song and seid among
'Lullay, my child, and slepe.'

'I may not slepe, but I may wepe,
I am so wo begone;
Slepe I wold, but I am colde,
And clothės have I none.'

Me thought I hard, the child answard,
And to his moder he said,
'My moder dere, what do I here,
In cribbe why am I laid?

'I was borne and laid beforne
Bestės, both ox and asse.
My moder mild, I am thy child,
But he my fader was.

'Adam's gilt this man had spilt;
That sin greveth me sore.
Man, for thee here shall I be
Thirty winter and more.

'Dole it is to see, here shall I be
  Hangėd upon the rode,
With baleis to-bete, my woundes to-wete,
  And yeve my fleshe to bote.

'Here shall I be hanged on a tree,
  And die as it is skill.
That I have bought lesse will I nought;
  It is my fader's will.

'A spere so scharp shall perse my herte,
  For dedes that I have done.
Fader of grace, whether thou has
  Forgeten thy litell sone?

'Withouten pety here shall aby,
  And make my fleshe all blo.
Adam, iwis, this deth it is
  For thee and many mo.'

27. *baleis*, scourges. 38. *blo*, pallid.
30. *skill*, reason.

LXIV

This endris night I saw a sight,
A stare as bright as day;
And ever among a maiden song,
'Lullay, by by, lullay.'

THIS lovely lady sat and song,
And to her child con say,
'My sone, my broder, my fader dere,
Why liest thou thus in hay?
My swetė brid, thus it is betid,
Thogh thou be king veray;
But nevertheles I will not cese
To sing, By by, lullay.'

The child than spak in his talking,
And to his moder said,
'I bekid am for heven king,
In cribbe thogh I be laid;
For aungeiles bright done to me light.
Thou knowest it is no nay.
And of that sight thou mayst be light
To sing, By by, lullay.'

'Now swetė sone, sin thou art king,
Why art thou laid in stall?
Why ne thou ordende thy bedding
In sum gret kingės hall?
Me thinketh it is right, that king or knight
Shuld lie in good aray;
And than among it were no wrong
To sing, By by, lullay.'

15. *bekid*, proclaimed.

'Mary moder, I am thy child,
  Thogh I be laid in stall;
Lordės and dukes shall worsship me
  And so shall kingės all.
Ye shall well see that kingės three
  Shall come the twelfthė day.
For this behest yeve me thy brest,
  And sing, By by, lullay.'

'Now tell me, swete son, I thee pray,
  Thou art me leve and dere,
How shuld I kepe thee to thy pay
  And make thee glad of chere?
For all thy will I wold fullfill,
  Thou weteste full well in fay;
And for all this I will thee kiss,
  And sing, By by, lullay.'

'My dere moder, whan time it be,
  Thou take me up on loft,
And settė me upon thy knee,
  And handell me full soft;
And in thy arme thou hill me warme,
  And kepė night and day;
If that I wepe, and may not slepe,
  Thou sing, By by, lullay.'

39. *pay*, liking.   49. *hill*, protect.

'Now swetė son, sin it is so,
  That all thing is at thy will,
I pray thee grauntė me a bone,
  If it be both right and skill,
That child or man that will or can
  Be mery upon my day,
To blisse hem bring, and I shall sing
  Lullay, By by, lullay.'

56. *skill*, reason.

LXV

Primus Pastor.

HAIL, comly and clene,
Hail, yong child!
Hail, maker, as I meene,
Of a maden so milde!
Thou has warėd, I weene,
The warlo so wilde;
The fals giler of teen,
Now goes he begilde.
Lo! he merys,
Lo! he laghės, my sweting.
A welfare meting!
I have holden my heting.
Have a bob of cherys!

Secundus Pastor.

Hail, sufferan Savioure,
For thou has us soght!
Hail, frely foyde and floure,
That all thing has wroght!
Hail, full of favoure,
That made all of noght!
Hail! I kneel and I cowre.
A bird have I broght
To my barne.
Hail, litel tinė mop!
Of oure crede thou art crop;
I wold drink on thy cop,
Litel day starne.

5. *warėd*, cursed.
6. *warlo*, warlock.
12. *heting*, promise.
16. *frely*, noble.
16. *foyde*, child.
23. *mop*, baby.

Tertius Pastor.

Hail, derling dere,
  Full of godhede!
I pray thee be nere
  When that I have nede.
Hail! Swete is thy chere;
  My hart woldė blede
To see thee sitt here
  In so poorė wede,
    With no pennys.
Hail! Put furth thy dall!
I bring thee bot a ball;
Have and play thee with all,
    And go to the tenis!

36. *dall*, hand.

LXVI

Terly terlow, terly terlow,
So merily the shepardes began to blow!

ABOUT the feld they piped full right,
Even about the middės of the night;
Adown from heven they saw cum a light.
Terly terlow.

Of angels there came a company
With mery songes and melody;
The shepardes anon gan them aspy.
Terly terlow.

'*Gloria in excelsis*' the angels song
And said that peace was present among
To every man that to the faith wold long.
Terly terlow.

The shepardes hied them to Bethleme,
To see that blessėd sonnės beme;
And there they found that glorious streme.
Terly terlow.

Now pray we to that mekė child,
And to his moder that is so mild
The which was never defiled.
Terly terlow.

17. *streme*, ray of light.

LXVII

Can I not sing but 'Hoy,'
Whan the joly shepard made so much joy?

THE shepard upon a hill he satt;
He had on him his tabard and his hat,
His tarbox, his pipe, and his flagat;
His name was called Joly Joly Wat,
For he was a gud herdės boy.
Ut hoy!
For in his pipe he made so much joy.

The shepard upon a hill was laid;
His dog to his girdell was taid;
He had not slept but a litill braid,
But '*Gloria in excelsis*' was to him said.
Ut hoy!
For in his pipe he made so much joy.

The shepard on a hill he stode;
Round about him his shepe they yode;
He put his hond under his hode,
He saw a star as rede as blode.
Ut hoy!
For in his pipe he made so much joy.

4. *tabard*, short coat.
5. *flagat*, flagon.
12. *braid*, time.
17. *yode*, went.

The shepard said anon right,
'I will go see yon farly sight,
Where as the angel singeth on hight,
And the star that shineth so bright.'
Ut hoy!
For in his pipe he made so much joy.

'Now farewell, Mall, and also Will!
For my love go ye all still
Unto I cum again you till,
And evermore, Will, ring well thy bell.'
Ut hoy!
For in his pipe he made so much joy.

'Now must I go there Crist was born;
Farewell! I cum again to morn.
Dog, kepe well my shepe fro ye corn,
And warn well 'Warroke' when I blow my horn!'
Ut hoy!
For in his pipe he made so much joy.

Whan Wat to Bedlem cum was,
He swet, he had gone faster than a pace;
He found Jesu in a simpell place,
Betwen an ox and an asse.
Ut hoy!
For in his pipe he made so much joy.

23. *farly*, marvellous.

'Jesu, I offer to thee here my pipe,
My skirt, my tar-box, and my scripe;
Home to my felowes now will I skipe,
And also look unto my shepe.'
Ut hoy!
For in his pipe he made so much joy.

'Now farewell, mine owne herdes man Wat!'
'Yea, for God, lady, even so I hat;
Lull well Jesu in thy lape,
And farewell, Joseph, with thy round cape!'
Ut hoy!
For in his pipe he made so much joy.

'Now may I well both hope and sing,
For I have bene at Cristes bering;
Home to my felowes now will I fling.
Crist of heven to his bliss us bring!'
Ut hoy!
For in his pipe he made so much joy.

53. *hat* = hight, am called.

LXVIII

Christo paremus cantica,
In excelsis gloria.

WHEN Crist was born of Mary free
In Bedlem in that faire citė,
Angelles song ever with mirth and glee
In excelsis gloria.

Herdmen beheld thes angelles bright
To hem apperėd with gret light,
And seid 'Goddes sone is born this night.'
In excelsis gloria.

This king is comen to save kinde,
In the scriptur as we finde;
Therefore this song have we in minde,
In excelsis gloria.

Then, Lord, for thy gret grace,
Graunt us the bliss to see thy face,
Where we may sing to thy solas
In excelsis gloria.

LXIX

Lullay, mine liking, my dere sone, mine sweting,
Lullay, my dere herte, mine owen dere derling!

I SAW a fair maiden
Sitten and singe,
Sche lullėd a litel child,
A swetė lording.

That echė lord is that
That made allė thinge;
Of allė lordės he is lord,
Of allė kingės king.

There was mekel melody
At that childės berthe;
Allė tho wern in hevenė bliss
They made mekel merthe.

Aungele bright they song that night,
And seiden to that child,
'Blessėd be thou, and so be sche
That is bothe meke and mild.'

Prey we now to that child,
And to his moder dere,
Graunt hem his blessing
That now maken chere.

7. *echė*, eternal.

LXX

Gloria tibi domine
Qui natus es de virgine!

A LITEL childe there is ibore,
Isprونge out of Jesses more,
To save alle us that were forlore.
Gloria tibi domine.

Jhesus that is so fulle of might
Ibore he was aboute midnight;
The angel songe with alle here might
Gloria tibi domine.

Jhesus is that childės name,
Maide and moder is his dame,
And so oure sorow is turned to game.
Gloria tibi domine.

Three kinges there came with here presence,
Of mirre and golde and frankencense,
As clerkės singe in here sequence
Gloria tibi domine.

Now sitte we downe upon oure knee,
And pray that child that is so free;
And with gode hertė now sing we
Gloria tibi domine.

4. *more*, stock.

LXXI

Tidinges, tidinges that be true,
Sorowe is paste and joye dothe renue.

QWHEREAS Adam causėd be sinne
Oure nature thus to be mortall,
A maiden sone dothe nowe begin
For to repaire us from that fall.
And that is true;
The name of him is Criste Jesu.

Sume of oure kinde hathe hadd suche grase
That sin his birthe they did him se
Bothe sonne and mother fase to fase
In the chefe citė calde Jure.
And that is true;
Bothe kinges and schepardes they it knue.

The prophettes thereof ware nothing dismaide,
Of that tidinges before that they hadde tolde;
For nowe it is full righte as they saide,
A clenė maide hathe borne a king in folde.
And that is true;
For he is borne to ware the purpull hue.

LXXII

Jesu, almighty king of bliss,
Assumpsit carnem virginis.

As holy kirkė makės mind,
Intravit ventris thalamum.
Fro heven to erthe to save monkind
Pater misit filium.

Of Mary milde Criste wolde be borne
Sine virili semine,
To save monkind that was forlorne
Prime parentis crimine.

To Mary come a messenger,
Ferens salutem homini;
Sche aunswerd him with mildė chere,
'*Ecce ancilla domini.*'

'Mekely on thee tho holy goste,
Palacium intrans uteri.
Of allė thing mekenes is moste
In conspectu altissimi.'

When he was borne that made all thing,
Pastor creator omnium,
Angellės they began to sing
'*Veni redemptor gencium.*'

Three kingės come on goid twelfth day,
Stella micante previa;
To seche that childe they toke tho wey,
Portantes sibi munera.

A sterne forth ladde theis kingės all,
Inquirentes dominum;
Lying in an assė stall
Invenerunt puerum.

For he was king of kingės hight,
Rex primus aurum optulit;
And allso lord and king full right,
Secundus rex thus pertulit.

For he was Godde, mon and king,
Mirra mortem retulit.
He hus all to hevenė bring,
Qui mortem cruce voluit.

LXXIII

Blessèd be that lady bright,
That bare a child of great might,
Withouten peine, as it was right,
Maid moder Marye.

GODDÈS sonne is borne;
His moder is a maid
Both after and beforne,
As the prophecy said.
With ay!
A wonder thing it is to see
How maiden and moder one may be;
Was there never nonne but she
Maid moder Marye.

This great lord of heaven
Our servant is becom,
Thorow Gabriels steven
Our kind hath benom.
With ay!
A wonder thing it is to see
How lord and servant one may be;
Was there never nonne but he,
Born of maid Marye.

16. *steven*, message. 17. *benom*, taken.

Two suns together
  They ought to shinė bright;
So did that fair ladye,
  Whan Jesu in her light.
    With ay!
A wonder thing is fall;
The lord that boughtė free and thrall
Is found in an assės stall
  By his moder Marye.

The sheperdes in her region
  They lokėd into heaven;
They see an angell comming down,
  That said with mildė steven,
    'With ay!
Joy be to God almight,
And pece in yerth to man is dite,
For God was born on Chrismes night
  Of his moder Marye.'

Three kinges of great noblay,
  Whan that child was born,
To him they tok the redy way
  And knelėd him beforn.
    With ay!
These three kinges cam fro fare,
Thorow leding of a stare,
And offered him gold, encence, and mure,
  And to his moder Marye.

32. *her*, their. 38. *dite*, prepared.

LXXIV

Nowel sing we now all and sum
For *rex pacificus* is cum.

IN Bedleem, in that fair cetė,
A child was born of a maden free,
That schall a lord and princė be
A solis ortus cardine.

Children were slain full grete plentė,
Jhesu, for the love of thee.
Wherfore here soulės savėd be,
Hostis Herodes impie.

As sunnė schineth throw the glass,
So Jhesu in his moder was.
Thee to serve now graunt us gras,
O lux beata trinitas!

Now God is comen to wurchepen us,
Now of Marye is born Jhesus.
Make we mery amongės us;
Exultet celum laudibus.

9. *here*, their.

LXXV

Singe we all, for time it is,
Mary hath born the flour-de-lyce.

FOR his love that bought us all dere,
Listen, lordinges that ben here,
And I will tell you in fere,
Where of cam the flour-de-lyce.

On Cristmas night, whan it was cold,
Our Lady lay amonge bestes bolde,
And there she bare Jesu, Joseph tolde,
And there of cam the flour-de-lyce.

Of that bereth witnesse Seint Johan,
That it was of much renown ;
Baptized he was in flome Jordan,
And there of cam the flour-de-lyce.

On Good Friday that child was slain,
Beten with skorges and all to-flain
That day he suffred muchė pain,
And there of cam the flour-de-lyce.

5. *in fere*, in company. 16. *to-flain*, flayed to pieces.
13. *flome*, river.

LXXVI

Nowel, el, el, el, el,
I thank it a maiden every del.

THE first day whan Crist was borne,
There sprong a rose out of a thorne,
To save mankind that was forlorne.
I thanke it a maiden every del.

In an oxstall the child was found;
In pore clothing the child was wound;
He sofered many a dedly wound.
I thanke it a maiden every del.

A garlond of thornes on his hed was sett;
A scharp spere to his hart was smet;
The Jewės seiden 'Take thee that!'
I thanke it a maiden every del.

The Jewes deden cryen her parlament;
On the day of jugėment
They werren aferd, they shuld hem schent.
I thanke it a maiden every del.

To the peler he was bounden;
To his hart a spere was stunggen;
For us he sofered a dedly wounden.
I thanke it a maiden every del.

2. *del*, deal, bit.

LXXVII

Moder, white as lily flour,
Your lulling lesseth my langour.

AS I up rose in a morning,
My thought was on a maidė ying,
That song aslepe with her lulling
Her derė sone, our Saviour.

As she him toke all in her lap,
He toke that maiden be the pap,
And toke thereof a right god nap,
And soke his fille of that licour.

To his moder than he gan say,
'For this milk me mustė deye;
It is my kind therewith to play,
My swete moder, my par amour.'

The maiden freely gan to sing,
And in her song she made morning,
How he that is our heven king
Shuld shed his blod with grete dolour.

'Your weping, moder, greveth me sore;
But I wold deye, ye wern forlore.
Do way, moder, and wepe no more!
Your lulling lesseth my langour.'

LXXVIII

'O my harte is wo!'
Mary she said so,
'For to see my dere son die,
And sones have I no mo.'

WHEN that my swetė sone
Was thirty winter old,
Than the traitor Judas
Wexėd very bold;
For thirty plates of money
His master he had sold.
But whan I it wist,
Lord, my hart was cold!

Upon Shere Thursday
Than truly it was,
On my sonnės deth
That Judas did compass.
Many were the fals Jewes
That folowed him by trace,
And there beffore them all
He kissed my sonnės face.

My son beffore Pilat
Brought was he,
And Peter said three times
He knew him not, parde.
Pilat said unto the Jewes
'What say ye?'
They criėd with one voice,
'*Crucifige, crucifige.*'

On Good Friday
  At the mount of Calvary
My son was don on the crosse,
  Nailėd with nailės three.
Of all the frendės that he had
  Never one could he see,
But jentill John the evangelist
  That still stode him by.

Though I were sorowfull,
  No man have at it wonder ;
For houge was the erth quake,
  Horible was the thonder.
I loked on my swete son
  On the crosse that I stode under ;
Then cam Lungeus with a spere
  And clift his hart in sonder.

LXXIX

SODENLY afraid,
Halfe wakinge halfe sleping,
And gretly dismayd,
A woman sate weping,
With favour in her face far passinge my reson
And of her sore weping this was the encheson.
Her sone in her lappe laid, sche seid, slein by treson,
If weping might ripe be, hit semed then in seson.
Jhesus, so sche sobbed,
So her sone was bobbed
And of his live robbed ;
Seinge this wordes as I sey thee,
'Who can not wepe, com lerne of me.'

I seid I coude not wepe, I was so hard herted.
Sche answerd me schortly with wordės that smarted,
'Lo, nature schall meve thee, thau must be converted,
Thine owne fader this night is dede?' This sche thwerted.
'Jhesus, so my sone is bobbed,
And of his live robbed,
For soth then I sobbed
Verifying this wordes, seing to thee,
Who can not wepe com lerne at me.

6. *encheson*, cause.
10. *bobbed*, mocked, scorned.
17. *thwerted*, retorted (?).

'Now breke hert, I thee praye! this cors lieth so rewlie,
So beten, so wounded, entreted so fuly.
What wight may behold, and wepe not? None truly,
To see my ded dere sone bledinge, lo, this newly.'
Ever stille sche sobbed,
So her sone was bobbed
And of his live robbed.
Newing these wordes, as I sey thee,
'Who can not wepe, com lerne at me.'

On me sche cast her ye, and seid 'See, man, thy brother!'
Sche kiste him and seid 'Swete, am I not thy moder?'
And swoninge sche felle; ther hit wold be no nother.
I not which more dedlie, the tone or the toder.
Yett sche revived and sobbed
How her sone was bobbed
And of his live robbed.
'Who can not wepe,' this is the lay,
And with that wordes sche vanisched away.

23. *rewlie*, pitiable. 32. *ye*, eye.

LXXX

Mary moder, cum and see!
Thy son is nailėd on a tree.

HIS body is wappėd all in wo,
Hand and fote he may not go.
Thy son, lady, that thou lovest so
Naked is nailed upon a tree.

The blessėd body that thou hast born,
To save mankind that was forlorn,
His body, lady, is all to-torn,
His hed with thornes, as ye may see.

Whan Johan his tale began to tell,
Mary wuld not lenger dwell
Till sche cam to that hill
There sche might her owen son see.

'My swetė son, thou art me dere,
Why have men hangėd thee here?
Thy hed is closėd with a brere.
Why have men so doo to thee?'

'Johan, this woman I thee betake;
Kepe this woman for my sake.
On the rode I hing for mannės sake,
For sinful men as thou may see.

3. *wappėd*, wrapped. 19. *betake*, entrust to.

'This game alone me mustė pley,
For sinfull soules that are to dey.
There is no man that gothe be the wey
  That on my peines will loke and see.

'Fader, my soule I thee betake,
My body deth for mannės sake;
To hell I go withouten wake,
  Mannės soule to makė free.'

Prey we all to that blessėd sone,
That he help us whan we not mon,
And bring us to bliss that is abone.
  Amen, amen, amen, for charite!

29. *wake*, funeral. 32. *mon*=*moun*, may.

LXXXI

Lully, lulley, lully, lulley,
The faucon hath borne my make away.

HE bare him up, he bare him down,
He bare him into an orchard brown.

In that orchard there was an halle,
That was hangėd with purpill and pall.

And in that hall there was a bede,
It was hangėd with gold so rede.

And in that bed there lithe a knight,
His woundės bleding day and night.

By that bede side kneleth a may,
And she wepeth both night and day.

And by that bede side there stondeth a stone,
Corpus Christi wreten there on.

2. *make*, mate.

LXXXII

Alas, my hart will brek in three.
Terribilis mors conturbat me.

ILLA juventus that is so nise
Me deduxit into vain devise;
Infirmus sum, I may not rise.
Terribilis mors conturbat me.

Dum juvenis fui litell I dred,
Sed semper in sinnės I ete my bred;
Jam ductus sum into my bed.
Terribilis mors conturbat me.

Corpus migrat in my soule;
Respicit demon in his roule,
Desiderat ipse to have his tolle.
Terribilis mors conturbat me.

Christus seipsum, whan he shuld die,
Patri suo his manhode did crye,
'*Respice me Pater* that is so hie.
Terribilis mors conturbat me.'

Quaeso jam the Trinity,
Duc me from this vanity
In celum, there is joy with thee.
Terribilis mors conturbat me.

12. *roule*, book.

LXXXIII

In what state that ever I be,
Timor mortis conturbat me.

AS I me walked in one morning,
I hard a birde both wepe and singe.
This was the tenor of her talkinge,
Timor mortis conturbat me.

I askėd this birde what he ment.
He said 'I am a musket gent;
For dred of deth I am nigh shent;
Timor mortis conturbat me.'

Jesu Crist, whan he shuld die,
To his Fader loud gan he crye;
'Fader,' he said, 'in Trinity,
Timor mortis conturbat me.'

Whan I shall die know I no day,
Therefore this songe sing I may;
In what place or contrey can I not say.
Timor mortis conturbat me.

8. *musket*, sparrow-hawk. 9. *shent*, destroyed.

LXXXIV

IN a valey of this restles minde
  I soughte in mounteine and in mede,
Trustinge a trewe love for to finde.
  Upon an hill than I took hede;
  A voice I herde, and neer I yede,
In huge dolour complaininge tho,
  'See, derė soule, how my sides blede,
Quia amore langueo.'

Upon this hill I fond a tree,
  Under the tree a man sittinge;
From heed to foot wounded was he;
  His hertė blood I segh bledinge;
  A semely man to ben a king,
A graciouse face to loken unto.
  I askede why he had peininge.
He seide '*Quia amore langueo.*

'I am true love that fals was nevere;
  My sister, mannes soule, I loved her thus;
Because we wolde in no wise discevere,
  I lefte my kingdom glorious.
  I purveide for her a paleis precious;
Sche fleith, I folowe, I soughte her so;
  I suffrede this peinė piteuous,
Quia amore langueo.

5. *yede*, went.

'I crowned her with bliss, and sche me with thorn;
I ledde her to chaumber, and sche me to die;
I broughte her to worschipe, and sche me to scorn;
I dide her reverence, and sche me vilonie.
To love that loveth is no maistrie.
Her hate made nevere my love her fo.
Axė me no questioun why,
Quia amore langueo.

'I wole abide till sche be redy;
I wole her sue if sche seie nay;
If sche be recheless, I wole be gredy,
And if sche be daungerus, I wole her praie.
If sche wepe, that hide I ne may,
Mine armės her hirėd to clippe her me to,
Crie oonės, 'I come;' now, soule, asay!
Quia amore langueo.

'I sitte on this hill for to see fer;
I loke into the valey my spouse to see;
Now renneth sche awayward, yet come sche me neer,
For out of my sighte may sche not flee.
Summe waite her pray to make her to flee;
I rennė bifore, and fleme her fo.
Returnė, my spouse, ayen to me,
Quia amore langueo.

35. *recheless*, reckless, careless. 46. *fleme*, put to flight.

'Fair lovė, lete us go pleye!
  Apples ben ripe in my gardaine.
I schal thee clothe in a newe aray;
  Thy mete schall be milk, hony, and win.
  Fair lovė, lete us go digne!
Thy sustenaunce is in my crippe, lo!
  Tarie thou not, my faire spouse mine,
Quia amore langueo.

'If thou be foul, I schall thee make clene;
  If thou be sik, I schall thee hele;
If thou moorne ought, I schall thee meene.
  Why wolt thou not, fair love, with me dele?
  Foundest thou evere love so leel?
What woldest thou, spouse, that I schulde do?
  I may not unkindely thee appele,
Quia amore langueo.

'What schall I do with my fair spouse,
  But abide her of my gentilness,
Till that sche loke out of her house
  Of fleischly affeccioun? Love mine sche is.
  Her bed is made, her bolster is bliss,
Her chaumber is chosen; is there none mo?
  Loke out on me at the window of kindeness,
Quia amore langueo.

'My love is in her chaumber. Hold youre pees;
  Make ye no noise, but lete her slepe.
My babe I wolde not were in disese;
  I may not heere my dere child wepe.
  With my pap I schall her kepe.
Ne merveille ye not though I tend her to.
  This hole in my side had nevere be so depe
But *quia amore langueo.*

'Longe thou for lovė nevere so high,
  My love is more than thine may be;
Thou wepest, thou gladest, I sitte thee by,
  Yet woldest thou oonės, leef, loke unto me!
  Schuldė I alwey fedė thee
With children mete? Nay, love, not so!
  I wole preve thy love with adversitė,
Quia amore langueo.

'Wexė not wery, mine ownė wife!
  What mede is it to live evere in coumfort?
In tribulacioun I regne moore rife
  Oftėtimės than in disport.
  In wele and in wo I am ay to supporte.
Mine ownė wife, go not me fro!
  Thy meede is markėd whan thou art mort,
Quia amore langueo.'

LXXXV

I HAVE set my hert so hie
  Me liket no love that lowere is,
And alle the paines that I may drie,
  Me thenk hit do me good iwis;
For on that lorde that loved us alle
  So hertely have I set my thowght,
It is my joye on him to calle,
  For love me hath in balus browght.
    Me thenk it do iwis.

3. *drie*=*dree*, endure.

LXXXVI

She may be called a sovereign lady,
That is a maid and beareth a baby.

A MAID peerless
Hath borne God's son.
Nature gave place,
When ghostly grace
Subdued reason.

As for beauty,
Or high gentry,
She is the flower
By God elect
For this effect,
Man to succour.

Of virgins queen,
Lodestar of light,
Whom to honour
We ought endeavour
Us day and night.

LXXXVII

'Ah my dear, ah my dear son,'
Said Mary, 'ah my dear,
Kiss thy mother, Jesu,
With a laughing cheer!'

THIS enders night
I saw a sight
All in my sleep;
Mary, that may,
She sang 'Lullay'
And sore did weep.

To keep she sought
Full fast about
Her son fro cold.
Joseph said 'Wife,
My joy, my life,
Say what ye wold.'

'No thing, my spouse,
Is in this house
Unto my pay;
My son, a king
That made all thing,
Lieth in hay.'

17. *pay*, liking.

'My mother dear,
Amend your cheer,
And now be still;
Thus for to lie
It is soothly
My Father's will.

'Derision,
Great passion,
Infinitely,
As it is found,
Many a wound
Suffer shall I.

'On Calvary
That is so high
There shall I be,
Man to restore,
Nailėd full sore
Upon a tree.'

LXXXVIII

In youth, in age, both in wealth and woe,
Auxilium meum a Domino.

THOUGH poets feign that Fortune by her chance
And her freewill doth oppress and advance,
Fortune doth miss her will and liberty.
Then trust to Virtue; let Fortune go!
Auxilium meum a Domino.

Of grace divine, with heavenly assistance,
If Virtue do remain, Virtue all way
When she list may call Fortune's chance again.
What force I then, though Fortune be my foe.
Auxilium meum a Domino.

11. *force*, care.

LXXXIX

PLEASURE it is
 To hear, iwis,
 The birdės sing.
The deer in the dale,
The sheep in the vale,
 The corn springing;
God's purveyance
For sustenance
 It is for man.
Then we always
To him give praise,
 And thank him than,
 And thank him than.

WILLIAM CORNISH.

MORAL LYRICS

I stond as still as ony stone,
The grace of God than he will send.
All thing may not cum anone,
But wane God will it may amend.
    Lex is leyd adowne,
    And *veritas* is but small;
    Amor is owt of towne,
    And *caritas* is gon with all.

The Boke of Brome.

MORAL

XC

UBI SOUNT QUI ANTE NOS FUEROUNT?

WERE beth they biforen us weren,
Houndės ladden and hauekės beren,
And hadden feld and wode,
The richė levedies in hoere bour,
That wereden gold in hoere tressour,
With hoere brighttė rode?

Eten and drounken and maden hem glad;
Hoere lif was al with gamen ilad;
Men keneleden hem biforen;
They beren hem wel swithė heye;
And in a twincling of an eye
Hoere soulės weren forloren.

Were is that lawing and that song,
That trayling and that proudė yong,
Tho hauekės and tho houndes?
Al that joye is went away,
That wele is comen to welaway
To manie hardė stoundes.

4. *hoere*, their.
6. *rode*, complexion.
10. *swithė*, very.
13. *lawing*, laughing.
18. *stoundes*, pains.

Hoere paradis they nomen here,
And nou they lien in hellė fere;
The fuir hit brennės hevere.
Long is ay and long is ho,
Long is wy and long is wo;
Thennės ne cometh they nevere.

Dreghy here man, thenne, if thou wilt,
A luitel pinė, that me the bit;
Withdrau thine eysės ofte.
They thi pinė be ounrede,
And thou thenkė on thi mede,
Hit sal the thinken softe.

If that fend, that foulė thing,
Thorou wikkė roun, thorou fals egging,
There ne there the haveth icast,
Oup, and be god championn!
Stond, ne fal namore adoun
For a luytel blast!

Thou tak the rodė to thi staf,
And thenk on him that thereoune yaf
His lif that wes so lef!
He hit yaf for the; thou yelde hit him!
Ayein his fo that staf thou nim,
And wrek him of that thef!

19. *nomen*, took.
20, 21. *fere*, *fuir*, fire.
21. *brennės*, burns.
25. *Dreghy*, endure.
26. *pinė*, pain.
27. *eysės*, ease.
28. *ounrede*, bitter.
29. *mede*, reward.
32. *roun*, secret, charm.
37. *rodė*, rood, cross.
38. *lef*, dear.
41. *nim*, take,

Of rightte bileve thou nim that sheld,
The wiles that thou best in that feld,
  Thin hond to strenkthen fonde!
    And kep thy fo with stavės ord,
    And do that traytre seien that word,
  Biget that murie londe!

Thereinne is day withouten night,
Withouten endė, strenkthe and might,
  And wreche of everich fo,
    Mid god himselwen echė lif,
    And pas and rest withoutė strif,
  Welė withouten wo.

Mayden moder, hevenė quene,
Thou might and const and owest to bene
  Oure sheld ayein the fende.
    Help ous sunnė for to flen,
    That we moten thi sone iseen,
  In joye withouten hende!
                Amen!

46. *ord*, point, tip.

XCI

LOLLAI, lollai, litil child!
  Whi wepistou so sore?
Nedis mostou wepe,
  Hit was iyarkid the yore
Ever to lib in sorow,
  And sich and mourne evere,
As thin eldren did er this,
  Whil hi alivės were.
    Lollai, lollai, litil child,
      Child, lolai, lullow!
    Into uncuth world
      Icommen so ertow.

Bestis and thos foules,
  The fisses in the flode,
And euch schef alivės
  Makid of bone and blode,
Whan hi commith to the world
  Hi doth ham silf sum gode,
Al bot the wrech brol
  That is of Adamis blode.
    Lollai, lollai, litil child!
      To kar ertow bemette;
    Thou nost noght this worldis wild
      Bifor the is isette.

4. *iyarkid*, prepared, ordained.
12. *ertow*, art thou.
15. *schef*, creature.
19. *brol*, child.

Child, if it betidith
  That thou ssalt thrive and the,
Thench thou wer ifostred
  Up thi moder kne;
Ever hab mund in thi hert
  Of thos thingės thre,
Whan thou commist, whan thou art,
  And what ssal com of the.
    Lollai, lollai, litil child,
      Child, lollai, lollai!
    With sorow thou com into this world,
      With sorow ssalt wend awai.

Ne tristou to this world;
  Hit is thi ful fo.
The rich he makith pouer,
  The porė rich also.
Hit turneth wo to wel,
  And ekė wel to wo.
Ne trist no man to this world,
  Whil hit turnith so.
    Lollai, lollai, litil child!
      The fote is in the whele.
    Thou nost whoder turne
      To wo other wele.

26 *the*, prosper.   29. *mund*, memory.

Child, thou ert a pilgrim
In wikidnis ibor;
Thou wandrest in this fals world;
Thou lokė the bifor.
Deth ssal com with a blast
Ute of a wel dim horre,
Adamis kin dun to cast,
Him silf hath ido befor.
Lollai, lollai, litil child!
So wo the worth Adam
In the lond of Paradis
Throgh wikidnes of Satan.

Child, thou nert a pilgrim,
Bot an uncuthe gist;
Thi dawės beth itold;
Thi iurneis beth icast.
Whoder thou salt wend,
North other est,
Deth the sal betide,
With bitter bale in brest.
Lollai, lollai, litil child!
This wo Adam the wroght,
Whan he of the appil ete,
And Eve hit him betacht.

54. *horre*, mist, fog, cloud. 72. *betacht*, gave.
63. *dawės*, days.

XCII

WYNTER wakeneth al my care;
Nou this levės waxeth bare;
Ofte I sike and mournė sare,
When hit cometh in my thoght
Of this worldes ioie, hou hit geth al to noht.

Nou hit is, and nou hit nys,
Also hit ner nere ywys.
That moni man seith, soth hit is,
Al goth bote Godės wille.
Allė we shulė deye, thah us like ylle.

Al that gren me greveth grene,
Now hit faleueth al by dene.
Jesu, help that hit be sene,
Ant shild us from helle,
For I not whider I shal, ne hou longe her duelle!

8. *soth*, truth. 10. *thah*, though.
12. *faleueth*, fades: *by dene*, at once.

XCIII

THE lif of this world
  Ys reulėd with wynd,
Wepinge, derknesse,
  And steriinge ;
With wind we blomen,
  With wind we lassun ;
With weopinge we comen,
  With weopinge we passun.
With steriinge we byginnen,
  With steriinge we enden,
With drede we dwellen,
  With drede we wenden.

3. *steriinge*, pang, throe.

XCIV

Memento homo quod sinis es
Et in cenerem reverteris.

ERTHE oute of erthe is wondirly wroghte,
Erthe has geten one erthe a dignite of noghte,
Erthe appon erthe hase sett alle his thoghte,
How that erthe appon erthe may be heghe broghte.

Erthe appon erthe wolde be a kinge;
Bot howe erthe to erthe sall, thinkes he no thinge.
When erthe bredes erthe, and his rentes home bringe,
Thane schalle erthe of erthe hafe full harde partinge.

Erthe appon erthe winnes castells and tourres,
Thane saise erthe unto erthe 'This is alle ourres';
When erthe appon erthe hase bigged up his bourres,
Thane shalle erthe for erthe suffere scharpe scourres.

Erthe gos appon erthe as golde appon golde.
He that gose appon erthe gleterande as golde,
Like as erthe never more go to erthe scholde,
And yitt schall erthe unto erthe ga rathere than he wolde.

Now why that erthe luffes erthe, wondere me thinke,
Or why that erthe for erthe scholde other swete or swinke;
For when that erthe appon erthe is broghte within brinke,
Thane shall erthe of erthe hafe a foulle stinke.

Mors Solvit Omnia.

XCV

BALADE DE BON CONSEYL.

FLEE fro the prees, and dwelle with sothfastnesse;
Suffyce unto thy thyng, though hit be smal,
For hord hath hate, and climbing tikelnesse,
Prees hath envye, and welė blent overal;
Savour no more than thee bihovė shal;
Werk wel thy self, that other folk canst rede;
And trouthė shal delivere, hit is no drede.

Tempest thee noght al crokėd to redresse,
In trust of hir that turneth as a bal.
Gret restė stant in litel besinesse;
And eek be war to sporne ageyn an al;
Stryve noght, as doth the crokkė with the wal.
Dauntė thy self, that dauntest otherės dede;
And trouthė shal delivere, hit is no drede.

That thee is sent, receyve in buxumnesse;
The wrastling for this worlde axeth a fal.
Her nis non hoom, her nis but wildernesse.
Forth, pilgrim, forth! Forth, beste, out of thy stal!
Know thy contree, look up, thank God of al;
Hold the hye wey, and lat thy gost thee lede;
And trouthė shal delivere, hit is no drede.

1. *prees*, crowd.
4. *blent*, blinded.
8. *Tempest*, vex.
12. *crokkė*, earthenware pot.

ENVOY.

Therfore, thou vache, leve thyn old wrecchednesse
Unto the world; leve now to be thral;
Crye him mercy, that of his hy goodnesse
Made thee of noght, and in especial
Draw unto him, and pray in general
For thee, and eek for other, hevenlich mede;
And trouthė shal delivere, hit is no drede.

GEOFFREY CHAUCER.

22. *vache*, animal.

XCVI

GENTILESSE.

THE firstė stok, fader of gentilesse,
What man that claymeth gentil for to be,
Must folowe his trace, and alle his wittės dresse
Vertu to sewe, and vyces for to flee;
For unto vertu longeth dignitee,
And noght the revers, saufly dar I deme,
Al were he mytre, croune, or diademe.

This firstė stok was ful of rightwisnesse,
Trewe of his word, sobre, pitous, and free,
Clene of his goste, and lovėd besinesse,
Ageinst the vyce of slouthe, in honestee;
And, but his heir love vertu, as dide he,
He nis noght gentil, thogh he richė seme,
Al were he mytre, croune, or diademe.

Vycė may wel be heir to old richesse;
But ther may no man, as men may wel see,
Bequethe his heir his vertuous noblesse
That is appropréd unto no degree,
But to the firstė fader in magestee,
That maketh him his heir, that can him queme,
Al were he mytre, croune, or diademe.

GEOFFREY CHAUCER.

20. *queme*, please.

XCVII

LAK OF STEDFASTNESSE.

SOM tyme this world was so stedfast and stable,
That mannės word was obligacioun,
And now hit is so fals and deceivable,
That word and deed, as in conclusioun,
Ben nothyng oon, for turnėd up so doun
Is al this world throgh mede and wilfulnesse,
That al is lost for lak of stedfastnesse.

What maketh this world to be so variable,
But lust that folk have in dissensioun?
Among us now a man is holde unable,
But if he can, by som collusioun,
Don his neighbour wrong or oppressioun.
What causeth this, but wilful wrecchednesse,
That al is lost, for lak of stedfastnesse?

Trouthe is put doun, resoun is holden fable;
Vertu hath now no dominacioun,
Pitee exyled, no man is merciable.
Through covetyse is blent discrecioun;
The world hath mad a permutacioun
Fro right to wrong, fro trouthe to fikelnesse,
That al is lost, for lak of stedfastnesse.

18. *blent*, blinded.

L'ENVOY TO KING RICHARD.

O prince, desire to be honourable,
Cherish thy folk and hate extorcioun !
Suffre no thyng, that may be reprevable
To thyn estat, don in thy regioun.
Shew forth thy swerd of castigacioun,
Dred God, do law, love trouthe and worthynesse,
And wed thy folk ageyn to stedfastnesse.

GEOFFREY CHAUCER.

24. *reprevable*, prejudicial.

XCVIII

NOW is wele and all thing aright
And Crist is come as a trew knight,
For our broder is king of might,
The fend to fleme and all his.
Thus the feend is put to flight,
And all his boost abated is.

Sithen it is wele, wele we do,
For there is none but one of two,
Heven to gete or heven forgo;
Oder mene none there is.
I counsaill you, sin it is so,
That ye wele do to win you bliss.

Now is wele and all is wele,
And right wele, so have I bliss;
And sithen all thing is so wele,
I rede we do no more amiss.

4. *fleme*, banish. 16. *rede*, advise.

XCIX

WOLD God that men might sene
Hertės whan they bene,
For thinges that bene untrew.
If it be as I wene,
Thing that semeth grene
Is ofte faded of hew.

Will is tak for reson;
Trew love is full geson;
No man sett be shame.
Trost is full of treson;
Eche man oderes cheson;
No man him seilfe will blame.

This warlde is variabell;
Nothing therein is stable,
Asay now who so will.
Sin it is so mutable,
How shuld me be stable?
It may not be thorow skill.

Whan brȯme will appelles bere,
And humloke hony in fere,
Than seke rest in lond.
With men is no pees;
Ne rest in hart is, no lese,
With few be see and sond.

8. *geson*, scarce.
11. *cheson*, accuse.
18. *skill*, reason.
24. *be see and sond*, by sea and sand.

Sithen there is no rest,
I hold it for the best,
God to be our frend.
He that is our Lord,
Deliver us out with his word,
And graunt us a good ende !

C

Gay, gay, gay, gay,
Think on dredful domės day!

EVERY day thou might lere
To helpe thy self while thou art here;
Whan thou art ded and leid on bere,
Crist help thy soule, for thou ne may!

Think, man, on thy wittės five;
Do sum good whil thou art on live;
Go to cherche, and do thee schrive,
And bring thy soule in good aray.

Think, man, on thy sinnės sevene;
Think how merie it is in hevene;
Prey to God with mildė stevene
To be thine helpe on domės day.

Lokė that thou non thing stere,
Ne non fals witnessė bere;
Think how Crist was stunge with spere,
Whan he deyed on Good Friday.

Lokė that thou ne slee non man,
Ne do non foly with non womman;
Think the blode from Jhesu ran
Whan he deyed withouten nay.

3. *lere*, learn.
13. *stevene*, voice.
15. *stere*, stir up, excite.

CI

God that allė mitės may
Helpe us at our ending daye.

THIS world, lordinges, I understonde,
May be likenėd to an husbonde
That taketh a ferme into his honde
To yeldė thereof sertein pay.

Spende we neither speche ne spille,
Neither for good ne for ille.
We schuln yeven acountės grille
Beforn our Lord on domės daye.

Levė lordinges, be ware of this,
For often time we don amiss;
There is non of us, iwis,
But that we trespasen every day.

This world, lordinges, is but a farye;
It fareth right as a neische weye,
That now is wet and now is dreye,
For sothe sertein as I you say.

Now is joye and now is bliss;
Now is balle and bitternesse;
Now it is, and now it nis;
Thus paseth this world away.

9. *grille*, painful.
11. *levė*, dear.
15. *farye*, enchanted place.
16. *neische*, soft.

Now I hoppe and now I singe;
Now I dauncė, now I springe;
Now I weile and now I wringe;
  Now is wele and now is way.

Now I hoppe and now I daunce;
Now I preke and now I praunce.
This day heil, tomorwe perchaunce
  We moun be ded and ley in clay.

At domės day whan we schul rise,
And come beforn our heye justise,
And yeven acountes of our servise,
  And payen up our lastė pay,

Help us, Mary, for than is nede;
Help to excusen our misdede;
As thou art moneyere at our nede,
  Help us than, and sey not nay!

26. *way*, woe.
37. *moneyere*, intercessor.

CII

Man, be ware, ere thou be wo ;
Think on pride and let him go !

PRIDE is out, and pride is in,
And pride is rote of every sinne,
And pride will never blinne
Till he hath brought a man in wo.

Lucifer was aungel bright,
And conqueror of meché might ;
Throw his pride he les his light
And fil doun into endeless wo.

Wenest thou for thy gaye clothing,
And for thine grete othės swering,
To be a lord or a king ;
Litil it schall availe thee to.

Whan thou schalt to cherchė glide,
Wermės schuln etė throw thy side,
And litil schall availe thy pride,
Or ony sinnes that thou hast do.

Prey to Crist, with blody side,
And othere woundės grile and wide,
That he foryevė thee thy pride
And thy sinnes that thou hast do.

20. *grile*, painful.

CIII

I durke, I dare, so well I may,
When I thinke on mine ending day.

I AM a child, and born full bare,
And bare out of this world schall fare;
Yet am I but wermės ware,
Thow I clothėd go never so gay.

Thow I be of mechė prise,
Fair of face, and holden wise,
Mine fleich schall faden as flour-de-lys,
Whan I am ded and leid in clay.

Whan I am ded and leid in stone,
I schall roten fleich and bone,
Fro mine frendes I schall gone.
Crist help mine soule whan I ne may!

Whan I schall all my frendes forsake,
Crist schild me fro the fendės blake!
To Jhesu Crist my soule I betake,
He be our help on domės day.

1. *durke*, lie in darkness: *dare*, lurk. 17. *betake*, give.

CIV

Be ware, squier, yeman, and page,
For servise is none eritage!

IF thou serve a lord of prise,
  Be not too boistous in thine servise,
Damne not thine soule in none wise,
  For servise is none eritage.

Winteres wether and wommanes thought
And lordės lovė chaungeth oft.
This is the sothe, if it be sought,
  For servise is none eritage.

Now thou art grete, tomorwe schall I,
As lordės chaungen here baly;
In thine welthe werk sekerly,
  For servise is none eritage.

Than serve we God in allė wise;
He schall us quiten our servise,
And yeven us giftės most of prise,
  Hevene to ben our eritage!

4. *boistous*, boisterous. 13. *sekerly*, securely.
12. *baly*, bailiff.

CV

Sinful man, for Godės sake,
I rede that thou amendės make.

THOW thou be king of tour and town,
Thow thou be king and were coroun,
I sette right not be thy renown,
But if thou wilt amendės make.

That thou hast here is othere menes,
And so it schall ben whan thou art hennes;
Thy soulė schall abeye thy sinnes,
But if thou wilt amendės make.

Thow thou be bothė stef and strong,
And many a man thou hast do wrong,
'Wellaway' schall be thy song,
But if thou wilt amendės make.

Man, be ware, the weye is sleder!
Thou schal slide thou wost not wheder;
Body and soule schul go togeder,
But if thou wilt amendės make.

Man, bere not thy hed too heye,
In pumpe and pride and velonie!
In helle thou schalt ben hangėd hie,
But if thou wilt amendės make.

2. *rede*, advise.
5. *not*, naught.
15. *sleder*, slippery.

CVI

God be with trewthė where he be!
I wolde he were in this cuntrė.

A MAN that schuld of trewthė telle,
With grete lordės he may not dwelle.
In trewė story as clerkės telle,
Trewthe is put in low degree.

In laydies chaumberes cometh he not;
There dare trewthė setten none fot.
Thow he woldė, he may not
Comen among the heye menė.

With men of lawe he hath non spas;
They loven trewthe in none plas;
Me thinketh they han a rewly grace
That trewthe is put at swich degree.

In holy cherche he may not sitte;
Fro man to man they schuln him flitte.
It reweth me sore in mine witte,
Of trewthe I have gret pitė.

Religious, that schulde be good,
If trewthe cum there, I holde him wood.
They schulden him rende cote and hood,
And make him bare for to flee.

10. *menė*=meinie, company.
13. *rewly*, pitiable.
20. *wood*, mad.

A man that schulde of trewthe aspie,
He must seken esilye
In the bosum of Marie,
  For there he is for sothe.

CVII

Abide I hope hit be the beste,
Sithe hasty man lakketh never wo.

LATE every man that wole have reste,
Ever ben avised what he wole do.

Preve or ye take ; thenke or ye feste ;
In wele be ware or ye be wo.

Under the busche ye shul tempeste
Abide til hit be over go.

For longe time your hert shal breste.
Abide, I consail you do so.

5. *Preve*, test.

CVIII

I may seyn, and so moun mo,
That in semenaunt goth gile.

SEMENAUNT is a wonder thing;
It begileth bothe knight and king,
And maketh maidenes of love-longing.
I warne you of that gile.

Semenaunt is a sly peintour,
It florcheth and fadeth in many a flour,
And maketh wommen to lesen here bright colour
Upon a litel while.

In semenaunt be thingės three;
Thought, speche, and previtė,
And trewthė schuld the fortė be;
It is hens a thousand mile.

Trewthe is fer and semeth hende;
Good and wikkit it hath in minde;
It fareth as a candele ende
That brenneth fro half a mile.

Many man faire to me he speketh,
And he wiste him well bewreke,
He had well levere mine hed to-breke
Than help me over a stile.

God that deyed upon the cross—
Ferst he deyed, sithen he ros—
Have mercy and pitė on us.
We leven here but a while.

2. *semenaunt*, semblance.
8. *florcheth*, flourisheth.
15. *fer*, far; *hende*, near.
20. *bewreke*, revenged.

CIX

Kepė thy tunge, thy tunge, thy tunge !
Thy wiked tunge werketh me wo.

THERE is none gres that groweth on ground,
Satenas ne peny round,
Wersse then is a wikked tunge,
That speketh bethe evil of frend and fo.

Wikked tunge maketh oftė strife
Betwixe a good man and his wife ;
Whan he schulde lede a merie life
Here white sidės waxen full blo.

Wikked tunge maketh oftė stauns
Bothe in Engelond and in Frauns.
Many a man with spere and launs,
Throw wikked tunge, to dede is do.

Wikked tungė breketh bone,
Thow the tungės self have none,
Of his friend he maketh his fon
In every place where that he go.

Good men that stonden and sitten in this halle,
I prey you bothe one and alle,
That wikked tungės fro you falle,
That ye moun to hevenė go.

10. *blo*, black and blue.
11. *stauns*, stoppage.
14. *dede*, death.
17. *fon*, foes.

CX

I hold him wise and well itaught,
Can bere an horn and blow it naught.

BLOWING was made for gretė game;
Of thy blowing cometh mekell grame;
Therefore I hold it for no schame
To bere a horne and blow it naught.

Hornes are made both loud and shill;
Whan time is, blow thou thy fill,
And whan nede is, hold thee still,
And bere a horne and blow it naught.

What so ever be in thy thought,
Here and see and sey right nought;
Then schall men sey thou art well taught
To bere a horne and blow it naught.

Of all the riches under the sun,
Than was there never beter wonne,
Than is a taught man for to conne
To bere a horne and blow it naught.

What so ever be in thy brest,
Stop thy mouth with thy fist,
And lok thou think well of had-I-wist,
And bere a horne and blow it naught.

And whan thou sittest at the ale,
And criest like a nighttingale,
Be ware to whom thou tellest thy tale,
But bere a horne and blow it naught.

4. *grame*, evil.
7. *shill*, shrill.
17. *conne*, know how.

CXI

Man, be ware and wise in dede;
Asay thy frend or thou hast nede.

UNDER a forest that was so long
As I me rode with mekell drede,
I hard a bird singing a song,
'Asay thy frend or thou hast nede.'

I there stode and hovèd still;
To a tree I teid my stede.
Ever the bird sang full shill,
'Asay thy frend or thou hast nede.'

Me thought it was a wonder noise;
Alwey nere and nere I yede;
And ever she song with loud vois,
'Asay thy frend or thou hast nede.'

I beheld that bird full long;
She bad me do as I thee rede,
Whether that thou do right or wrong,
Asay thy frend or thou hast nede.

The birdè sat upon a tree;
With fethers gray than was her wede;
She seid 'And thou wilt do after me,
Asay thy frend or thou have nede.'

9. *shill*, shrill.
12. *yede*, went.
16. *rede*, advise.

Of me I trow she was agast;
She toke her flight in length and brede;
And thus she sang whan she showed last,
'Asay thy frend or thou have nede.'

Away full fast she gan her highe.
God graunt us well our lives to lede!
For thus she sang, whan she gan flie,
'Asay thy frend or thou have nede.'

CXII

IN a time of a somers day,
The sune shon full merily that tide,
I took my hawke me for to play,
My spaniell renning by my side.
A feasaunt henne than gan I see;
My houndės put her sone to flight;
I lett my hawke unto her flee;
To me it was a deintė sight.

My faucon flewe fast unto her pray;
My hound gan rennė with glad chere;
And sone I spurnėd in my way;
My leg was hent all in a breer.
This breer forsothe it did me gref,
Iwis it made me to turn ayė,
For he bare writing in every leff,
This Latin word *Revertere*.

I haled and pulled this breer me fro,
And rede this word full merily.
My hart fell down unto my toe,
That was before full likingly.
I lett my hawke and feasaunt fare;
My spaniell fell down unto my knee;
It took me with a sighing fare,
This new lessun *Revertere*.

11. *spurnėd*, tripped.
12. *hent*, caught.
14. *ayė*, again.
23. *fare*, demeanour.

Liking is moder of sinnės all,
  And norse to every wiked dede;
To much mischefe she maketh men fall,
  And of sorow the daunce she doth lede.
This hawke of youth is high of porte;
  And wildness maketh him wide to flee,
And ofte to fall in wiked sorte;
  And then is best *Revertere*.

CXIII

I am as lighte as any roe
To preise womene where that I go.

TO onpreise womene it were a shame,
For a woman was thy dame.
Our blessèd lady bereth the name
Of all womene where that they go.

A woman is a worthy thing ;
They do the washe and do the wringe ;
'Lullay, lullay !' she dothe thee singe ;
And yet she hath but care and wo.

A woman is a worthy wight ;
She serveth a man both daye and night ;
Thereto she putteth alle her might ;
And yet she hath but care and wo.

CXIV

Wimmen beth bothe goude and truwe;
Witnesse on Marie.

WIMMEN beth bothe goud and schene,
On handės, fete, and facė clene;
Wimmen may no beter bene.
Witnesse on Marie.

Wimmen beth gentel on her tour;
A wimman bare oure Saviour;
Of all this world wimman is flour.
Witnesse on Marie.

Wirchip we wimmanės face,
Where we set hem on a place;
For wimman is the well of grace.
Witnesse on Marie.

Love a wimman with hertė truwe,
He nil chongė for no newe;
Wimmen beth of wordės fewe;
Witnesse on Marie.

Wimmen beth goud, withoute lesing;
Fro sorwe and care hi wol us bring;
Wimman is flour of allė thing,
Witnesse on Marie.

3. *schene*, fair. 20. *hi*, they.
16. *he*, she.

CXV

O DEATH, rock me a sleep,
  Bring me to quiet rest,
Let pass my weary guiltless ghost
  Out of my careful breast.
Toll on the passing bell;
Ring out my doleful knell;
Thy sound my death abroad will tell,
  For I must die,
  There is no remedy.

My pains who can express?
  Alas, they are so strong;
My dolours will not suffer strength
  My life for to prolong.
Toll on the passing bell;
Ring out my doleful knell;
Thy sound my death abroad will tell,
  For I must die,
  There is no remedy.

Alone in prison strong
  I wail my destiny.
Woe worth this cruel hap that I
  Must taste this misery!
Toll on the passing bell;
Ring out my doleful knell;
Thy sound my death abroad will tell,
  For I must die,
  There is no remedy.

Farewell, my pleasures past,
  Welcome, my present pain!
I feel my torment so increase
  That life cannot remain.
Toll on the passing bell;
Ring out my doleful knell;
Thy sound my death abroad will tell,
  For I must die,
  There is no remedy.

Cease now the passing bell;
  Ring out my doleful knoll,
For thou my death dost tell.
  Lord, pity thou my soul!
    Death doth draw nigh.
    Sound dolefully;
    For now I die,
    I die, I die.

TRIVIAL LYRICS

Fetes bel chere,
Drink to thy fere,
Vesse le bavere,
And singe nouwelle.

Selden B. 26.

TRIVIAL

CXVI

THE COMPLEINT OF CHAUCER TO HIS EMPTY PURSE.

TO you, my purse, and to noon other wyght
Compleyne I, for ye be my lady dere!
I am so sory, now that ye ben light;
For certės, but ye make me hevy chere,
Me were as leef be leyd upon my bere;
For whiche unto your mercy thus I crye
'Beth hevy ageyn, or ellės mot I dye!'

Now voucheth sauf this day, or hit be nyght,
That I of you the blisful soun may here,
Or see your colour lyk the sonnė bright,
That of yelownesse haddė never pere.
Ye be my lyf, ye be myn hertės stere,
Quene of comfort and of good companye;
Beth hevy ageyn, or ellės mot I dye!

Now purse, that be to me my lyvės light
And savėour, as doun in this worlde here,
Out of this toun help me throgh your myght,
Syn that ye wole not been my tresorere;
For I am shave as nye as any frere.
But yet I pray unto your curtesye,
Beth hevy ageyn, or ellės mot I dye!

12. *stere*, helm, rudder.

L'ENVOY DE CHAUCER.

O conquerour of Brutės Albioun,
Which that by lyne and free eleccioun
Ben verray king, this song to you I sende;
And ye, that mowen al myn harm amende,
Have mynde upon my supplicacioun!

GEOFFREY CHAUCER.

CXVII

L'ENVOY DE CHAUCER A BUKTON.

MY maister Bukton, whan of Criste our kyng
Was axėd, what is trouthe or sothfastnesse,
He nat a word answerde to that axyng,
As who saith 'No man is al trewe,' I gesse.
And therfor, thogh I hightė to expresse
The sorwe and wo that is in mariage,
I dar not wryte of hit no wikkednesse,
Lest I my self falle eft in swich dotage.

I wol nat seyn how that hit is the cheyne
Of Sathanas, on which he gnaweth ever,
But I dar seyn, were he out of his peyne,
As by his wille, he wolde be boundė never.
But thilkė doted fool that eft hath lever
Y-cheynėd be than out of prison crepe,
God lete him never fro his wo dissever,
Ne no man him bewaylė thogh he wepe!

But yit, lest thou do worsė, tak a wyf;
Bet is to wedde than brenne in worsė wyse.
But thou shalt have sorwe on thy flessh, thy lyf,
And ben thy wyvės thral, as seyn these wyse;
And if that holy writ may nat suffyse,
Experience shal thee techė, so may happe,
That thee were lever to be take in Fryse
Than eft to falle of weddyng in the trappe.

5. *hightė*, promised.

ENVOY.

This litel writ, proverbės, or figure
I sendė you; tak kepe of hit, I rede.
Unwys is he that can no wele endure.
If thou be siker, put thee nat in drede.
The Wyf of Bathe I pray you that ye rede
Of this materė that we have on honde.
God grauntė you your lyf frely to lede
In fredom; for ful hard is to be bonde.

GEOFFREY CHAUCER.

CXVIII

How hey! it is none lese,
I dare not seyn, whan sche seith 'Pes!'

YING men, I warne you everichone,
Eldė wivės tak ye none,
For I myself have one at home.
I dare not seyn, whan sche seith 'Pes!'

Whan I cum fro the plow at none,
In a reven dich mine mete is done;
I dare not asken our dame a spone.
I dare not seyn, whan she seith 'Pes!'

If I aske our damė bred,
Sche taketh a staf and breketh mine hed,
And doth me rennen under the led.
I dare nat seyn, whan sche seith 'Pes!'

If I aske our damė fleich,
Sche breketh mine hed with a dich;
'Boy, thou art not worth a reich.'
I dare not seyn, whan sche seith 'Pes!'

If I aske our damė chese,
'Boy,' sche seith, 'all at ese!
Thou art not worth half a pese.'
I dare not seyn, whan sche seith 'Pes!'

1. *lese*, false.
13. *led*=*lead*, vat.
17. *reich*, rush.

CXIX

Care away, away, away,
Care away for ever more!

ALL that I may swink or swete,
My wife it will both drink and ete;
And I sey ought, she will me bete;
Careful is my hart therefor.

If I sey ought of her but good,
She loke on me as she ware wod,
And will me clout about the hod;
Careful is my hart therefor.

If she will to the gud ale ride,
Me must trot all by her side,
And whan she drink I must abide;
Careful is my hart therefor.

If I say it shall be thus,
She sey 'Thou liest, charll, I wous;
Wenest thou to overcome me thus?'
Careful is my hart therefor.

If ony man have such a wife to lede,
He shall know how *Judicare* cam in the crede;
Of his penans God do him mede!
Careful is my hart therefor.

CXX

In sorow and care he lede his life,
That have a schrow ontill his wife.

YING men, I rede that ye be ware,
That ye cum not in the snare;
For he is brout in mechė care,
That have a schrow onto his wife.

In a panter I am caute;
My fote is penned, I may not out.
In sorow and care he is put,
That have a schrow onto his wife.

With a quene yef that thou run,
Anon it is told into the town.
Sorow he hath both up and down,
That have a schrow onto his wife.

3. *rede*, advise.
7. *panter*, net.
11. *quene*, quean, wench.

CXXI

A, a, a, a,
Yet I love where so I go.

IN all this warld nis a meriar life
 Than is a yong man withouten a wife ;
For he may liven withoughten strife,
 In every place where so he go.

In every place he is loved over all,
Among maidens grete and small,
In dauncing, in piping, and renning at the ball,
 In every place where so he go.

They lat light be husbondmen,
Whan they at the ballė renne ;
They cast her lovė to yong men,
 In every place where so he go.

Than sey maidens 'Farewell, Jacke !
Thy love is pressed all in thy pake ;
Thou berest thy love behind thy back,'
 In every place where so he go.

13. *her*, their.

CXXII

THE bachelor most joyfully
    In pleasant plight doth pass his days;
Good fellowship and company
    He doth maintain and keep always.
With damsels brave he may well go;
The married man cannot do so;
If he be merry and toy with any,
His wife will frown, and words give many,
Her yellow hose she straight will put on,
So that the married man dare not displease his
        wife Joan.

CXXIII

PASTIME with good company
  I love and shall, until I die.
Grudge who lust, but none deny.
So God be pleased, thus live will I.
  For my pastance,
  Hunt, sing and dance,
  My heart is set.
    All goodly sport
    For my comfort
  Who shall me let?

Youth must have some dalliance,
Of good or ill some pastance.
Company me thinks the best,
All thoughts and fancies to digest;
  For idleness
  Is chief mistress
  Of vices all.
    Then who can say
    But mirth and play
  Is best of all?

5. *pastance*, pastime.

Company with honesty
Is virtue, vices to flee;
Company is good and ill,
But every man has his freewill.
  The best ensue,
  The worst eschew!
  My mind shall be,
    Virtue to use,
    Vice to refuse;
  Thus shall I use me.

HENRY THE EIGHTH.

CXXIV

Women, women, love of women
Maketh bare pursės with some men.

SOME be mery, and some be sad;
Some be besy, and some be bad;
Some be wild, by Seint Chad!
Yet all they be not so.
For some be lewd, and some be shrewd.
Go, shrew, where so ever ye go!

Some be wise, and some be fond;
Some be tame, I understond;
Some will take bred at a mans hond.
Yet all they be not so, etc.

Some be wroth, and cannot tell wherefore;
Some be scorning evermore;
And some be tuskėd like a bore.
Yet all they be not so, etc.

Some will be dronken as a mouse;
Some be croked and will hurt a louse;
Some be fair and good in a house.
Yet all they be not so, etc.

Some be snouted like an ape;
Some can nother play ne jape;
And some of them be well shape.
Yet all they be not so, etc.

Some can prate withouten hire ;
Some make bate in every shire ;
Some can play check mate with our sire.
Yet all they do not so, etc.

Some be browne, and some be white ;
And some be tender as a chike ;
And some of them be chiry ripe.
Yet all they be not so, etc.

Some of them be treue of love,
Benethe the gerdelle, but not above ;
And in a hode above can chove.
Yet all they do not so, etc.

Some can whister, and some can crie ;
Some can flater, and some can lie ;
And some can sette the mouth awrie.
Yet all they do not so, etc.

He that made this songe full good
Came of the northe and of the sothern blode,
And somewhat kine to Robin Hode.
Yet all we be not so, etc.

CXXV

WELCOM be ye whan ye go,
And farewell whan ye come;
So faire as ye there be no mo
As brighte as bery broune.
I love you verrily at my to,
Nonne so moche in all this toune;
I am right glad when ye will go,
And sory when ye will come.

And whan ye be other fare,
I pray for you sertaine,
That never manner horsse ne mare
Bringe you to town agein.
To praise youre beutė I ne dare,
For drede that men wille seyn;
Farewelle, no more for you I care,
But pray you of my songe have no desdein.

CXXVI

LORD, how shall I me complain
  Unto mine own lady dere,
For to tell her of my pain
  That I fele this time of the yere?
  My love, if that ye will here,
Though I can no songės make,
  So your love changeth my chere,
That when I slepe I may not wake.

Though love do me so mikell woe,
  I love you best, I make a vow,
That my shoo bindeth my little toe,
  And all my smarte it is for you.
  Forsothe, me thinketh it will me slo,
But ye sumwhat my sorow slake,
  That barefot to my bedde I go,
And when I slepe I may not wake.

Whosoever wist what liff I lede,
  In mine observaunce in diveres wise;
From time that I go to my bedde
  I ete no mete till that I rise.
  Ye might tell it for a gret emprise,
That men thus morneth for your sake;
  So mikell I think on your service,
That when I slepe I may not wake.

7. *chere*, countenance.

In the morning when I rise shall,
  Me list right well for to dine,
But comonly I drink noon ale,
  If I may get any good wine.
  To make your hart to me encline
Such tormentės to me I take;
  Singing dothe me so mikell pine
That when I slepe I may not wake.

I may unneth boton my sleves,
  So mine armės waxen more;
Under my hele is that me greves,
  For at my hart I fele no sore;
  Every day my girdell goth out a bore;
I cling as doth a wheton cake;
  And for your love I sigh so sore,
That when I slepe I may not wake.

Therefore, but ye quit me my hire,
  Forsoth I not what I shall done,
And for your love, lady, by this fire,
  Old glovės will I werė none.
  I laugh and sing and make no mone,
I wex not lene as any rake,
  Thus in langour I leve alone,
And when I slepe I may not wake.

26. *me list*, I wish.
33. *unneth*, scarcely.
37. *bore*, hole.
38. *cling*, shrink.
42. *not*, know not

My dublet is more than it was,
  To love you first when I began,
It must be wider, by my lace,
  In each a stedė by a span.
  My love, sith I becam your man
I have riden thorow many a lake,
  One milėway morning I can
Yet when I slepe I may not wake.

Thus in langour I am lent.
  Long or you do so for me,
Take good hede to mine entent,
  For this shall my conclusion be.
  Me thinketh I love as well as ye,
Never so coy though ye it make ;
  By this ensample ye may see,
That when I slepe I may not wake.

CXXVII

Kyrie, so *kyrie*,
Jankin singeth merie,
With *eleyson*.

AS I went on Yole day
In oure prosession,
Knew I joly Jankin,
Be his merie tone.
Jankin began the offis
On the Yolė day;
And yit me thinketh it dos me good,
So merie gan he say
Kyrieleyson.

Jankin red the pistil
Full faire and full well,
And yit me thinketh it dos me good,
As ever have I sel.
Jankin at the *Sanctus*
Craketh a merie note,
And yit me thinketh it dos me good,
I payėd for his cote.
Jankin craketh notės
An hunderid on a knot,
And yit he hakketh hem smallere
Than wortės to the pot.
Kyrieleyson.

13. *pistil*, epistle.
16. *sel*, happiness.
24. *wortės*, herbs.

Jankin at the *Agnus*
  Bereth the *Pax* brede;
He twinkelėd, but said nought,
  And on mine fote he trede.
Benedicamus Domino,
  Crist from schame me schilde!
Deo gracias thereto.
  Alas, I go with childe.
    Kyrieleyson.

CXXVIII

Bring us in good ale, and bring us in good ale;
For our blessèd Lady sake bring us in good ale!

BRING us in no browne bred, for that is made of brane,
Nor bring us in no white bred, for therein is no gane,
But bring us in good ale!

Bring us in no befe, for there is many bones,
But bring us in good ale, for that goth downe at ones,
And bring us in good ale!

Bring us in no bacon, for that is passing fate,
But bring us in god ale, and gife us enought of that;
And bring us in good ale!

Bring us in no mutton, for that is often lene,
Nor bring us in no tripes, for they be seldom clene,
But bring us in good ale!

Bring us in no egges, for there are many schelles,
But bring us in good ale, and gife us nothing elles;
And bring us in good ale!

Bring us in no butter, for therein are many heres,
Nor bring us in no pigges flesch, for that will make us bores,
But bring us in good ale!

Bring us in no podinges, for therein is all Godes
good,
Nor bring us in no venesen, for that is not for our
blod;
But bring us in good ale!

Bring us in no capons flesch, for that is oftė dere,
Nor bring us in no dokes flesch, for they slober in
the mere,
But bring us in good ale!

CXXIX

Doll thy ale, doll, doll thy ale, doll !
Ale make many a man to have a doty poll.

ALE make many a man to stik at a brere ;
Ale make many a man to ly in the miere ;
And ale make many a man to slepe by the fiere.
With doll !

Ale make many a man to stombel at a stone ;
Ale make many a man to go dronken home ;
And ale make many a man to breke his tone.
With doll !

Ale make many a man to draw his knife ;
Ale make many a man to make grete strife ;
And ale make many a man to bete his wife.
With doll !

Ale make many a man to wet his chekes ;
Ale make many a man to ly in the stretes ;
And ale make many a man to wet his shetes.
With doll !

Ale make many a man to stombell at the blokkes ;
Ale make many a man to make his hed have knokkes ;
And ale make many a man to sit in the stokkes.
With doll !

1. *Doll*, warm, mull.
2. *doty*, foolish.
9. *tone*, toes.

Ale make many a man to rine over the falows;
Ale make many a man to swere by God and Allhalows;
And ale make many a man to hang upon the galows.
With doll!

23. *rine*, run.

CXXX

TAPSTER, fille another ale.
Anonne have I do.
God sende us good sale.
Avale the stake, avale.
Here is good ale ifounde.
Drinke to me,
And I to thee,
And lette the cuppe go rounde.

CXXXI

How, butler, how !
Bevis a tout !
O fill the boll, jentill butler,
And let the cup rout !

JENTILL butler, bellamy,
Fill the boll by the eye,
That we may drink by and by,
With 'How, butler, how !
Bevis a tout !
Fill the boll, butler,
And let the cup rout !'

Here is metė for us all,
Both for grete and for small.
I trow we must the butler call,
With 'How, butler, how !'

I am so dry I cannot speke ;
I am nigh chokėd with my mete ;
I trow the butler be aslepe.
With 'How, butler, how !'

Butler, butler, fill the boll,
Or ellės I beshrewe thy noll.
I trow we must the bell toll,
With 'How, butler, how !'

If the butler's name be Water,
I wold he were a galow claper ;
But if he bring us drink, the rather
With 'How, butler, how !'

2. *bevis=buvez.*

CXXXII

FILL the cup, Philip,
And let us drink a dram,
Once or twice about the house,
And leave where we began.

I drink to you, sweet heart,
So much as here is in,
Desiring you to follow me,
And do as I begin.

And if you will not pledge,
You shall bear the blame;
I drink to you with all my heart,
If you will pledge me the same.

CXXXIII

Back and side go bare, go bare,
  Both hand and foot go cold,
But belly, God send thee good ale enough
  Whether it be new or old !

BUT if that I may have truly
  Good ale my belly full,
I shall look like one, by sweet Saint John,
  Were shorn against the wool.
Though I go bare, take ye no care,
  I am nothing cold,
I stuff my skin so full within
  Of jolly good ale and old.

I cannot eat but little meat,
  My stomach is not good ;
But sure I think that I could drink
  With him that weareth an hood.
Drink is my life ; although my wife
  Some time do chide and scold,
Yet spare I not to ply the pot
  Of jolly good ale and old.

I love no roast but a brown toast,
  Or a crab in the fire ;
A little bread shall do me stead ;
  Much bread I never desire.
Nor frost, nor snow, nor wind I trow,
  Can hurt me if it wold,
I am so wrapped within and lapped
  With jolly good ale and old.

I care right nought, I take no thought
  For clothes to keep me warm ;
Have I good drink, I surely think
  Nothing can do me harm.
For truly than I fear no man,
  Be he never so bold,
When I am armed and throughly warmed
  With jolly good ale and old.

But now and than I curse and ban,
  They make their ale so small ;
God give them care and evil to fare !
  They stry the malt and all.
Such peevish pew, I tell you true,
  Not for a crown of gold
There cometh one sip within my lip,
  Whether it be new or old.

Good ale and strong maketh me among
  Full jocund and full light,
That oft I sleep and take no keep
  From morning until night.
Then start I up and flee to the cup ;
  The right way on I hold ;
My thirst to staunch, I fill my paunch
  With jolly good ale and old.

40. *stry*, destroy.

And Kit my wife, that as her life
  Loveth well good ale to seek,
Full oft drinketh she, that ye may see
  The tears run down her cheek.
Then doth she troll to me the bowl,
  As a good malt-worm shold,
And say 'Sweet-heart, I have take my part
  Of jolly good ale and old.'

They that do drink till they nod and wink,
  Even as good fellows should do,
They shall not miss to have the bliss
  That good ale hath brought them to.
And all poor souls that scour black bowls,
  And them hath lustily trolled,
God save the lives of them and their wives,
  Whether they be young or old!

CXXXIV

Wolcum, Yole, thou mery man,
In worchepe of this holy day!

WOLCUM be thou, hevenė king,
Wolcum, born in one morwening,
Wolcum, for whom we schall sing,
Wolcum, Yole!

Wolcum be ye, Stevene and Jon,
Wolcum, Innocentes everichone,
Wolcum, Thomas, marter one,
Wolcum, Yole!

Wolcum be ye, good Newe Yere,
Wolcum, Twelfthe Day, both in fere,
Wolcum, seintės lefe and dere,
Wolcum, Yole!

Wolcum be ye, Candelmesse,
Wolcum be ye, quene of bliss,
Wolcum bothe to more and lesse,
Wolcum, Yole!

Wolcum be ye that arn here,
Wolcum alle and make good chere,
Wolcum alle another yere,
Wolcum, Yole!

12. *in fere*, together. 13. *lefe*, dear.

CXXXV

Good day, good day,
My lord sire Cristėmasse, good day !

GOOD day, sire Cristėmas our kinge,
For every man bothe olde and yinge
Is glad and blithe of youre cominge.
Good day !

Godės sone so moche of might,
Fram heven to erthė doun is light,
And borne is of a maide so bright.
Good day !

Heven and erthe and also helle,
And alle that ever in hem dwelle,
Of youre cominge they beth ful snelle.
Good day !

Of youre cominge this clerkės finde,
Ye comė to save all man kinde,
And of here balės hem unbinde.
Good day !

All maner of merthės we wole make,
And solas to oure hertės take,
My semely lordė, for youre sake.
Good day !

13. *snelle*, alert. 17. *balės*, troubles.

CXXXVI

Make we mery bothe more and lasse,
For now is the time of Cristėmas!

LETT no man cum into this hall,
Grome, page, nor yet marshall,
But that sum sport he bring with all;
For now is the time of Cristėmas!

If that he say he can not sing,
Some oder sport then lett him bring,
That it may please at this festing;
For now is the time of Cristėmas!

If he say he can nought do,
Then for my love aske him no mo,
But to the stokkes then let him go;
For now is the time of Cristėmas!

CXXXVII

Caput apri refero
Resonans laudes domino.

THE borės hede in hondes I bringe,
With garlondes gay and birdes singinge.
I pray you all, helpe me to singe,
Qui estis in convivio.

The borės hede, I understonde,
Is cheffe service in all this londe,
Where so ever it may be fonde,
Servitur cum sinapio.

The borės hede, I dare well say,
Anon after the twelfthė day
He taketh his leve, and goth away;
Exivit tunc de patria.

CXXXVIII

Ivy chefe of treis it is.
Veni coronaberis.

THE most worthie she is in towne;
He that seith other, do amisse;
And worthy to bere the crowne.
Veni coronaberis.

Ivy is soft and meke of speche;
Ageinst all balė she is blisse.
Well is he that may her reche.
Veni coronaberis.

Ivy is green, with coloure bright,
Of all treis best she is;
And that I preve well now be right.
Veni coronaberis.

Ivy bereth beris black.
God graunt us all his blisse,
For there shall we nothing lack!
Veni coronaberis.

CXXXIX

HOLVER and Heivy made a grete party,
Who schuld have the maistry
In londės where they go.

Than spak Holver 'I am frece and joly ;
I will have the maistry
In londės where we go.'

Than spak Heivy 'I am loud and proud ;
And I will have the maistry
In londės where we go.'

Than spak Holver, and set him downe on his knee,
'I prey thee, jentil Heivy,
Sey me no veleny
In londės where we go.'

4. *frece*, fresh, quick.

CXL

Alleluia, alleluia,
Alleluia, now sing we !

HERE commes holly, that is so gent ;
To pleasse all men is his intent.
Alleluia.

But, lord and lady of this hall,
Who so ever ageinst holly call,
Alleluia,

Who so ever ageinst holly do crie,
In a lepe shall he hang full hie.
Alleluia.

Who so ever ageinst holly do sing,
He maye wepe and handės wring.
Alleluia.

9. *lepe*, noose.

CXLI

Nay, nay, Ivy!
It may not be, iwis,
For Holly must have the mastry
As the maner is.

HOLLY bereth beris,
Beris rede enough;
The thristilcok, the popingay
Daunce in every bough.
Welaway, sory Ivy!
What fowlės hast thou,
But the sory howlet
That singeth 'How how'?

Ivy bereth beris
As blak as any sloe.
There commeth the woode colver,
And fedeth her of tho;
She lifteth up her taill
And she cakkės or she go;
She wold not for an hundred pound
Serve Holly so.

Holly with his mery men
They can daunce in hall;
Ivy and her jentell women
Can not daunce at all,
But like a meine of bullokės
In a water fall,
Or on a hot somers day
Whan they be mad all.

15. *colver*, pigeon.
16. *tho*, them.
18. *cakkės* = Lat. cacat.
25. *meine*, company.

Holly and his mery men
  Sitt in cheires of gold;
Ivy and her jentell women
  Sitt without in fold,
With a paire of kibėd
  Helės caught with cold.
So wold I that every man had
  That with Ivy will hold!

33. *kibėd*, covered with chilblains.

CXLII

THE merthe of alle this londe
  Maketh the gode husbonde,
  With eringe of his plowe.
Iblessed be Cristės sonde,
That hath us sent in honde
  Merthe and joye enowe.

The plowe gothe mony a gate,
Bothe erly and eke late,
  In winter in the clay,
Aboute barly and whete,
That makethe men to swete.
  God spede the plowe all day!

Browne Morel and Gore
Drawen the plowe full sore
  All in the morweninge;
Rewarde hem therefore
With a shefe or more
  Alle in the eveninge.

Whan men biginne to sowe,
Full well here corne they knowe
  In the mounthe of May.
However Janiver blowe
Wether hie or lowe,
  God spede the plowe alle way!

4. *sonde*, message.

Whan men biginnethe to wede
The thistle fro the sede
  In somer whan they may,
God lete hem well to spede;
And longe gode life to lede,
  Alle that for plowe men pray.

CXLIII

Prenegard, prenegard!
Thus bere I mine baselard.

LESTENETH, lordinges, I you beseke!
There is none man worth a leke,
Be he sturdy, be he meke,
But he bere a baselard.

Mine baselard hath a schede of red,
And a clene loket of led;
Me thinketh I may bere up mine hed,
For I bere mine baselard.

My baselard hath a wrethen hafte.
Whan I am full of alė caughte,
It is grete dred of manslaughte,
For then I bere mine baselard.

My baselard hath a silver chape;
Therefore I may bothe gaspe and gape.
Me thinketh I go like none knape,
For I bere a baselard.

My baselard hath a trencher kene,
Fair as rasour scharp and schene.
Evere me thinketh I may be kene,
For I bere a baselard.

2. *baselard*, a short dagger. 7. *schede*, sheath.
8. *loket*, band across the scabbard. 11. *wrethen*, twisted.
15. *chape*, butt of the scabbard. 17. *knape*, knave.

As I yede up in the strete,
With a cartere I gan mete.
'Felawe,' he seide, 'so mote I the,
  Thou schalt forego thy baselard.'

The cartere his whippe began to take,
And all mine fleich began to quake,
And I was lefe for to ascape;
  And there I left mine baselard.

Whan I cam forth onto mine damme,
Mine hed was broken to the panne;
Sche seide I was a praty manne,
  And well coude bere mine baselard.

25. *the*, thrive.
29. *lefe*, glad.
32. *panne*, skull.

CXLIV

AS I came by a grene forest side,
I met with a forster that badde me abide,
With 'Hey go bet, hey go bet, hey go howe!'

Underneath a tree I did me set,
And with a grete hert anone I met;
I badde let slippe, and said 'Hey go bet!'
With 'Hey go bet, hey go bet, howe!'

I had not stande there but a while,
For the mountenaunce of a mile,
There came a grete herte, without gile.
'There he gothe, there he gothe, hey go howe!
We shall have sporte and game enowe!'

Talbot my hounde with a mery taste
All about the grene wode he gan cast.
I toke my horne and blew him a blast,
With 'Tro-ro-ro-ro, tro-ro-ro-ro!'
With 'Hey go bet, hey go bet, hey go howe!
There he gothe, there he gothe, hey go howe!
We shall have sport and game enowe!'

CXLV

I am a jolly foster, I am a jolly foster,
And have been many a day;
And foster will I be still,
For shoot right well I may.

WHEREFORE should I hang up my bow
Upon the green wood bough?
I can bend and draw a bow,
And shoot well enow.

Wherefore should I hang up mine arrow
Upon the green wood lind?
I have strength to make it flee,
And kill both hart and hind.

Wherefore should I hang up my horn
Upon the green wood tree?
I can blow the death of a deer as well
As any that ever I see.

Wherefore should I tie up my hound
Unto the green wood spray?
I can luge and make a suit
As well as any in May.

1. *foster*, forester. 10. *lind*, linden, lime.
19. *luge*, lodge, discover the 'lodge' of a buck.
19. *suit*, pursuit.

CXLVI

I HAVE been a foster long and many day;
My locks ben hoar.
I shall hang up my horn by the green wood spray;
Foster will I be no more.

All the whiles that I may my bow bend
Shall I wed no wife.
I shall bigg me a bower at the woodės end,
There to lead my life.

1. *foster*, forester. 7. *bigg*, build.

CXLVII

Hoyda, hoyda, jolly rutterkin,
Hoyda, hoyda, like a rutterkin,
Hoyda, hoyda, hoyda, hoyda,
Like a rutterkin, hoyda !

RUTTERKIN is come unto our town
In a cloak without coat or gown,
Save ragged hood to cover his crown,
Like a rutterkin, hoyda, hoyda !

Rutterkin can speak no English ;
His tongue runneth all on buttered fish,
Besmeared with grease about his dish,
Like a rutterkin, hoyda, hoyda !

Rutterkin shall bring you all good luck,
A stoup of beer up at a pluck,
Till his brain be as wise as a duck,
Like a rutterkin, hoyda, hoyda !

W. CORNISH, JR.

CXLVIII

I HAVE a gentil cok
  Croweth me day;
He doth me risen erly
  My matines for to say.

I have a gentil cok;
  Comen he is of grete;
His comb is of red corel,
  His tail is of get.

I have a gentil cok;
  Comen he is of kinde;
His comb is of red corel,
  His tail is of inde.

His leggės ben of asour,
  So gentil and so smale;
His sporės arn of silver white
  Into the wortėwale.

His eynen arn of cristal,
  Loken all in aumber;
And every night he percheth him
  In mine ladyes chaumber.

12. *inde*, indigo.
16. *wortėwale*, the skin of the claws.
18. *loken*, set; lit., locked.

CXLIX

I HAVE twelfė oxen that be faire and brown,
And they go a grasing down by the town.
With hey! with how! with hey!
Saweste not you mine oxen, you litill prety boy?

I have twelfė oxen, and they be faire and white,
And they go a grasing down by the dyke.
With hey! with how! with hey!
Saweste not you mine oxen, you litill prety boy?

I have twelfe oxen, and they be faire and blak,
And they go a grasing down by the lak.
With hey! with how! with hey!
Saweste not you mine oxen, you litill prety boy?

I have twelfė oxen, and they be faire and rede,
And they go a grasing down by the mede.
With hey! with how! with hey!
Saweste not you mine oxen, you litill prety boy?

CL

Draw me nere, draw me nere,
Draw me nere, ye joly juggelere!

HERE beside dwelleth
  A riche barons doughter;
She wold have no man
  That for her love had sought her.
    So nise she was.

She wold have no man
  That was made of molde,
But if he had a mouth of gold
  To kisse her whan she wold.
    So dangerus she was.

There of hard a joly juggeler
  That laid was on the grene,
And at this ladys wordės
  Iwis he had gret tene.
    An angred he was.

He juggeled to him a well good stede
  Of an old hors bone,
A sadill and a bridill both,
  And set himself thereon.
    A juggeler he was.

16. *tene*, vexation.

He priked and praunsėd both
  Beffore that lady's gate;
She wend he had ben an angell
  Was come for her sake.
    A prikker he was.

He priked and praunsėd
  Beffore that lady's bowr;
She wend he had ben an angel
  Come from heven towre.
    A praunser he was.

Four and twenty knightės
  Lade him into the hall,
And as many squirės
  His hors to the stall,
    And gaff him mete.

They gaff him ottės
  And also hay;
He was an old shrew
  And held his hed away.
    He wold not ete.

The day began to passe,
  The night began to come,
To bed was brought
  The fair jentell woman,
    And the juggeler also.

25. *wend*, thought.

The night began to passe,
  The day began to springe,
All the birdės of her bowr
  They began to singe,
    And the cokoo also.

'Where be ye, my mery maidens,
  That ye come not me to?
The joly windows of my bowr
  Look that you undo,
    That I may see!

'For I have in mine armės
  A duke or elles an erle.'
But whan she lookėd him upon,
  He was a blere-eyed chorle.
    'Alas!' she said.

She lade him to an hill,
  And hangėd shuld he be.
He juggeled himself to a mele pok;
  The dust fell in her eye;
    Begiled she was.

God and our Lady
  And swetė Seint Johan
Send every giglot of this town
  Such another leman,
    Even as he was.

65. *pok*, bag.
70. *giglot*, wench.
71. *leman*, lover.

CLI

My heart of gold as true as steel,
As I me leanèd to a bough,
In faith but if ye love me well,
Lord, so Robin lough !

MY lady went to Canterbury,
The saint to be her boot ;
She met with Kate of Malmesbury :
Why sleepest thou in an apple root ?

Nine mile to Michaelmas,
Our dame began to brew ;
Michael set his mare to grass,
Lord, so fast it snew !

For you, love, I brake my glass,
Your gown is furred with blue ;
The devil is dead, for there I was ;
Iwis it is full true.

And if ye sleep, the cock will crow,
True heart, think what I say ;
Jackanapes will make a mow,
Look, who dare say him nay ?

I pray you have me now in mind,
I tell you of the matter ;
He blew his horn against the wind ;
The crow goeth to the water.

4. *lough,* laughed.

Yet I tell you mickle more ;
  The cat lieth in the cradle ;
I pray you keep true heart in store ;
  A penny for a ladle.

I swear by Saint Katharine of Kent,
  The goose goeth to the green ;
All our doggės tail is brent,
  It is not as I ween.

Tirlery lorpin, the laverock sang,
  So merrily pipes the sparrow,
The cow brake loose, the rope ran home,
  Sir, God give you good-morrow !

CLII

ME liketh ever the lengere the bet
  By Wingester, that joly sitė ;
The ton is god and wel iset ;
  The folk is comely on to see ;
The aier is god bothe inne and oute ;
  The sitė stent under an hille ;
The riverės renneth all aboute ;
  The ton is rueled apon skille.

Benedicamus Domino. Alleluia Alleluia-a.

SOME ASPECTS OF MEDIÆVAL LYRIC

BY E. K. CHAMBERS

'*Scripsi haec carmina in tabulis.*
Mon ostel est en mi la vile de Paris.
May I sugge namore, so wel me is ;
Yef I deye for love of hire, duel hit ys.'

Harl. MS. 2253.

SOME ASPECTS OF MEDIÆVAL LYRIC

THE written lyric of the Middle Ages is generally the work of the minstrel or of the *trouvère*, who represent successive stages in the developement of the poet as a self-conscious artist. Both naturally write down their songs; the minstrel to aid his own memory and to preserve a professional stock-in-trade, which he may wish to sell or lend to another; the *trouvère* out of creative vanity, to secure from his friends and from those who come after him the

'monumentum ære perennius'.

But beyond *trouvère*-song and beyond minstrelsy lies the folk-song out of which they both grew, and which long continues to exist side by side with them. Folk-song is rarely written down, at least until it has already been contaminated with literary elements; and the reconstruction of its primitive features by the disentangling of these elements, with what aid history, psychology, and the comparative study of barbarous peoples may afford, is an important function of the anthropologist. His investigations trace the beginnings of lyric to the instinct of emotional self-expression, rhythmic with those quickened dilations and contractions of the heart which are the physiological accompaniments of emotion. Such expression proves to be readily punctuated by the external rhythms of folk-activities which occupy the limbs and leave the spirit free to brood or to exult; rhythms of labour, in the pull of the oar, the swing of the sickle or the flail, the rock of the cradle, the rise and fall of the batlet, the twisting of the spindle, the throw of the shuttle in the loom; or rhythms of play, when the nervous energies, released from the ordinary claims, are diverted into unremunerative channels, and under the rare stimulus of meat and wine the idle feet of the chorus, grouped around the altar of sacrifice or the fruit-laden tree, break into the uplifting of the dance.

The primitive method of folk-song may have been that of mere improvisation, bringing something of definite form and content into half-inarticulate outcry and gradually yielding place in its turn to habits of more deliberate composition. At a very early stage the differentiation must have established itself between the leader of retentive memory and nimble resource who sets the strain and the throng who listen and beat time until the recurring moments when they get the signal to strike in with some rehearsed or familiar burden. And as functions are distinguished and the original homogeneity of the folk begins to break up, it is from the song-leader that the minstrel, and after the minstrel the *trouvère*, takes his starting-point and establishes himself as the recognised exponent of the old songs and the recognised 'maker' of the new. Obviously during this process the dependence of poetry upon the throng gradually disappears. The rhythms of the *trouvère's* verses are marked, not by the pulse of flying feet, but by the chords of viol or of lute; and the emotions which dictate them tend more and more to become personal instead of communal, those which a man tells to his own heart in solitude, rather than those which he is moved to cry aloud in company by his sympathy with the crowd of which he forms a part. The burden or *refrain*, no longer an essential element of the song, drops out of use or is retained solely as a literary ornament. But in its survival it is significant of its origin. The forms of art are conservative; and, with whatever change of temper and intention, the *trouvère*, and even more the minstrel, who is far less completely disengaged from the folk than the *trouvère*, is apt to continue the themes and conventions which were first shaped by the folk and still, through all modifications, carry their birth-marks upon them. One other feature of the transition is notable. Art-poetry, whether of the minstrel or the *trouvère* variety, is mainly, if not wholly, masculine poetry. The relation of the minstrel to the *comitatus*, the literary advantage of the clerk, are perhaps sufficient between them to account for this. But it involves a distinct breach with the traditions of the folk, for whom woman, not man, is the characteristic singer. This also is intelligible, since woman's are the greater number of the more leisured and rhythmical of the folk-occupations, and to her, the primitive sower of the seed and planter of herbs, has always been assigned the chief part in that persistent ritual of agriculture, at whose high seasons the festival excitement finds its ready outlet in the dance.

The earliest written love-poetry of the northern *trouvères* discovers art-song in the very act of passing out of the *cantica diabolica amatoria et turpia* of *rustici* and *rusticanæ* in the *ballationes* of their holiday *chori*, which for centuries past had been a scandal to the discipline of the Church and which a preacher, who may be Cæsarius of Arles, does not hesitate to denounce as a survival of the *observatio paganorum*.[1] The moment is so fundamental for the understanding of all subsequent literature in England as well as in France, that it is important to dwell upon it. The second half of the twelfth century, in which the texts begin, already acknowledges the establishment under Provençal influence of that official *chanson d'amour* or *chanson courtois*, which ultimately succeeded in impressing itself upon the imagination of the Renaissance no less than upon that of the Middle Ages, and may be said to have fixed the type of literary romantic sentiment from the *Canzoniere* of Petrarch to *The Angel in the House*. The characteristics of this poetry are familiar enough. It has practically but one theme, that of the

[1] See the series of prohibitions quoted in my *Mediaeval Stage*, i. 161.

amour courtois or *fine amour;* which it expounds with a literary skill and frequent delicacy of feeling, that do not save it in the end from the reproach of being cloistered, or from the monotony inseparable from the repeated treatment of the same situation in the light of the same ideals.

> 'Qu'onques ne fis chançon jor de ma vie,
> Se fine amor nel m'enseigna avant.'
>
> (Gace Brulé, xiii. 3.)

The love of the *trouvère* is conceived on the analogy of feudal relations. He vows himself to the service of a mistress, who becomes his liege lady. He is in her *baillie*, her *seignorie*. He must render her the submission of a vassal, and his devotion is amply rewarded by any favour she may choose to bestow upon him. Moreover his loyalty implies not only submission but endurance. His love is for life, and there must be no turning aside. He must love *sens trichier*, through absence, through cruelty, through the misrepresentations of the *gent malparlière*, a terrible folk—

> 'Qu'a maint amant ont fait ire et oltrage.'
>
> (Renals de Couci, ed. Brakelmann, vii. 38.)

The lady, indeed, is most often unkind, and love has to be its own reward. Then the poets go pensively, for love has them in prison, and their songs are sad with tears. But they love on, all the same.

> 'J'aim par costume et par us,
> La, ou je ne puis ataindre.'
>
> (Blondels de Nesle, ed. Brakelmann, xi. 1.)

They are but as children crying for stars; and they know it.

> 'Empris ai greignor folie
> Que li fols enfes qui crie
> Por la bele estoile avoir,
> Qu'il voit halt el ciel seoir.'
>
> (Renals de Couci, iv. 5.)

But they are glad to have it so; they glory in their foolishness, for after all foolishness is only another name for loyalty.

'Coment que je m'en desespoir,
Bien m'a amors guerredoné,
Ce que je l'ai a mon pooir
Servie senz deslealté,
Que roi m'a fait de folie.'

(Renals de Couci, iv. 9.)

Tradition has it that the object of the *trouvère's* worship was often the wife of the patron who protected his art. Certainly there is much deference in the *chansons* to the great romantic exemplar of Tristan and Iseult at the court of King Mark. But since the *trouvère* was not prone to conceal his verses, and since, without any assumption of a particularly high moral standard at courts under the ægis of Eleanor of Aquitaine, it is obvious that patronage has its limits, the conclusion suggests itself that in many cases *amour courtois* must have been a literary convention rather than a passionate reality. This indeed is a problem which recurs at many later stages in the history of amorous poetry; and it stands to reason that no solution of universal application can ever be found for it. The actual formulæ of the *chansons*, like those of the Elizabethan sonnets, may cover a variety of personal relations, from somewhat shameless intrigue to married chastity. There were Donnes and Habingtons already in the twelfth century. Equally well there may be nothing to cover but a mere courtly game. In any case this literature is generally reticent, so far as regards the expression of the physical side of love. It is an exception when a *trouvère* writes on the eve of a crusade—

'Or me laist Deus en tel honor monter,
Que cele ou j'ai mon cuer et mon penser
Tiegne une nuit entre mes braz nuete,
Ains que j'aille oltre mer!'

(Renals de Couci, viii. 5.)

There is not even much insistence upon corporeal beauty. Many stanzas are devoted to refining on the psychology of love, and but comparatively few to the celebration of the *bels gens cors* and the *bel oir vair et riant et cler*. The whole literature, indeed, for all its undeniable grace and charm, is self-conscious. The *trouvères* are more in love with love than with their mistresses. They will die, of course, unless the lady shows *merci*; but they take a long time doing it, and in the meantime they find consolation in thinking out intricate arrangements of rhyme for their verses, and sending them abroad to make known their sufferings and their constancy to others of the select few who, like themselves, are sworn to the cult of the *bels sires Deus*. Euphuism ever walks hand in hand with Romance, and there is significance in the phrases which Blondels de Nesle finds to sum up the ideal of himself and his fellows.

'A la joie apartient
D'amer molt finement,
Et, quant li lius en vient,
Li doners largement;
Encor plus i covient
Parler cortoisement;
Qui ces trois voies tient
Ja n'ira malement.'

(Blondels de Nesle, xiv. 9.)

How far all this is from the folk! not only because folk-song is never self-conscious and never desires to convert the natural way of a man with a maid into mere sentiment, but also because the whole relation between the sexes, as it is represented in the *chansons*, could only have been imagined in the artificial social conditions of courts, wherein it is possible for the real economic subjection of women to be glossed over with an appearance of consideration and respect. The *amour courtois*, in which man is a suppliant, is not the love of the folk, in which the cry for love and the service of love are always on the side of the woman, any more than it is the purged love of the future between two independent human souls coming together out of the depths of their dignity and their isolation.

But the *chanson courtois* does not exhaust the possibilities of mediæval French love-poetry. Existing side by side with it in the twelfth century, even outliving it and enduring into and beyond the Renaissance, we find another strain of song, which may be distinguished as the *chanson populaire*. This, according to M. Gaston Paris, probably came into existence in the region of Poitou and Limousin, and represents a stock out of which the more developed art-poetry of Provence itself, no less than that of Northern France, had its origin. Little of it can be assigned to famous or even to known *trouvères*; much of it is anonymous and may be in part the work of minstrels. Its themes and forms differentiate themselves very clearly from those of the *chanson courtois*. A notable feature is afforded by the dance-songs, called in the earlier documents *rotrouenges* and in the later *chansons de carole*, *rondets*, or *rondets de carole*. Of these there must once have been many, but only a few dating from the twelfth or early thirteenth century are preserved in their entirety; the rest solely through their *refrains* or burdens, which are freely adapted and quoted in *chansons* of other types and in romances. The burden is of course essential to the dance-song. The primitive form may have consisted of nothing but single lines of text alternating with the burden. Afterwards the number of lines in the *couplet* or stanza was increased, and one or more of these was made to rhyme with the burden. So long as it continued to be popular, the *rondet* retained great freedom of arrangement; ultimately, through its adoption for musical purposes, it became in its turn literary and hardened into fixed forms, such as the *rondel* and the *balade*. The documents seem to distinguish from the *chansons de carole* a group of poems known as *chansons d'histoire*, which tell short love-stories in assonant stanzas with burdens, and bear a close analogy to the English and Scottish ballads. It is not quite clear in what exactly the distinction consists. Possibly the *chansons d'histoire* are in origin just dance-songs with a narrative instead of a purely lyrical content. But they are also sometimes called *chansons de toile*, and in the twelfth century they appear to have been ordinarily sung, not at a dance, but by a company of women over their needlework. In any case it must not be assumed that the *chansons de carole* were never narrative. The extant *refrains* are mostly lyrical, but there are also fragments dealing with the adventures of certain popular personages; with Robin, the typical rustic lover, with 'la bien faite Aalis', with Emmelot, whose mother kept her at home from the dance—

> 'C'est la jus c'on dit es pres,
> Jeu et bal i sont criés;
> Enmelos i veut aler,
> A sa mere en aquiert gres.
> Par dieu, fille, vous n'ires,
> Trop y a de bachelers.'
>
> (Bartsch, ii. 90.)

From dance-songs may perhaps have been developed the *aubes*, lyric dialogues of lovers parting in the morning, into which is often introduced the cry of the *gaite* or watchman from the castle hard by. But the greater number of the *chansons populaires* belong to a class which may perhaps be best described as *chansons d'aventure*. These are not, as they stand, dance-songs, and although they often use burdens, these are not essential to their structure. They have a narrative setting. The poet tells how he went abroad, generally on a spring morning, and what befell him by the way. Sometimes his part is limited to that of a reporter. In one group of poems, known as the *chansons de mal mariée*, he overhears a woman's complaint against married life. In others it is the lovesong of a girl, or her regret at having no lover, or at the absence of her lover, or at her immurement in a nunnery. But sometimes he is himself more directly concerned in the adventure. He takes part in a dialogue; or in a very common and widespread type of such poetry he makes love, and after good or ill success rides away.

The distinction between the *chanson courtois* and the *chanson populaire* must not be pressed into an absolute one. We have not here to do with folk-song in the strict sense. The tokens of the castle are clear enough. The *aube* has its *gaite* in the background. The maidens of the *chansons d'histoire* work silken embroideries in a bower. The singers of the *chansons d'aventure* describe themselves as *chevaliers* or *vassals*. Even the dance-songs probably come to us from those *caroles* which the same documents that preserve their burdens record as an amusement of high society.

> 'Es ombres sont aléez dessous les oliviers.
> La karole commenchent que les cors ont legiers'
>
> (*Gui de Nanteuil*, 2441.)

says one romancer; and another—

> 'Dames et chevaliers ensemble se meslerent
> Et pristrent main à main, et puis si carolerent,
> Et grassieusement deus des dames chanterent.'
>
> (*Brun de la Montaigne*, 1838.)

What one claims for the *chanson populaire* is, not that it is folk-song, but that it rests upon folk-song, and that the forms and motives which it adapts still inevitably reflect the manners and the sentiments of the folk by whom they were fashioned. What, indeed, are the *caroles* of lords and ladies themselves but the survival under altered social conditions of precisely those *ballationes vel saltationes aut caraulae* of village girls against which the Church had for so many centuries made war? They have features common in folk-dances to this day. They are danced hand to hand, in a *ronde* or ring. They have leaders and a chorus, who divide the song and the burden between them. They are in the open air, on a lawn 'dessous les oliviers.'

Students of social history have noticed that in the earlier documents women alone take part in the *caroles*. That is significant, when the place of women in folk-literature is borne in mind. And it is precisely in keeping with the general character of the *chanson populaire*, which invariably and in complete contradiction to the tone of the *chanson courtois* approaches love from the woman's point of view. The yearning, the surrender, the rapture, the endurance, the submission, the regret of woman's love; these are the arguments throughout of *chansons d'histoire*, of *aubes*, and of *refrains*. I have not of course forgotten that the great bulk of the literature before us is made up of *chansons d'aventure*, and that in these, at least, the man speaks. It is precisely at this point that the process of adapting folk-themes to the needs of a masculine art-poetry betrays itself. And surely the disguise is transparent enough, if you bear in mind that in the simplest and probably the earliest type of *chanson d'aventure*, that to which M. Jeanroy gives the name of *chanson dramatique*, the minstrel or *trouvère*, as already pointed out, is nothing more than a mere reporter. All that he contributes is the briefest of narrative introductions, and the substance of the song remains the passion or complaint of a woman which he has overheard—

'L'autrier aloie pensant
A un chant
Que je fis.
Trouvai dame soupirant
Et criant
A haus cris.
Tout ainsi, ce m'est avis,
S'escria—
Li jalous
Envious
De corrous
Morra;
Et li dous
Savourous
Amourous
M'avra.' (Bartsch, i. 51.)

One can hardly doubt that the judgement of M. Gaston Paris is sound, when he puts together this dominant note of womanhood in the *chanson populaire* and the spring settings which the *chansons d'aventure* affect, and finds the well-head of French amorous poetry in the spring festivals, mainly celebrated by women, which remain deeply rooted in European agricultural custom as it survives in countless observances of Midsummer or May.[1] Remembering the ecclesiastical pronouncements, he goes on to suggest that to the tradition of such days belonged something of sexual license inherited from earlier stages of ethical developement, and that the 'regina avrilloza' of the Limousin *carole* claimed, as it were, by right to bid defiance to the 'jelos,' and to solace herself with the 'leugier bachelar.' Perhaps too much stress should not be laid upon this. Folk-song may become wanton, especially upon a holiday, without being consciously or unconsciously atavistic. The fact remains, however, that the reticence of the *chanson courtois* finds no echo in the sensuous and unabashed temper of the *chanson populaire*—

'Soufres, maris, et si ne vous anuit,
Demain m'ares et mes amis anuit.

Je vous deffenc k'un seul mot n'en parles ;
Soufres, maris, et si ne vous mouves,
La nuis est courte, a par mains me rares,
Qant mes amis ara fait sen deduit.

Soufres, maris, et si ne vous anuit,
Demain m'ares et mes amis anuit.'

(Bartsch, i. 22.)

It is full-blooded southern love, abandoning itself beneath the white moon and to the music of the nightingale, such as startles one on the very threshold of European literature in the *Pervigilium Veneris*, and burns still, after how

[1] Cf. *Mediæval Stage*, Book II.

many centuries, in the heart-throbs of the great Provençal *alba*—

> 'Bels dous amics, fassam un joc novel,
> Ins el jardi on chanton li auzel,
> Tro la gaita toque son caramel.
> Oi Deus, oi Deus, de l'alba! Tan tost ve!'
> (Bartsch, *Chrest. Prov.* 109.)

The nightingale, indeed, plays a conspicuous part in all this poetry. His song is the symbol of amorous passion, and he himself is appealed to as the confident and adviser of lovers, the go-between who bears messages from heart to heart. He has a right to his place, for in France his coming, like that of the swallow in Greece, the stork in Germany, and the cuckoo in England, is the signal to the folk that summer is at hand, and that the time for the high revel has come.

Naturally enough, the courtly adapters have drawn more freely upon the amorous elements in the festival songs than upon the invocations of the summer itself which accompanied them in the village ritual. But examples of these also are to be found in the rich store of *refrains* preserved in the singular romance of *Guillaume de Dole*. One of these is specifically described as sung on May morning by citizens who 'aporterent lor mai' from the wood—

> 'Tout la gieus sor rive mer,
> Compaignon, or dou chanter.
> Dames i ont bauz levez:
> Mout en ai le cuer gai.
> Compaignon, or dou chanter
> En l'onor de mai.'
> (v. 4154.)

The other is of precisely similar character—

> 'Tendez tuit voz mains a la flor d'esté,
> A la flor de liz.
> Por Deu, tendez i.'
> (v. 5099.)

These complete the connection of the *caroles* and the *chanson populaire* to which they belong with the folk-festivals. To them, one may conjecture, originally belonged the title of *reverdie*, song of earth's *renouveau*, which in fact is used in a more general sense as indicating a light-hearted ditty. It is to be observed that the descriptive passages, of blossoming trees and luting birds, which occur in the introductions to the *chansons d'aventure*, are just of the nature to be expected on the theory that these represent an adaptation of the manner of more primitive spring songs. The original *chanson* has no need to explain its own circumstances. But the adapter strives to reproduce the environment as well as the theme, and it is only in his narrative setting that he can do this. The same principle may be pushed further. A large number of those *chansons d'aventure* which are not purely *chansons dramatiques* have a character which has earned them the name of *pastourelles*. The scenes are placed amongst shepherds and shepherdesses; and is not this precisely because it was amongst shepherds and shepherdesses that the literary models of which the poets are making use were found? You have to deal with a deliberate attempt to preserve local colour. The *pastourelle*, one feels, is the most sophisticated variety of the *chanson populaire*, the nearest to the *chanson courtois*. The authors are already a long way from the folk when they begin to make pictures of it like this. In the substance of the poems, too, the class-distinction between the *vassal* and the *pastorel* is very clearly felt. And the courtly temper of minstrel and *trouvère* is beginning to remould the folk-material. The poet now sings more often of his own love than of a woman's love overheard. And it is a light love; the seriousness of the folk-poetry, with its strain of elemental passion, is relaxed. Quite a number of *pastourelles* are by known *trouvères* who have taken part in the *chanson courtois* itself. They have their *aventures* as they come and go *pensis com fins amourous*. Apparently a passage with Marion or Ermenjon was no bar to *aimer sens trichier*, although it is to the credit of Jehans Erars that he refused an *amor novele* even when offered in such circumstances. Technically, again, the *pastourelle* is freely handled. It uses a burden or not, at pleasure. Often a number of *refrains* occur in a single piece; an arrangement which implies a clear departure from the original choric intention which produced the *refrain*. Or for sung words is substituted a *dorenlot*, or nonsense-burden, a collection of inarticulate syllables, such as 'turuluruta' or 'chivalala,' meant as a conventional imitation of the notes of a rustic pipe. Here, once more, is the device of an adapter.

If, now, we accept the *chanson populaire* as a half-way stage in the movement of the poetic impulse from folk-song to the fully developed art-song represented by the *chanson courtois*, it becomes apparent that even the *chanson courtois* itself is not wholly forgetful of its remoter past. Atmosphere and sentiment have changed until they are hardly recognisable; but the tradition of the spring setting still endures, and as of old it is the nightingale who, in the *renouveau* of all things, calls upon the poet also to renew, no longer the glad hymn of anticipated foison, but the sad plaining of a cherished love which may neither attain nor die.

'Li roisignors anonce la novele
Que la saisons del dolz tens est venue,
Que tote riens renaist et renovele,
Que li pré sont covert d'erbe menue.
Por la saison, qui se change et remue,
Chascuns, fors moi, s'esjoïst et revele;
Las! car si m'est changie la merele,
Qu'on m'a geté en prison et en mue!'

(Blondels de Nesle, xiii. 1.)

Art, indeed, is at once the most revolutionary and the most conservative of human activities.

The perversity of history renders it impossible to trace any direct developement of art-song out of folk-song in England analogous to that which took place in France. There is no post-classical European poetry older than that of the Anglo-Saxons; but this, in its surviving texts, is already clear of the folk. A small and early portion of it is the work of minstrels interested in epic and the glorification of kings; the bulk has taken on a uniformly religious and didactic colouring at the hands of clerks. There is no love-poetry, and the nearest approach to lyric is in certain reflective pieces more properly to be called elegiac. They are philosophic poems, broodings over life in its entirety, rather than expressions of its passionate moments of joy and sorrow, and they have a well-defined tendency towards pessimism which impresses itself as a distinctive note of the Anglo-Saxon temper. Life really is a serious thing to these dwellers in a desolate region. It gives little joy when it is here, save the stern joy of battle, and it rapidly passes into nothingness. One recalls Bede's image of the sparrow flying into the radiant hall and out again into the whirl of frost and snow from whence it came. There is little hint of folk-song beyond a few historic lays, and at the Conquest the vernacular goes underground for a couple of centuries, and England becomes for literary purposes a province of France. From the blossoming time of the *chanson populaire* and the *chanson courtois* no English secular lyric is preserved to us, although Giraldus Cambrensis affords testimony in an amusing story to its existence.[1] The latter part of the thirteenth century brings three snatches, caught up, as was so often the case in France itself at this time, into musical settings. Two of these (Nos. I and III) are laments, probably amorous in character and still impregnated with the Anglo-Saxon melancholy; the third, the famous *Cuckoo Song* (No. II), is not folk-song, but a learned composer's adaptation of a *reverdie* or chant of welcome to the spring. Finally, just at the beginning of the fourteenth century, comes a sudden group of poems of and about love, most of which form part of a miscellaneous collection gathered out of French, Latin, and various dialects of English, and written down

[1] See the passage from his *Gemma Ecclesiastica* quoted in the notes to No. VI.

somewhere in the south-west of the country, possibly at Leominster Abbey. With these the silence is broken indeed (Nos. IV–VII). The love-songs are those of a man, not a woman. The general tone is closely akin to that of the French *trouvères*. The lovers are parted from their ladies, or these are unkind, and they sing of the pains and yearning of love, rather than of love's exultation. 'Derne love' has them in his 'baundoun'. They 'sorewe ant syke' and 'waxe grene' for love, and will die or 'walke wod' unless they have some comfort. They are thrashed about in the mill-dam of love—

'For wowyng al forwake,
Wery so water in wore'.

The derivation of all this is unmistakeable. The nightingale, the *renouveau* of leaf and grass, the sudden remembered pang; all are there—

'When the nyhtėgalė singes,
The wodės waxen grene,
Lef ant gras ant blosmė springes
In Averyl, I wene;
Ant love is to myn hertė gon
With onė spere so kene,
Nyht ant day my blod hit drynkes,
Myn hertė deth to tene.'

The song has been sung from Arragon to Arras ere now.

Yet, as compared with the typical *trouvères*, these writers wear their rue with a difference. The ambiguous Platonic relationships of the regular *amour courtois* are missing. The poet is wooing, not a wedded wife, but a 'byrd' or a 'mai', and his will is clearly for the natural end of unsophisticated love. He is frank enough about it—

'Hevene y tolde al his
That o nyht were hire gest.'

There are little personal touches. One 'wommon woneth by west'; the country-side wherein another hath no equal is 'bituenė Lyncolne ant Lyndeseye, Norhamptoun ant

Lounde'. The hawthorn name of this is Alysoun, of that Johon. And there is a good deal more of physical description than the courtly *trouvères*, always intent upon the metaphysics of love to the disregard of its sensuous aspects, allow themselves. It is the serene western type—

'With lossom eyė, grete and gode,
With browen blysfol under hode.'

The 'bel oil vair' of *chanson* and romance is repeated in 'that swetė thing, with eyenen gray'; but Alysoun has black eyes which contrast with her fair hair and brown brows. A damsel of Ribbesdale is depicted with the precision of a miniature—

'Hire hed when ich biholde upon,
The sonnėbeem aboutė noon
  Me thohtė that y seye;
Hyre eyyen aren grete ant gray ynoh,
Ant lussum, when heo on me loh,
  Ybend wax eyther breye.

. . . .

Heo hath browės bend an heh,
Whyt bytuene ant nout to neh,

. . . .

Hire chyn ys cloven, ant eyther cheke
Whit ynoh ant rode on eke,
  Ase rosė when hit redes.

Heo hath a mury mouht to mele,
With lefly redė lippės lele,
  Romaunz forte rede.

. . . .

Hyre tyttės aren an under bis
As apples tuo of parays,
  Ou self ye mowen seo.'

This becomes a detestable way of writing later on, with the seventeenth-century cataloguers of feminine charms, but in the fourteenth century it at any rate shows that the poet has his eye on the object.

The lines just quoted form part of a *chanson d'aventure*,

and another poem in the manuscript belongs definitely to the same type. It is a dialogue in which the singer finds 'a wel fayer fenge' in a 'fryht', woos her, and is bidden to 'go his gates' exactly as in a *pastourelle*. Certainly the English poems have their affinities to the *chanson populaire* as well as to the *chanson courtois*. They derive, indeed, not from the courtly heyday of *trouvère* poetry so much as from the aftermath, itself touched with popular elements, which was produced amongst the great *bourgeois* towns of Northern France. It was with the Adans de le Hale, not the Thibauts de Champagne, that our monk was in touch during the *wanderjahre* in which he first heard the songs that he afterwards wrote down amongst the apple-blossoms of his Herefordshire priory. And his gatherings contain more than one of those controversial pieces for and against womanhood, which were the outcome of a sceptical *bourgeois* reaction against the rigorous idealism of the *amour courtois*. The authors of his poems probably belonged, like himself and like Adan de le Hale, to the order of *clerici vagantes*. It is a clerk and not a *chevalier* for whom the lady of the dialogue (No. VII) is ready to defy 'fader, moder, and al my kun'. And thus may be explained the trilingual character of the collection, culminating in lines which are illuminating almost to the point of autobiography.

'*Dum ludis floribus velut lacinia,*
Le dieu d'amour me tient en tiel *angustia* ;
Merour me tient de duel e de *miseria*,
Si je ne la ay *quam amo super omnia.*

Ejus amor tantum me facit fervere,
Qe je ne soi *quid possum inde facere* ;
Pur ly covent *hoc saeculum relinquere*,
Si je ne pus l'amour de li *perquirere.*

Ele est si bele e gente dame *egregia*,
Cum ele fust *imperatoris filia* ;
De beal semblant *et pulcra continencia*
Ele est la flur *in omni regis curia.*

Quant je le vey, je su *in tali gloria,*
Come est la lune *coeli inter sidera.*
Dieu la moi doint *sua misericordia*
Beyser et fere *quae secuntur alia !*

Scripsi haec carmina in tabulis ;
Mon ostel est en mi la vile de Paris.
May y sugge namore, so wel me is !
Yef hi deye for love of her, duel hit ys.'

(Wright, *S.L.P.* xxiii.)

To the ecclesiastical training of the writers may perhaps be ascribed certain touches of pedantic symbolism, whereby a mistress is designated in a string of tropes as 'lilie of largesse, parvenke of prouesse, selsecle of suetnesse,' and the like, after a manner familiar in hymns to the Virgin.

It remains to be asked how far the fourteenth-century poems give a distinctively English note, and whether they can be supposed to draw any direct inspiration from English folk-song. English enough is a tendency to alliteration, showing itself especially in the passages of pedantry just referred to ; and English, I think, is a certain seriousness and brooding melancholy which affords love-ecstasies more convincing either than the conventions of the *trouvères* or than the *chansons d'aventure*, about which there is always a suspicion of Gallic irony. But these belong to the Anglo-Saxon literary tradition, and of folk-song there is but little to be found. There are only two burdens used. One of these, indeed, may be taken up from folk-song ; it is alien from the poem to which it is attached, and its motive of woman's love in absence recurs in the *Western Wind* (No. XXXI) of a Tudor song-book, and in the ballad of *The Unquiet Grave.*

' Blow, northerne wynd,
Sent thou me my suetyng !
Blow, northerne wynd,
Blou, blou, blou !'

In another poem (No. v) the amorous element is subordinated to a *reverdie* more elaborate, like the *Cuckoo Song* itself, than is usual in the French models. But on the whole the poets, with their masculine love and their rhythmical accomplishment, do not stand very near to the folk. They have the freshness of the primal world upon them, no doubt, but after all it is the business of the art-poet to keep this freshness and yet to sing his own song. And the sentiment is individual, not communal. Out of his personal fancy a man writes—

'Ich wolde ich were a threstelcok,
A bountyng other a laverok,
Swetė bryd !
Bi tuene hire curtel ant hire smok
Y wolde ben hyd.'

There is a literary past behind one who endeavours to sum up a thousand poetic introductions in the single line—

'Lenten ys come with love to toune.'

And what curious sympathy with far-off Catullus shaped this exquisite love-letter across the English cowslips ?

'Fayrest fode upo loft,
My gode luef, y the greete
As felė sythe ant oft
As dewes dropės beth weete,
Ase sterrės beth in welkne ant grasės sour ant suete.'

The delightful promise of the Leominster manuscript is, alas ! not maintained. The macaronic verses (Nos. VIII and IX) of a Cambridge manuscript are perhaps less interesting for any sheer poetic quality than as a renewed reminder of the cosmopolitan character of mediæval literature. There must have been popular songs in the fourteenth century for Absolon to sing to his rubible, but edacious time has reduced them to tantalising fragments. Amongst aimless scribbles on a blank leaf of *Rawlinson MS*. D. 913 is the following—

'Icham of Irlaunde and of the holy londe of Irlande.
Gode sire, pray ich ye,
For of saynte Charite,
Come ant daunce wyt me in Irlaunde.'

We would dance gladly did we but know the tune. Another scrap on the same page has also its air of romantic suggestion—

'Maiden in the mor lay, in the mor lay, sevenyht full.
Welle was hire mete, wat was hire mete?
The primerole ant the violet.'

Of an entire poem in *Bodley MS.* 692, only the first two lines are legible—

'Joly cheperte of Aschell down
Can more on love than al this town.'

With the fifteenth century emerge the ballads; but these, although they contain lyric as well as narrative elements, and certainly bring us, in some kind or degree, into contact with the folk, open up too many serious questions for treatment as a side-issue here. An isolated masterpiece, at the end of the century, is *The Nutbrown Maid* (No. XIX). This has affinities to the ballads, to which outlaws and the greenwood are dear; but it is primarily lyric, and may have been written for recitation in alternative chant by two minstrels. Its double burden and the fact that the woman bears the brunt of the emotion hint at an inspiration from folk-song. It continues the tradition also of the Leominster manuscript. There is an advance in freedom of handling and mastery of rhythm; but the ring of sincerity and wholesome conviction is the same. The professed purpose of the poem connects itself with the old dispute as to the qualities of women which the *amour courtois* had provoked. The actual form has its precedent in the earlier dialogue between the lady and the clerk (No. VII), and even the greenwood note is there anticipated.

Literary poetry during the fifteenth century is, of course, wholly under the domination of Chaucer; and Chaucer, English though he is and thoroughly in touch with the folk in *The Canterbury Tales*, does not draw his lyric from native sources. His *balades* and *rondels* (Nos. X–XIV) represent a fresh wave of continental influence. 'The note, I trowe, ymakèd was in Fraunce.' These are exotic forms, worked out by French musicians on the basis of the French *caroles*, which became the literary fashion as the *grands chansons* died away. What Chaucer really did was to divert the fifteenth century from lyric to narrative; but so far as Lydgate and Occleve and their fellows write lyric at all, they follow his models, and show but little spontaneity. The English versions of poems by Charles of Orleans and others (Nos. XVI and XVII) are something of an accident and hardly come into account; and the resource, pungency, and versatility of Skelton (Nos. XX to XXII) were too rarely turned in a lyrical direction. Skelton, however, was contemporary with a renascence of song under the early Tudors, for which we have to thank the musicians. *The Cuckoo Song* and other isolated examples survive to show that the thirteenth-century part-song had its English as well as its continental vogue, and that both courtly and popular poetry were drawn upon to provide secular themes for such compositions. But the great age of English counterpoint was in the fifteenth century, and was due to the growth in importance under the patronage of Henry VI, himself no mean musician, of the domestic choir which maintained the services of the royal chapel. A school of composers arose, of whom the most famous was John Dunstable; and for a while England led the musical developement of France and Flanders. The work of this school was mainly religious and largely liturgical, and such of its amorous productions as have survived are unfortunately mutilated. But we owe to it the well-known *Agincourt* song and that of *God Speed the Plow*, which is included

(No. CXLII) in this collection. After the death of Dunstable the school lost its European hegemony, and became, from a musical point of view, unprogressive. But the habit of composition endured, and song-books of the reigns of Henry VII and Henry VIII show a considerable activity in the setting of light and amorous ditties (Nos. XXIII–XLIV). Henry VIII (Nos. XXIII, XXIV, CXXIII) had himself some taste for music, although modern critics deny him musical talent; and, with his, the outstanding names are those of Robert Fairfax and William Cornish (Nos. XXV, LXXXIX), both of whom were Gentlemen of the Chapel. It must not, of course, be taken for granted that the authors of settings were necessarily also the authors of the words set. But probably it was so in some cases. Cornish, for example, was certainly a literary man as well as a musician. He was Master of the Children of the Chapel, and in this capacity devised masks and interludes, in which he appeared before the king with his fellows and the children.

It must be admitted that the general character of the Tudor songs is a little disappointing. They hardly foreshadow a new literary age. The Renascence lingers, while they re-echo conventions which have already grown familiar during the mediæval centuries. Here, dressed out in the more complicated harmony of pricksong, are the very vows and laments of *amour courtois* (Nos. XXIII, XXIV, XXVI, XXXV, XXXIX, XLIII, XLIV), which the *trouvère* chanted so long ago to the simple accompaniment furnished by the *vielle* of his *jougleur*. Here are bits of the allegory dear to the fourteenth century (No. XXV). Here once again are the overheard complaints of women (Nos. XXVII, XXXI) and the pastoral dialogues of the *chansons d'aventure* (Nos. XXVIII, XXIX). The nightingale is still 'jargonning' in the spring (Nos. XXXII, XXXIII). Courtly and popular elements appear in about equal degree. Burdens are not unusual; the Amyas snatch of Cornish's allegory (No. XXV) seems alien to the structure of the poem, and recalls the greenwood motive of *The Nutbrown Maid* and the ballads. Looking back on the Leominster manuscript and comparing its temper with that of the Tudor lyrists, one is conscious of a loss of seriousness and conviction. 'Derne love' has given place to the light love of a frivolous court, where you wear your heart upon your sleeve and must not have the ill manners to let real feeling spoil the game. Irresponsible lightheartedness—'Pastime with good company,' as Henry put it—is the ideal of the day. The deeper accents of emotion, with much else that is of the soul of literature, come back with Wyatt; but Wyatt, though he rubbed elbows with the writers of the song-books, lies outside the scope of this collection and of these observations.

The English religious lyric of the Middle Ages far exceeds in bulk that of the love-lyric. And it declares itself earlier. Some twelfth-century fragments pass under the name of St. Godric, once a sea-roving chapman and afterwards a hermit of Finchale in Durham. The thirteenth and early fourteenth centuries afford quite a respectable harvest in half a dozen manuscripts, including that of Leominster already dwelt upon. One of these comes from as far as Kildare, in Ireland, and is written in an Anglo-Irish dialect. The dominant feature of this poetry is its elegiac quality. It takes its impulse from the contemplation of things as a whole and the conviction of their inherent uncertainty. It is full of the vanity of life and the nothingness of man—

> 'Of this worldes ioie, hou hit geth al to noght.'

It abounds in metaphors for the fleeting character of human happiness, which glides away 'also the schadewe' or 'so wyndės bles' or 'so the scheft is of the cleo.' The world is 'bot a brotil tre' and 'the ax is at the rote.' It 'faleweth so doth medowė gras,' as said the Psalmist—

> 'This world is love is gon awai,
> So dew on grasse in somer is dai.'

Glories and splendours may not endure. As to the rest, so the message is to those—

> ' that sittet ischrud
> With skarlet and with palle.'

The laughter of youth, the beauty of woman, the strength of knight and baron, the state of queens; all must vanish. Where are the great sovereigns and the great lovers of the past?

> ' Hwer is Paris and Heleyne,
> That weren so bryht and feyre on bleo?
> Amadas, Tristram and Dideyne,
> Yseude and allė theo,
> Ector with his scharpė meyne,
> And Cesar riche of worldės feo?
> Heo beoth iglyden ut of the reyne,
> So the scheft is of the cleo.'

Ubi nunc fidelis ossa Fabricii manent? Boethius had asked the question long ago; and long afterwards it resounds in Villon's famous *ballade*, and even in the song of Elizabethan Nash—

> ' Queens have died young and fair;
> Dust hath closed Helen's eye.'

It is all vanity, saith the poet, as the preacher had said before him. Even 'Henry ure kyng,' no less than Absalon, shall be dimmed—

> ' Ne may hit never his waraunt beo,
> Gold ne seolver, vouh ne gray.'

Man is no more than earth upon earth, and the phrase becomes the text of a whole group of poems, linking themselves with that favourite pictorial representation of mediæval pessimism, the Dance of Death. The singer dwells with grim interest upon the last tragic horrors of mortality, when the rosy flesh is but 'wermės fode,' and man 'that was so modi and so strong' is impotent on his bier any longer to protect his own—

'Nu lith the clei-clot
Al so the ston,
And his freondės striveth
To gripen his iwon.'

And after death comes the judgement. The future is dark in the next world, as in this—

'I not whider I shal, ne hou longe her duelle.'

There is the 'murie londe', but there is also the dread alternative of—

'the lothė hous
That to the fende is wrohte.'

It is perhaps a consolation that even in these grim regions the irony of fate pursues the great ones of the earth, no less than common folk.

'Moni of thissė riche,
That wereden foh and grei,
An rideth uppė stede
And uppen palefrai,
Heo schulen attė dome
Suggen weilawei.'

Weilawei! It is the keynote, the constantly iterated burden, of all this *macabre* desperate song.

Professedly it is Christian poetry, but the colour of its sentiment is no essential part of the Christian attitude towards life. Perhaps we have to do with a matter of racial temperament rather than of creed, and it is the Anglo-Saxon melancholy that inspires so keen a sense of the transitoriness and uncertainty of all mortal things. It speaks, as it were, with the least qualification in the lullaby (No. XCI) of the Kildare manuscript. By this sad lilt the very child in his cradle is taught that sorrow is the law of life. Weeping he comes into the world, and with good cause, for the world will be his foe, as it has ever been the foe of his 'eldren'. His foot is in the wheel, and he is beginning a pilgrimage, at the end of which death out of 'a wel dim horre' awaits him. It is the very cry of pagan Lear, as he feels the foundations of his life crumbling around him—

> 'Thou knowest, the first time that we smell the air,
> We wawl and cry . . .
> When we are born, we cry that we are come
> To this great stage of fools.'

Of course, it is largely a matter of emphasis. Even the lullaby takes its Christian turn; it is through Adam's apple and the wickedness of Satan that death came into the world. And the consciousness of the vanity of things fits in well enough with one aspect of Christian doctrine. It is a reading of life which Christianity had had to meet and to absorb into itself at an earlier stage. The poets, as we have seen, could draw from the *Psalms* and from *Ecclesiastes*. They could draw also from more than one patristic writing *De Contemptu Mundi*. A more immediate source is the so-called *Poema Morale*, which dates from the second half of the twelfth century. This is not cast in lyric form, but the lyrics repeat many of its ideas and its phrases. It is a poem of regret for a misspent life, which expands into an exposition of the last things and of the scheme of salvation. Obviously the sentiment becomes more definitely Christian when the philosophical despair is supplemented by a sense of personal sin, and still more when the hope of redemption is suggested as a consolation. The lullaby lacks both of these, but the latter at least is seldom altogether omitted in a thirteenth-century lyric. Only it is present in different proportions. Sometimes there is a mere perfunctory bidding of Christ or the Virgin to be 'bote', in a final stanza, which hardly affects the tenour of the whole; sometimes this element is elaborated, until the pessimism and even the expression of personal contrition fall into the background, and the poem takes the shape of a hymn or a prayer. Herewith comes in, directly or through the French, the influence of Latin hymnology, which supplies models both for structure and for diction.

At this stage the appeal is generally to Christ and the Virgin themselves, rather than to the saints. An address to 'holy Thomas of heoveriche' as 'help in Engelaunde' is quite exceptional. And the approach is a direct one; there is little flavour of ecclesiasticism, or dwelling on church and sacraments as avenues of grace. Certain objective elements of description and incident begin to make their appearance with such themes as the Annunciation, the *Stabat Mater*, and the Five Joys of Mary. It can hardly be said that the ethical tone of the lyrics is strenuous. The monastic shrinking from the world is more in evidence than the virile desire to conquer it. The soul is too often content with a passive acquiescence in its own salvation through the merits of others; and one welcomes the rarer intervention of a more vigorous temper—

> 'Oup, and be god champioun !
> Stond, ne fal namore adoun
> For a luytel blast !'

Other examples of individual lyric emotion disengaging itself from the common theme are afforded by two poems in the Leominster manuscript, which are imitations, but not translations, of the *Iesu, dulcis memoria!* of St. Bernard of Clairvaux. Here the feeling of personal adoration breaks away from the formal 'bidding', and the burden of the whole is the constant motive of the mystics, the passion of the soul for the divine object. The aspiration is not merely for salvation at the end, but for the love of Christ for its own sake, as an abiding comfort here and now.

The dependence of the English upon the Latin hymns would be unmistakeable, even without the tags of Latin which indicate a habit of translating the couplets of a caudated poem, while leaving the *caudæ* themselves in the original. It is even more interesting to trace a very distinct influence of the contemporary secular lyric. Thus the Virgin is addressed, not only by such obvious names as

'Moder milde', 'Maiden moder', 'Moder and virgyne', or by the symbolic appellations of 'Quene of evene', 'Quene of storre', 'Flur of parays', and the like, but also in language bearing the closest resemblance to that which the *trouvères* were in the habit of addressing to their mistresses. She is 'Mi leovė swetė lefdi' or 'Lavedi so fair and so hende'. One poet calls her—

'My dayės blis, my nyhtės rest.'

Another sings—

'Nou is fre that er was thral,
Al thourh that levedy gent ant smal.'

Nor do the parallels stop here. The structure and conventions of amorous poetry are deliberately adapted and turned to pious uses in songs of spiritual love-longing, *chansons d'aventure* of the soul.

'Ase y me rod this ender day
By grenė wodė to seche play,
Mid herte I thohte al on a may,
Suetest of allė thinge.'

The 'may' is the Virgin, and the poem goes on to tell of her Five Joys. For these poets the old setting of the *renouveau* has found a new meaning.

'When y se blosmės springe,
Ant herė foulės song,
A suetė lovė-longynge
Myn hertė thourh out stong;
Al for a lovė newe,
That is so suete ant trewe,
That gladieth al mi song.'

But it is Jesus whom the singer has 'cheosen to lemmon'. In another piece the theme of 'Somer is comen and winter gon' is similarly diverted, while in the Leominster manuscript a love-song and its religious parody are preserved side by side. Such give and take between the divine and the secular is of course no rarity in literature. It were easy to quote examples from the comedies of Hrotsvitha to the *Gude and Godlie Ballatis* and beyond. In the case of the lyrics the earliest intermediaries were doubtless the *scholares vagantes*, who stole mundane melodies for their hymns as readily as they profaned the churches by fitting improper words to the liturgical chants. But by the end of the thirteenth century one has also to take account of the activity of the Franciscan friars, and to remember that St. Francis, a *trouvère* in his youth and a poet to the end, was careful to enjoin upon his brothers the duty of becoming *ioculatores Domini* and turning song to the service of heaven. It is at least curious that the only two names to which religious lyrics attach themselves in this century are both those of Minorites. One is that of 'Frere Michel Kyldare' who wrote one at least of the Anglo-Irish poems; the other that of Thomas de Hales, whose *Cantus quem composuit ad instanciam cuiusdam puellae deo dicatae* is perhaps the most complete example of the tendency under discussion. A 'maydė Cristes' has bidden the poet—

> 'That ich hire wurche a luveron';

and so, after a typical exposition of the vanity of the world, some passages from which I have already had occasion to quote, he advises her to let Christ be her lover—

> 'Mayde, if thu wilnest after leofmon,
> Ich techė the enne treowė king.'

Christ has sent her his 'sonde' and desires 'forto beo the cuth'. All the joys of his 'leovemon', including the 'derewurthe gemme' of 'maydenhod', are set out.

The same strain of religious poetry endured into the fourteenth century. The lyrical element in the Kentish poems of William of Shoreham is of little account. A more significant name is that of the Yorkshire hermit and precursor of Wyclife, Richard Rolle of Hampole, who seems to have adopted the deliberate Minorite practice of endeavouring to sanctify song. 'Nec lira laetitiae quam lubrici laudabant mihi libebat,' he says in his barbarous Latin, 'sed et cantum carnalium concito calcavi, ad Christum convertens quod cantabatur. Cantilenas quidem de feminis fecerunt; hoc reputavi rursum ruinam.' Rolle was a systematic mystic, and represents the impulse to sing as an echo of a divine *canor* forming a particular stage in the mystical path. He seems to have begun with short snatches of song interspersed amongst his prose treatises, and afterwards to have expanded these into more elaborate poems, of which a collection is preserved under the name of *Cantica Divini Amoris*. Amongst other pieces assigned to him on conjecture is a lengthened and amalgamated version of the two imitations of St. Bernard of Clairvaux in the Leominster manuscript. Whether this conjecture be sound or not, it is precisely the tradition of such poetry that he continues. All his verse is of 'love-longing', filled with that sense of personal contact between the soul and the divine object which appears to lie at the heart of the mystical apprehension. His subjective reading of religion and a certain personal austerity of outlook give him affinities rather to Protestant than to typically Catholic sentiment. He conceives of love, not as softness, but as fire; to him, as to the *trouvères*, although in another sense, it is 'derne love'.

'For now, lufe thow, I redė, Cryste, as I thee tell,
And with aungels take thy stedė; that joy loke thou noght sell!
In erth thow hate, I rede, all that thy lufe may fell,
For luf es stalworth as the dedė, luf es hard as hell.'

(Horstman, i. 77.)

Rolle's literary quality has been exaggerated by uncritical admirers; and, as a matter of fact, this collection does not find room for him. But a vein of real lyric sweetness runs through his rather harsh northern utterance; and even his homeliness of speech is not without its occasional charm.

'Owre setels heven ar within; me lyst sytt in myne,'

he says; and the red-litten windows of a Yorkshire

farmhouse arise before you as an image of the new Jerusalem. In his mood he is strongly alliterative, and not least in his most objective poem, a meditation on the Passion—

'My fender of my fose sa fonden in the felde,
Sa lufly lyghtand at the evensang-tyde;
Thy moder and hir menyhe unlacėd thy scheld;
All wepėd that thar were, thy woundės was sa wyde.'

(Horstman, i. 72.)

Alliteration is a feature of his Latin also, and he perhaps represents the beginning of a tendency, natural enough as the English folk came more and more into contact with literature, which culminated in the marked alliterative revival by Langland and his fellows at the end of the century. This revival itself touches upon lyric in *Pearl*, although the exquisite threnody is too long and too elegiac to be properly classed as a lyric. Rolle seems to have founded something of a school, through such disciples as William of Nassington; and his influence is the most notable one in the large accumulations of religious poetry garnered in the Thornton, Vernon, Simeon, Lambeth, and other manuscripts of the fifteenth century. Here, however, we may trace a growing ecclesiasticism, together with literary influences which show themselves in elaborate Chaucerian stanza-forms and Latin refrains. The beautiful *Quia Amore Langueo* (No. LXXXIV) stands out of a mass of verse of no great moment.

But this amazing fifteenth century, whose official poets sleep so contentedly in the shadow of Chaucer, shows itself, in the less exalted sphere of popular literature, full of surprises. To the miracle plays and the ballads it adds the carols. At the end of a tedious versifying of the whole duty of man by John Awdlay, a blind chaplain of Haghmon, in Shropshire, comes a sudden change of key. The gladdened scribe marks it with red letters—

'I pray yow, sirus, boothe moore and lase,
Sing these caroles in Cristėmas,'

Then follow twenty-five short poems, some at least of which have the genuine lyric ring, while all are shown by their lilting burdens to be intended for utterance in song (Nos. LVII, CXXXIV). One of them is 'mad of King Herrė'; others are on moral themes, or in honour of the Virgin. But there is a group belonging to the range of high feasts which fall in the twelve nights from Nativity to Epiphany; and the introductory couplet makes it sufficiently clear that the primary purpose of the whole collection was for service in the Christmas season. They are, in fact, examples of a kind of song which is familiar in the popular literature of all European countries, and has lasted to quite modern times, in England under Awdlay's very name of carols, and in France under that of *noëls*. Part of Awdlay's volume was composed in the year 1426. Some of the carols may be of rather earlier date. Two of them recur, with many others of similar structure, in an anonymous Sloane manuscript of about the same period. It is convenient and, as will be seen, historically correct, to confine the use of the term carol to short poems, furnished with a burden and intended for singing. Of these the bulk of the Sloane manuscript is made up; but it also contains Latin verses, at least one regular ballad, and a few lyrics in ballad metre, which share the general character of the carols, and are in some cases of rare beauty (Nos. L, LIV, LVI). One of the carols preserves historical allusions which suggests that it was written in the last half of the fourteenth, rather than at the beginning of the fifteenth century. Carols continue to be plentiful for the next hundred years after Awdlay's time. They are to be found scattered through numerous manuscripts. Two considerable gatherings of them are set as part-songs for two or three voices in music-books of the Dunstable school. At the end of the fifteenth century they still form the principal element in another collection, curiously like that of the Sloane manuscript after an interval of at least fifty years, which is now in the Bodleian.

About 1524 Richard Hill, a London tradesman, brought a number of them together, with much other poetry both secular and religious from literary sources, in his commonplace book. Skelton and the musicians of Henry the Eighth's court occasionally wrote and set them; and printed books of *Christmas Carolles*, of which fragments only survive, were produced by the London stationers until well into Elizabeth's reign. It is interesting to find Awdlay's poems enduring, not only in both the song-books, but also in Richard Hill's miscellany. Most of the best carols are, however, anonymous, and the vast compilation made by the Franciscan James Ryman about 1494 chiefly serves to show how savourless a thing popular poetry can become in the adapting hands of a pious and unimaginative ecclesiastic. If Ryman is interesting at all, it is only as continuing the old Franciscan tradition of religious minstrelsy. Awdlay himself has a special devotion to St. Francis, but the abbey of Haghmon, in which he wrote, was an Augustinian and not a Minorite house.

Thomas Wright, who first edited the Sloane and Bodleian manuscripts, regarded them as the professional repertories of minstrels; and indeed there is a specious air of minstrelsy about their frequent appeals to the 'more and lasse' and the 'lordings' present in hall and bower. But while they contain a small proportion of secular, satirical, and even improper pieces, their general tone is far too uniformly didactic and religious to be at all characteristic of minstrelsy. These qualities and the Latin tags with which they abound inevitably suggest that the authors were clerks, although, likely enough, clerks of the errant persuasion. Some of the Latin verses, indeed, belong definitely to the Goliardic cycle. Even John Awdlay leaves the impression of looking back on a misspent youth. And the addresses to the 'lordings' are obviously capable of another explanation. They may be those not of minstrels, but of wassailing neighbours who make their rounds at Christmastide to drink a cup and take a gift and bring good fortune upon the house. It is not necessary to labour here the folk character of a custom which, like the kindred ritual of mumming or mask, has its origin in the sacrificial perambulations of pagan festival.[1] The earliest *noëls* were no doubt wassailing songs. In an Anglo-Norman one of the thirteenth century, the singers hail the 'seignors' of the 'hostel' which they visit, and announce that they have come 'pur quere Noël,' who, as they understand, holds his yearly revel there. The song has its burden—

> 'Deu doint à tuz icels joie d'amurs,
> Qui à danz Noël ferunt honors.'

But in the last stanza this is varied, and two English words introduced—

> 'Si jo vus di trestoz *Wesseyl !*
> Dehaiz eit qui ne dirra *Drincheyl !*'
> (Wright, *S.C.C.* i.)

The English carols of the fifteenth century do not wholly miss the festive note. There are carols of 'my lord sire Cristèmasse,' or of 'Yole, thou mery man' (Nos. CXXXIV–CXXXVI), carols of the wassail (Nos. CXXVIII, CXXIX, CXXXI, CXXXIII) and the boar's head (No. CXXXVII), carols of the contest of holly and ivy (Nos. CXXXVIII–CXLI), which seems to symbolize some ancient opposition of the sexes in the folk festival. It is easy to understand how the religious element in Christmas at last prevailed and gave its own colouring to the majority of the ditties. But the religious element is the superadded and not the primitive one. The very name of carol is significant; for here, no less than in the amorous *caroles* of twelfth-century France, are represented the mingled dance and song of the village *chorus*, hailing with rhythmic exultation the coming of the summer or the winter holiday. An interesting confirmation of this relationship is afforded by the metrical

[1] Cf. *Mediaeval Stage*, i. 253, 400.

structure of the carols. Their form varies considerably, but the commonest type of all, to which almost precisely half the examples in the two earliest manuscripts belong, consists of a triplet upon a single rhyme, followed by a *cauda* which is linked by a second rhyme to one or more lines of the burden. Exactly the same arrangement is to be found in several twelfth- or thirteenth-century French *caroles*, including that quoted on page 269.[1] It is an intermediate stage between the elaborated *rondel* and the simpler scheme of the *chanson d'histoire*, in which a monorhymed *couplet*, originally perhaps of a single line, is followed by a *refrain* upon another rhyme, without any connecting link. It lends itself admirably to the methods of a dance-song shared between a leader and a *chorus*, since the change of rhyme in the *cauda* serves literally as a cue to the *chorus* that it is their turn to break in with the burden. Sometimes the whole of the *cauda*, and not merely its rhyme, is repeated from stanza to stanza, and it becomes in effect a second or inner burden. The burden or 'fote' itself remains a characteristic of the carols, long after both the dance accompaniment and the strict division of lines between a leader and a *chorus* have been forgotten.

Space fails for any sufficient analysis of the literary quality of the carols. There are perhaps enough of them in this volume to speak for themselves. The contrast which they present to the more ecclesiastical modes of mediæval religious poetry is remarkable. The Anglo-Saxon pessimism, the oppression of imminent mortality, the brooding sense of personal sin, pass into the background, if they do not altogether disappear. These singers approach their religious themes with something of the light-hearted simplicity of the first shepherds. They greet the coming of a Saviour without trepidation, as a gay and wonderful event.

'Mary is quene of allė thinge,
And her sone a lovely kinge,'

[1] Cf. Bartsch, i. 22–27, 50; ii. 48, 91.

they chant; or with an even more naive blending of familiarity and awe—

'Blessėd be God this game is begonne,
And his moder emperesse of helle.'

Even the thought of the sin of Adam leads to its *Deo gracias.* All is for the best—

'Ne hadde the appil takė ben,
The appil taken ben,
Ne haddė never our lady
A ben hevenė quene.'

Philosophic contemplation puts on the gnomic manner of the folk. The garnered wisdom of life is summed up in proverbial phrases of unassailable homespun—

'For there is none but one of two,
Heven to gete or heven forgo;
Oder mene none there is.'

Or again—

'Now is joye and now is bliss;
Now is balle and bitternesse;
Now it is and now it nis;
Thus paseth this world away.'

The world, indeed, is 'but a chery ffayre', in the pretty metaphor of the Shropshire orchards; and the poets are content to take it for granted and to make the best of it, without repining. As compared with the ecclesiastical verse, again, the carols are markedly objective and pictorial in their apprehension of things. They are the lyric counterpart of the miracle plays; and probably they betray the actual influence of the constant visualisation of biblical scenes and personages in the periodical representations of Nativity or of Passion. Those who sang them and those who listened had looked on 'Bethlem, that faier borow' and on 'Herowd, that mody king' and the 'three kinges of great noblay', Caspar, Melchior, and Balthasar, marching in each one with his train. They could recall how Gabriel 'sat on knee, and seide *Ave!*'

and how Mary 'stod stille as ony ston', and how the 'angeles cam out of here toure' to behold, clustering no doubt upon a flight of steps, as one sees them in Jean Fouquet's miniature of the *Miracle of St. Apollonia.* In the carols, as in the miracle plays, the personality of the Virgin is hung about with a tender humanity. There is a series of lullabies (Nos. LXIII, LXIV, LXXVII), some of which contain dialogues between the Mother and Child comparable to those later dialogues at the Crucifixion, which also figure in our collection (No. LXXX) and are a recognised variety of the *Planctus Mariae.* To trace the development of these lullabies and their relation to the lullaby of a purely human mother in the Anglo-Irish manuscript of the early fourteenth century (No. XCI) would be in itself a tempting theme.

Like the love-songs of the *chanson populaire*, the carols are not wholly of the folk, nor is the folk wholly forgotten in them. They bring up an image of the spacious coloured burgess life of which they formed a part. The flames of the Yule-log flicker upon the hearth, and the roasted crab bobs in the wassail-bowl of spiced ale. The skin-clad mummers, with their grotesque fool, have but just left the hall. Already the chanted question comes nearer and nearer along the crooked mediæval street—

'What tithingis bringst us, messangere,
Of Cristės birth this new eris day?'

And the clear voices peal out the exultant answer to the tingling stars—

'Suche wonder tithingis ye mow here,
That maydon and modur is won i fere,
And lady is of hye aray.'

Even so 'as he lay seke in his langure' had John the blind Awdlay written it for his countrymen, in the quiet dormitory of his 'abbay here be west'.

E. K. C.

Sept. 1906–*Feb.* 1907.

SOURCES OF TEXTS

LIST OF BOOKS

NOTES AND INDEX

'Se what folowth to them that love mynstrels.'

Lambeth MS. 306.

SOURCES OF TEXTS

I.—MANUSCRIPTS

London.

(*a*) British Museum.

Additional 5465. Parchment; blank paper inserted where leaves are missing; 11½ × 8½. Belonged to Robert Fairfax, Gentleman of the Chapel Royal and organist of St. Albans, ob. 1529, and may be in his hand. In 1618 it belonged to General Fairfax, from whom it passed to Ralph Thoresby of Leeds (see his *History of Leeds*, 517), and at his sale to Mr. Jno. White of Newgate Street. It contains words and music throughout; the composers include R. Fairfax, G. Banistre, W. Cornishe jun., Turges, Tudor, W. Newark, R. Davy, Sir Thos. Phelyppis, Sheringham, Browne; these range from Henry VI to Henry VIII. Used by Hawkins as 'Thoresby's MS.'; often called 'the Fairfax MS.' Described by Burney, *History of Music*, ii. 539; Briggs, *Songs and Madrigals*, Introduction, xv. Extracts printed by Ritson, Rimbault, and by Flügel in *N.L.* Edited in *Archiv*, cvi, 48; cix, 70, by B. Fehr, who prints all that is not in the above. [Nos. XXXIV, XXXV, XXXVI, LXXXVII, CXLVII.]

Additional 5665. Chiefly paper; some parchment leaves inserted; 10 × 7. MS. note, 'Presented by J. Ritson Esq. 7 August 1795.' Latin and English songs, with music throughout; the poems probably belong to the reigns of Edward IV, Henry VII, and the early years of Henry VIII; the composers include Henry VIII, R. Smart, John Trouluffe, Ric. Mower, Sir T. Pakke, H. Petyr, Edm. Sturges, John Cornish, Sir W. Hawte. Extracts in Ritson (as from his 'Folio MS.'), Stafford Smith, Wright, *S.C.C.*, Rimbault, and Flügel, *N.L.* Edited in *Archiv*, CVI, 262, by B. Fehr, who prints all that is not in the above. [No. CXLVI.]

Additional 26,737. Paper, 11½ × 7½. Collectanea concerning Yorkshire. Lyrics only on ff. 106*b*–108*b*. XVI cent. [No. CXV.]

Additional 31,922. Parchment, 12 × 8½. Music throughout, with and without words of lyrics. The composers include Henry VIII, W. Cornish, T. Farding, Cowper, Fluyd, W. Daggere, Rysbye, Pygott. At least one of the poems is by Sir Thomas Wyatt; this may be dated 1518–1528. Another poem can be exactly dated Jan. 1–Feb. 22, 1511. The MS. is said to have belonged to Henry VIII; it is certainly well decorated. In the XVI cent. it appears to have belonged to several families in the parish of Benenden, in Kent (perhaps that of Sir H. Guildford among others); it bears bookplates of Thomas Fuller, M.D., and Archibald, 11th Earl of Eglinton; a later owner was Sir Charles Montolieu Lamb. It was lent by Mrs. Lamb, of Beauport Park, Sussex, to William Chappell, who described it in *Archaeologia*, xli. 371, in 1867. The British Museum purchased it in 1882. Also described in Briggs, *Songs and Madrigals*, Introduction xvi. Edited by Flügel in *Anglia*, xii. 226; he also prints extracts in *N.L.* [Nos. XXIII–XXVIII, XXX, CXXIII, CXLV.]

Cottonian Vesp. A. xxv. Paper (parchment copy of Benedictine rule inserted), 8¼ × 6¼. Poems and ballads, mainly religious, but with secular and jovial poems as well; chiefly in one hand; 69 items, of which 52 are English poems. At the end is 'Finis per me, William Asheton clericum.' One poem is dated 1578; on f. 1 is a note 'Divers things of Henry VIII time'; and certain poems are in the early Tudor manner. Was 'quondam peculium Hen. Savill, ex dono Anstis Arm̄'. Extracts in Wright, *S.C.C.*, and *Rel. Ant.* Edited by Böddeker in *Lemcke's Jahrbuch* (Neue Folge), ii. 81, 210, 347; iii. 92; he prints all the lyrics. [No. CXXXII.]

Egerton 613. Parchment, $8\frac{3}{4} \times 5\frac{3}{4}$. A few English lyrics of the XIII or early XIV cent. on the first few leaves. The remainder is a miscellany in prose and verse, English and Norman-French; epistles, religious and moral poems. The MS. bears the name 'Wm. Bentham Esq of Gower Street'; it was purchased by the British Museum in 1836. The lyrics printed in *Rel. Ant.* and some by Morris, *O.E.M.* (1872). [No. XLVI.]

Harleian 682. Parchment, $7\frac{3}{4} \times 5\frac{1}{2}$. English Poems ascribed to Charles, Duke of Orleans; c. 1450. Edited by G. W. Taylor for the Roxburghe Club, 1827. [Nos. XVI, XVII.]

Harleian 913. Parchment, $5\frac{1}{2} \times 3\frac{3}{4}$. English, Latin, and French, in various hands; written apparently in Gray Abbey, a Franciscan house, in Kildare; Anglo-Irish dialect; c. 1308–1318. One poem by 'Frere Michel Kildare.' Belonged in 16th century to George Wyse, mayor of Waterford; in 1697 to Bishop More of Norwich, but did not go with his bequest to Cambridge. Described in T. Crofton Croker's *Popular Songs of Ireland*, and edited by W. Heuser. Some poems in *Rel. Ant.* and Furnivall, *E.E.P.* [No. XCI.]

Harleian 978. Parchment, $7\frac{1}{2} \times 5\frac{1}{4}$. Chiefly Latin and French, prose and verse. MS. note on flyleaf, signed 'F. M[adden]., Apr. 1862,' says 'In all probability the earlier portion of this volume was written in the Abbey of Reading about the year 1240 . . .' Music ff. 1–15. The 'Cuckoo-Song' is on f. 11*b*. Described in *O.H.M.*, i. 327. [No. II.]

Harleian 2252. Paper, 11 × 7½. In various hands. Bears the name of John Colyn, citizen and mercer of London, living in the parish of St. Mary Wolnoth; temp. Henry VIII. Some poems in *Rel. Ant.*, Wright, *S.C.C.*, and Hazlitt-Ritson. Copied by Flügel for *Anglia* series. [Nos. XXXVII, XXXVIII.]

Harleian 2253. Parchment, 11½ × 7½. Miscellany of Latin, Anglo-French, and English verse and prose, in various hands. Wright conjectured it to be from Leominster Abbey, Herefordshire; the collector a clerk; Böddeker supposes him to have been a *vagans*. The poems are in Southern English, often translated from other dialects. An allusion to the death of Edward I shows that the MS. was not complete in 1307. Some of the English poems printed by Wright, *S.L.P.*; all the English poems by Böddeker, who gives (ix) a complete list of contents. Ten Brink, vol. i, has good estimate of literary value of MS. Variants of some of the non-erotic lyrics appear in Egerton 613, Digby 86, and other MSS. [Nos. IV, V, VI, VII, XLVIII, XLIX, XCII.]

Harleian 4294. Paper, 11¾ × 7¾. English lyrics, mostly in the same hand; fifteenth century. [No. CXIII.]

Harleian 5396. First part non-lyrical, ff. 1–270, parchment; second part, ff. 271–311, paper, 8½ × 5½, with MS. note 'A Collection of Ancient Poems with some other Memorandums dated ye 34 year of K. Hen. VI. 1456.' Extracts in Wright, *S.C.C.* [Nos. LXII, LXVII.]

Harleian 7322. Parchment, 6¾ × 4¾. In several hands, of various dates in the XV century. Lyrics occur quoted in sermons; some printed by Furnivall, *P.R.L.* [No. XCIII.]

Harleian 7358. Paper, $6 \times 4\frac{3}{4}$. Verses, riddles, etc., in Latin and English. XV cent. [No. CXIV.]

Harleian 7578. Ff. 83–117, paper : whole MS. as now bound is $12\frac{1}{4} \times 8\frac{1}{2}$. Note on f. 83 in Ritson's writing 'An oblong paper book, given in 1717/18, to Mr. [Humphrey] Wanley, by James Mickleton Esquire of Gray's Inn, containing the treble part of a collection of old songs &c set to musick, used within and about the bishop[ric] of Durham, in the time of queen Elizabeth, with the names of the composers : imperfect.' Extracts in Ritson (1790) ; and by B. Fehr in *Archiv*, cvii. 57. [Nos. XL, XLI.]

Lansdowne 379. Paper, $8 \times 5\frac{1}{2}$. Two carols on f. 38. XV cent. [No. LXXI.]

Royal Appendix 58. Paper, $8\frac{1}{2} \times 6$. Music throughout, including compositions by Cornish and Cowper ; 27 with words, some incomplete. One poem is on the marriage of Margaret to James IV in 1503 ; Flügel places the MS. in the first decade of the XVI cent. and before Addl. 31922, which contains variants of some of the poems. Extracts in Stafford Smith, Chappell, Rimbault, Briggs' *Songs and Madrigals*, and Flügel, *N.L.*; the last has also edited the whole of the words in *Anglia*, xii. 256. [Nos. XXVI, XXXI–XXXIII.]

Sloane 2593. Paper, $5\frac{3}{4} \times 4\frac{1}{2}$. Songs and carols, seventy-four in number, of which three are in Latin, and the rest in English. Mainly religious or moral, but some trivial and satirical. Wright considered it to be the song-book of a minstrel (cf. Eng. Poet. e. 1) ; the last folio bears the name 'Johannes Bardel' or 'Bradel,' written in the same hand as the rest of the MS. Wright traces one poem to 1362–9, but probably this and others were traditional when written down ; he dates the handwriting temp. Henry VI. According to Bradley-Stratmann, the MS. was written in

Warwickshire at the beginning of the XV cent. Variants of some poems appear in Eng. Poet. e. 1. Extracts in Ritson (1790), Wright, *Carols* (1836), and *S.L.P.*, *Rel. Ant.*, and Fehr in *Archiv*, cvii. 48. Edited complete by Wright for the Warton Club in 1856; and by B. Fehr in *Archiv*, cix. 33; who does not print poems extracted as above, but is ignorant of the Warton Club print. [Nos. L, LI, LIV–LVI, LXIX, LXXVII, C–CIII, CIV–CVI, CVIII, CIX, CXVIII, CXXVII, CXXXIV, CXLIII, CXLVIII.]

(*b*) Dyce Library, Victoria and Albert Museum.

Dyce 45. Paper, $7\frac{3}{4} \times 5\frac{1}{2}$. English and Latin extracts, in various hands. Late XV to early XVI cent. The MS. is quoted by Dyce as in his possession, Skelton, i. vii. The lyrical contents are chiefly religious parodies of secular poems. Two are signed 'Wynton' and 'Smythe.' [No. CXXXIII.]

(*c*) Lambeth Palace Library.

Lambeth 853. Vellum, small quarto. One of the collection presented by Archbishop Tenison. Written about 1430. Short description in H. J. Todd's Catalogue of the Lambeth MSS. (1812), 195. Extracts in Furnivall, *P.R.L.*; edited Furnivall, *H.V.* [No. LXXXIV.]

Oxford.

(*a*) Bodleian Library.

Ashmolean 191. § IV of the MS., ff. 191–6, contains six songs with music, on paper, $8\frac{1}{2} \times 6$; dated 1445 by E. W. B. Nicholson. First lines of words in Black's *Catalogue of Ashm. MSS.*, 159. Described in *E.B.M.*, i. xx. Facsimiles and transcripts also in *E.B.M.* [No. XVIII.]

Ashmolean 1393. Two carols on verso of last leaf, parchment, $5\frac{3}{4} \times 4$. Described in *E.B.M.*, i. xix. Facsimiles and transcripts also in *E.B.M.* [No. LXX, and note on XLVI.]

Digby 86. Parchment, $8\frac{1}{4} \times 5\frac{3}{4}$. Poems in Latin, Anglo-Norman, and English, southern dialect; 'written in Worcester Priory, finished sometime between 1272 and 1283' (*E.B.M.*, i. xii.). Described, with extracts, by Stengel; notes on its relation to Harl. 2253 in Böddeker, vii and 456. Some poems from it in Horstmann-Furnivall, ii. 753. [No. XC.]

Douce 139. Parchment, $9\frac{7}{8} \times 7\frac{3}{8}$. Several MSS. bound together. Douce states that it belonged to Sir Robert Cotton; this is doubted by Madan. Fol. 5, containing the lyric and its music, is of the second half of the XIII cent. Described in *O.H.M.*, ii. 100, by Madan, iv. 534, and in *E.B.M.*, i. xv. [No. III.]

Douce 302. Parchment, $10\frac{7}{8} \times 7\frac{7}{8}$. Religious poems and legends by John Awdlay, a blind and deaf *capellanus* in Haghmon (Haughmond) Abbey, in Shropshire; he describes himself on f. 35 as 'the furst prest to the lord Strange,' *i.e.* Richard Lestrange, Lord Strange of Knockin. Some of the poems are dated 1426, and the MS. may be not much later. It passed through the hands of William Wyatt, a minstrel of Coventry, and John Barker, 'a chanon of Lawnd.' Its contents, says Madan (iv. 585–6), are very fully described in the 1840 [Bodleian] Catalogue. Halliwell printed extracts in the Percy Society publications, vol. 14, in 1844. A new complete edition is in preparation by J. E. Wülfing for the *E.E.T.S.* [No. LVII and note on CXXXIV.]

Douce 381. Parchment and paper, $16\frac{7}{8} \times 13\frac{1}{4}$. Divided by Madan, iv. 614, into eleven sections, A–K;

section H only concerns us. This is ff. 20–23, French and English lyrics with music; dated 'about 1425' by E. W. B. Nicholson and Sir E. Maunde Thompson. Described by Madan as above (see also v., Corrections xxvii) and in *E.B.M.*, i. xix. See *O.H.M.*, ii. 128. [No. LXXXV.]

Eng. Poet. e. 1. Paper, 6 × 4¼. 'Seventy six songs, religious and other, including some Christmas carols and drinking songs, presumably collected for the use of a professed minstrel' (Madan, v. 679). Written partly in English, partly in Latin, partly in both. In several hands; two pieces of music (facsimiles in *E.B.M.*). Variants of several poems in Sloane 2593. Dated 1460–80 by Madan, and 'about 1485–90' by Nicholson in *E.B.M.* Belonged in 1847 to Thomas Wright, but was then lost, and was said to have been taken away by the bookbinder to whom it was entrusted (Chappell, 43, note). It was bought for the Bodleian in 1887 at the sale of the library of Joseph Mayer, who was a patron of Wright's. Described by Madan as above, and in *E.B.M.*, i. xxiv. Edited complete by Wright in 1847 as No. LXXIII of the Percy Society publications (misquoted XXIII by Flügel, Fehr, and others, owing to an error in the Brit. Mus. Catalogue). [Nos. LXI, LXIII, LXIV, LXVI, LXXIII, LXXVI, LXXVII, LXXX, LXXXIII, XCVIII, XCIX, CX, CXI, CXIX–CXXI, CXXIV, CXXVIII, CXXIX, CXXXVIII, CXXXIX, CXL.]

Rawlinson C. 813. Paper, 8¼ × 6. Early XVI century. English poems and prophecies. Two in Halliwell's *Nugae Poeticae*, 1844. Ballad No. 111 in Child is from this MS. [No. XXIX.]

Rawlinson G. 22. Parchment, 8½ × 6. 'The Book of Psalms in Latin,' etc. Bequeathed to Bodleian by Dr. Richard Rawlinson in 1755. Nicholson says it was written in East Midlands in the latter half of the XII cent. The English lyric 'Mirie it is' is dated about 1225 by A. S. Napier and E. W. B. Nicholson. Described in *E.B.M.*, i. xi. § 5; Madan, iii. 344; iv, Corrections xi; v, Corrections x. [No. I.]

Selden B. 26. 'Several MSS., apparently bound together after they came into the possession of the library' [in or about 1659]; ff. 3–33, parchment, 10¼ × 7, contains 52 English and Latin carols and songs with music in 2, 3, and 4 parts. Nicholson traces eleven different hands in the music and nine in the words; Southern English; about 1450. One tune by John Dunstable, who died 1453. Variants of four lyrics and tunes in T.C.C., O. 3. 58; including the Song on Agincourt, transcribed hence by or for Samuel Pepys, now in his collection of Ballads, i. 3. Described in *E.B.M.*, i. xx–xxiii, and *O.H.M.*, ii. 133 (from musical point of view). [Nos. LIX, CVII, CXXV, CXXX, CXXXV, CXLI.]

(*b*) Balliol College Library.

Balliol 354. Paper, 11½ × 4. Commonplace book of Richard Hill, who describes himself as 'seruant with Mr. Wyngar, alderman of London.' John Wyngar, grocer, was alderman in 1493, mayor 1504, and died 1505. Richard Hill married in 1518 Margaret, daughter of Harry Wyngar, haberdasher, 'dwellyng in bowe parishe in London,' and the births of his seven children are recorded in the MS. from 1518 to 1526. The MS. is a miscellany of the widest character, English, French, and Latin, poems, romances, fabliaux, extracts from Gower and Sir Thomas More, receipts, legal notes, London customs, etc. Some pieces, signed by Hill, must be in his own hand; so probably is most of the MS. The latest date in it is 1535, but part must have been written before 1504.

Rimbault, 120, refers apparently to the MS. in 1851, (see notes on CXXXI), and said he intended to print it entire. Chappell (1855–59), 50, notes that this MS. had been 'recently found in the library . . . , where it had been accidentally concealed, behind a bookcase, during a great number of years.' Extracts printed by Flügel, *W.L.*, in 1894; and thence by Pollard, 1903; also in Flügel, *N.L.* Edited, almost complete, with full table of contents, by Flügel in *Anglia*, xxvi, 94, printing 126 items. [Nos. XIX, LX, LXVI, LXVII, LXXV, LXXVIII, LXXXI, LXXXII, LXXXIII, CXII, CXXIV, CXXVI, CXXXI, CXXXVI, CXXXVII, CXLI, CXLIX, CL.]

Cambridge.

(*a*) University Library.

Camb. Ff. i. 6 (No. 1139). Paper, quarto. Imperfect, carelessly written in various hands, containing poetry of the XV cent., Chaucer, Gower, Hoccleve, romances, and lyrics. Described in the Catalogue of the Cambridge MSS., ii. 286. Extracts in *Rel. Ant.* (3 poems signed 'A. Godwhen'). [No. XVIII.]

Camb. Gg. iv. 27 (No. 1526). Parchment, folio. Handwriting of early XV century; contains chiefly Chaucer, prose and verse; also the romance of King Horn; as well as three macaronic English-French poems. Described in Catalogue, iii. 272. First stanzas of above 3 poems quoted by Ellis, ii. 463 (see note on VIII). [Nos. VIII, IX.]

(*b*) Trinity College Library.

T.C.C., B. 14. 39 (James, no. 323). Parchment, $7\frac{1}{8} \times 5\frac{3}{8}$. XIII cent.; Skeat says 'a Norman scribe.' (Bound with B. 14. 40, James, no. 324, of the XIV and XV centuries.) Poems in English, Latin, and French.

Some items appear also in the contemporary MSS., Jesus College, Oxford, I. xxix, and Cottonian Calig. A. ix; see Morris, *O.E.M.*, 158–163. The whole MS., including B. 14. 40, was transcribed in 1843 by Sir Frederick Madden, which transcript is now B. 14. 40*a*. The MS. was missing from the library 1863–1896. It was used by Hickes for his *Thesaurus*. Extracts in *Rel. Ant.* On the French pieces in it, see *MSS. Français de Cambridge* by Paul Meyer in *Romania* (1903). Described, with list of contents, in James, i. 438. [Nos. XLV, XLVII, and note on XLVI.]

T.C.C., O. 3. 58 (James, no. 1230). Parchment roll 7 inches wide, and 6 feet 7 inches long. One side bears a Latin ecclesiastical treatise; the other 13 carols and poems with music, perhaps by John Dunstable (see Bodl. Selden B. 26). Of the XV cent.; the forms of the words indicate northern origin. A variant of the Agincourt song is the only secular poem. The MS. was presented in 1838 to the College by H. O. Roe Esq. Described in James, iii. 247. Edited with a facsimile and added vocal parts by J. A. Fuller Maitland and W. S. Rockstro in 1891 (see List of Books). [Nos. LII, LIII, LXXIV.]

T.C.C., O. 9. 38 (James, no. 1450). Paper, $11\frac{7}{8} \times 4\frac{3}{8}$. Commonplace Book of Glastonbury, once owned by a Glastonbury monk. Of the XV and XVI centuries, in various hands. Described in James, iii. 495. Extracts in Wright, Skeat, and Furnivall, *H.V.* [Nos. LXXIX, and note on CXII.]

Edinburgh.

Advocates' Library.

Advoc. Lib. 19. 3. 1. Paper, $8\frac{3}{4} \times 6$. It is lettered on the back 'Metrical Romances and Moralizations' (see

Rel. Ant. ii. 76). A flyleaf bears a list of contents, not exhaustive, in Sir Walter Scott's hand. Late XV cent. Described by K. Breul, *Sir Gowther* (1886), l. Two lyrics printed from it by Breul in *Englische Studien*, xiv. 401–2. [Nos. LVIII, LXXII, and note on LXIV.]

Lincoln.

Cathedral Library.

Linc. A. i. 17. (Thornton MS.). Paper, $11\frac{1}{2} \times 8\frac{1}{4}$, imperfect at beginning and end. Compiled by Robert Thornton of East Newton, Yorkshire, about 1440; and remained in possession of the Thornton family till the beginning of the seventeenth century. It contains an important collection of romances, Arthurian and other, religious and moral poems, medical recipes, &c. Used and described by Sir Frederick Madden in his *Syr Gawayne*, Introduction, l.: described also by J. O. Halliwell, *The Thornton Romances* (Camden Soc., 1844), Introduction xxv; Horstman, *Richard Rolle of Hampole*, i. 184. [No. XCIV.]

Privately Owned.

Howard de Walden MS. The MS. appears from a note to have been given on 12 December, 1418, to an anonymous possessor by Master Thomas Turke, formerly vicar perpetual of Brading, Isle of Wight, then a Carthusian at Henton, Somerset. Various notes refer to places in Somerset and Dorset. Most of the contents have music. The MS. was sold at Sotheby's, 14 December, 1903 (lot 678) and again in 1904; see Madan, v, Corrections xxviii under no. 21956. Privately printed as *Music, Cantelenas, Songs, etc.* (see List of Books). [No. CLII.]

Porkington MS. (*No. 10*). At Brogyntyn, near Oswestry, Shropshire; owned by Lord Harlech (family name Ormsby-Gore). Parchment and paper, $5\frac{3}{8} \times 4\frac{1}{4}$, written in various hands of the latter half of the XV cent. Calendar ff. 2–3 ends with 'ye batel of Achyngcourte' (1415). Halliwell says 'a table of eclipses calculated for the period from 1462 to 1481.' Collection of poems and ballads; list of contents in Sir Thomas Phillipps' *Manuscripts at Porkington*. It contains a version of *Sir Gawayne* printed by Sir F. Madden; see his Introduction lviii. Described by Halliwell, *E.E.M.*, who prints extracts. Selections in *Rel. Ant.* [No. CXXVI, and notes on XCIV and CXXXVII.]

II.—PRINTED BOOKS

Wynkyn de Worde (1521). [Colophon] ¶ Thus endeth the Christmasse carolles newely enprinted at Londō in the fletestrete at the sygne of the sonne by wynkyn de worde. The yere of our lord M.D. xxi.

[A single leaf, $5 \times 3\frac{1}{2}$. Formerly Douce Fragment 94[b], now Rawl. 4°. 598 (10). Contains two carols only, 'A caroll of huntynge' and 'A caroll bringyng in the bores heed.' Reprinted in *Anglia*, xii. 587.] [No. CXLIV, and note on CXXXVII.]

Bassus. ¶ Bassus. In this boke ar cōteynyd XX sōges. IX of IIII partes and XI of thre partes. [A list of titles follows.] Anno domini M. CCCCC. XXX. Decimo die mensis Octobris.

[Printed by Wynkyn de Worde. Only copy known is British Museum shelf mark K. 1. e. 1, catalogued under 'Book.' The words reprinted by Flügel in *Anglia*, xii. 589, and Imelmann in Shakespeare-Jahrbuch (1903), xxxix. 121.] [Nos. LXXXVI, LXXXVIII, LXXXIX.]

KELE. ¶ Christmas carolles newely Inprinted. [Woodcut of crucifixion.] *Colophon*, ¶ Inprynted at London, in the Powltry, by Rychard Kele, dwellyng at the longe shop vnder saynt Myldrede's Chyrche.

Bliss supposed it to be 'a part of at least three volumes of carols as there are three different sets of signatures' . . . 'probably printed between 1546 and 1552 . . .'

[Extracts in Bliss (see List of Books). In 1819 Dibdin mentions it in his edition of Ames's and Herbert's *Typographical Antiquities* as 'in the possession of the Revd. H. Cotton, of Christ Church, Oxford,' who was the compiler of the two series of the *Typographical Gazetteer*. In 1833 Sandys says 'I have understood this curious volume to be in the possession of Sir Francis Freeling.' In *Hand Lists of English Printers*, part iii, issued by the Bibliographical Society, the book is said to be at Christ Church ; but after enquiring for the book there and in the *Gentleman's Magazine*, February, 1906, p. 74, we have failed to discover its present resting-place.] [No. CLI, and note on LXXVIII.]

LIST OF BOOKS

*** This List, which makes no claim to bibliographical completeness or accuracy, mainly includes (*a*) collections of mediæval English lyrics, (*b*) special dissertations upon English lyric poetry, (*c*) a few books dealing with contemporary French and Latin lyrics.

Anglia. Anglia; Zeitschrift für englische Philologie enthaltend Beiträge zur Geschichte der englischen Sprache und Literatur. Halle a.S. [Begun in 1877.]

Archiv. Archiv für das Studium der neueren Sprachen und Litteraturen. Begründet von Ludwig Herrig. Braunschweig [previously Elberfeld]. [Begun in 1846.]

Arber. The Dunbar Anthology, 1401–1508 A.D. Edited by E. Arber. [*British Anthologies*, i.] 1901.

Ashby. George Ashby's Poems. Edited by Mary Bateson. *E.E.T.S.*, Extra Series, 1899. [Texts from Camb. Univ. Lib. Mm. iv. 42, and T.C.C., R. 3. 19.]

Audelay. The Poems of John Audelay. . . . Edited by J. O. Halliwell. *Percy Society*, 1844. [Texts from Douce 302.]

Aust. Beiträge zur Geschichte der mittelenglischen Lyrik. Von. J. Aust. [In *Archiv*, lxx. 253.]

Bartsch. Chrestomathie Provençale (x^e^–xve Siècles). Par K. Bartsch. Sixième Édition entièrement refondue par E. Koschwitz. Two vols. 1903–4.

Bartsch. Romanzen und Pastourellen. Von K. Bartsch. 1870.

BLISS. Bibliographical Miscellanies. Edited by P. Bliss. 1813. [Texts from R. Kele's *Christmas Carolles;* see Sources of Texts, p. 311.]

BÖDDEKER. Altenglische Dichtungen des MS. Harl. 2253. Von K. Böddeker. 1878.

BÖDDEKER. Englische Lieder und Balladen aus dem 16. Jahrhundert. Von K. Böddeker. [In Lemcke's *Jahrbuch*, Neue Folge, (q.v.), ii. 81, 210, 347; iii. 92.] [Texts from Cott. Vesp. A. xxv.]

BRAKELMANN. Les plus anciens chansonniers français. Par Jules Brakelmann. Paris, 1870–1891 [Part I]; Marburg, 1896 [Part II].

BRAMLEY AND STAINER. Christmas Carols New and Old. Edited by H. R. Bramley and John Stainer. [1871.]

BRIGGS, *Madrigals*. Madrigals by English Composers of the Close of the Fifteenth Century. With a preface by H. B. Briggs. *P.M.M.S.*, 1893.

BRIGGS, *Musical Notation*. The Musical Notation of the Middle Ages. By H. B. Briggs. *P.M.M.S.*, 1890.

BRIGGS, *Songs and Madrigals*. A Collection of Songs and Madrigals by English Composers of the Close of the Fifteenth Century. Part of introduction signed H. B. B. *P.M.M.S.*, 1891.

BULLEN. Carols and Poems. Edited by A. H. Bullen. 1886.

Captain Cox, his Ballads and Books; or, Robert Laneham's Letter. Edited by F. J. Furnivall. *Ballad Society*, 1871; *New Shakspere Society*, 1887.

CHAMPOLLION-FIGEAC. Les Poésies du duc Charles d'Orléans. Par Aimé Champollion-Figeac. 1842.

CHAPPELL. The Ballad Literature and Popular Music of the Olden Time. By William Chappell. The airs harmonized by G. A. Macfarren. Two vols. (but continuous pagination). [1855–1859.]

In some copies the title begins with 'Popular Music,' &c. See also WOOLDRIDGE-CHAPPELL.

CHAUCER. The Complete Works of Geoffrey Chaucer. Edited by W. W. Skeat. Six vols., 1894.

Supplementary vol. vii, see SKEAT.

CHILD. The English and Scottish Popular Ballads. Edited by Francis James Child. Five vols., 1882–1898.

COURTHOPE. A History of English Poetry. By W. J. Courthope. Five vols. published, 1895–1905.

DANIEL. Thesaurus Hymnologicus Sive Hymnorum Canticorum Sequentiarum circa Annum M.D. usitatarum Collectio amplissima. Edidit H. A. Daniel. Five vols. 1841–56.

D'HÉRICAULT. Poésies completes du duc Charles d'Orléans. Edited by C. d'Héricault. Two vols., 1874.

DU MÉRIL. Poésies populaires latines antérieures au xiie siècle. Par E. Du Méril. 1843.

DU MÉRIL. Poésies populaires latines du moyen âge. Par E. Du Méril. 1843.

E.B.M. Early Bodleian Music. Sacred and Secular Songs together with other MS. Compositions in the Bodleian Library, Oxford : ranging from about A.D. 1185 to about A.D. 1505. With an Introduction by E. W. B. Nicholson, and Transcriptions into Modern Musical Notation by J. F. R. Stainer and C. Stainer. Edited by Sir John Stainer. Two volumes (vol. i, facsimiles, vol. ii, transcriptions), 1901.

E.E.T.S. Early English Text Society.

Ellis. Early English Pronunciation. By A. J. Ellis. *Chaucer*, *E.E.T.*, and *Philological Societies*, 1869.

England and Pollard. The Towneley Plays. Re-edited from the unique MS. by G. England. With side-notes and introduction by A. W. Pollard. *E.E.T.S.*, 1897.

Englische Studien. Englische Studien. Herausgegeben von Dr. E. Kölbing. Heilbronn. [Begun in 1877.]

Erskine. The Elizabethan Lyric. A Study by John Erskine. 1903.

Fehr. Weitere Beiträge zur englischen Lyrik des 15. und 16. Jahrhunderts. By Bernhard Fehr. [In *Archiv*, cvii. 48; texts from Sloane 1212, 2593, 3501, and Harl. 367, 541, 7578.] 1901.

Fehr. Die Lieder der Hs. Add. 5665. By Bernhard Fehr. [In *Archiv*, cvi. 262.] 1901.

Fehr. Die Lieder des Fairfax MS. (Add. 5465 Brit. Mus.) By Bernhard Fehr. [In *Archiv*, cvi. 48.] 1901.

Fehr. Die Lieder der Hs. Sloane 2593. By Bernhard Fehr. [In *Archiv*, cix. 33.] 1902.

Flügel. Liedersammlungen des xvi Jahrhunderts, besonders aus der zeit Heinrichs VIII. By Ewald Flügel. [In *Anglia*, xii. 225, from Addl. 31922; *ib.* 256, from Royal Appx. 58; *ib.* 585, from W. de Worde's *Christmasse Carolles*, &c.; xxvi. 94, from Balliol 354.]

Flügel, *N.L.* Neuenglisches Lesebuch. Herausgegeben von Ewald Flügel. Band I, 1895.

Flügel, *W.L.* Englische Weihnachtslieder aus einer Handschrift des Balliol College zu Oxford. By Ewald Flügel. [In *Forschungen zur deutschen Philologie. Festgabe für Rudolf Hildebrand.* 1894. Texts from Balliol 354.]

Frere. Bibliotheca Musico-Liturgica. By W. H. Frere. *P.M.M.S.*, 1894–1901.

Fuller Maitland. English Carols of the Fifteenth Century, from a MS. Roll in the Library of Trinity College, Cambridge. Edited by J. A. Fuller Maitland. With added vocal parts by W. S. Rockstro. [1891 ; text from T.C.C., O.3.58.]

Furnivall, *E.E.P.* Early English Poems and Lives of Saints. Edited by F. J. Furnivall. [In *Transactions of the Philological Society*, 1858, part ii ; texts from Harl. 913, Egerton 613, and Addl. 22283. 1862.]

Furnivall, *H.V.* Hymns to the Virgin and Christ. Edited by F. J. Furnivall. *E.E.T.S.*, 1867. [Texts from Lambeth 853.]

Furnivall, *P.R.L.* Political, Religious, and Love Poems, from Lambeth 306 and other sources. Edited by F. J. Furnivall. *E.E.T.S.*, 1866 ; re-edited with additions 1903.

Gasté. Chansons normandes du quinzième siècle. Par A. Gasté. 1869.

Gollancz. Pearl: An English Poem of the Fourteenth Century. Edited with a Modern Rendering by I. Gollancz. 1891.

Grove. A Dictionary of Music and Musicians (A.D. 1450–1889). Edited by Sir George Grove. With Appendix, edited by J. A. Fuller Maitland.

Guy. Essai sur la Vie et les Oeuvres littéraires du Trouvère Adan de le Hale. Par Henry Guy. 1898.

Halliwell, *E.E.M.* Early English Miscellanies, in Prose and Verse. Edited by J. O. Halliwell. *Warton Club*, 1855. [Texts from Porkington MS.]

Hawkins. A General History of the Science and Practice of Music. By Sir John Hawkins. Five vols., 1776.

HAZLITT—RITSON. Ancient Songs and Ballads from the reign of King Henry the Second to the Revolution. Collected by Joseph Ritson, Esq. Third Edition carefully revised by W. Carew Hazlitt. 1877.

See s.v. RITSON.

HEIDER. Untersuchungen zur mittelenglischen erotischen Lyrik (1250–1300). Von O. Heider. 1905. [Halle dissertation.]

HEUSER. Die Kildare Gedichte. Von W. Heuser. 1904. [*Bonner Beiträge zur Anglistik*, xiv; texts from Harl. 913.]

HOCCLEVE. Hoccleve's Works. *E.E.T.S.*, 1892–1897. [I. The Minor Poems, edited by F. J. Furnivall. II. The Minor Poems, part II, edited by I. Gollancz. III. The Regement of Princes, &c., edited by F. J. Furnivall.]

HORSTMAN—FURNIVALL. The Minor Poems of the Vernon MS. *E.E.T.S.*; Part I, edited by C. Horstman, 1892; Part II, edited by F. J. Furnivall, 1901 [with some poems from Digby 2 and 86].

HUGHES-HUGHES. Catalogue of Manuscript Music in the British Museum. By A. Hughes-Hughes. Vol. I, Sacred Vocal Music, 1906. [Vol. II, Secular Vocal Music, not yet published.]

HUSK. Songs of the Nativity, being Christmas Carols, Ancient and Modern. By W. H. Husk. [1868.]

IMELMANN. Zur Kenntnis der vor-Shakespearischen Lyrik: I. Wynkyn de Worde's 'Song Booke,' 1530. Von R. Imelmann. [In *Shakespeare-Jahrbuch*, xxxix. 121.] 1903.

Jahrbuch, Lemcke's. Jahrbuch für romanische und englische Sprache und Litteratur. Herausgegeben von Ludwig Lemcke. Neue Folge, 1874, *etc.*

Jahrbuch, Shakespeare-. Jahrbuch der deutschen Shakespeare-Gesellschaft. 1864, *etc.*

JAMES. Catalogue of the Western MSS. in the Library of Trinity College, Cambridge. By Montague Rhodes James. Four vols., 1900–1904.

JEANROY. Mélanges d'Ancienne Poésie Lyrique. Chansons, Jeux Partis, et Refrains Inédits du xiij^{e} Siècle. Publiés et annotés par A. Jeanroy. [*Extrait de la Revue des Langues romanes.*] 1902.

JEANROY. Les Origines de la Poésie lyrique en France au Moyen-Age. Par A. Jeanroy. 1889. New edition, with additions, 1904.

KLUGE. Mittelenglisches Lesebuch. Von F. Kluge. 1904.

LEWIN. Das mittelenglisches Poema Morale. Von H. Lewin. 1881.

LYDGATE. A Selection from the Minor Poems of Dan John Lydgate. Edited by J. O. Halliwell. *Percy Society*, 1840.

MADAN. Summary Catalogue of the Western Manuscripts in the Bodleian Library. By Falconer Madan. [Vol. iii, 1895; vol. iv, 1897; vol. v, 1905; no other vols. yet published.]

MAPES. The Latin Poems commonly attributed to Walter Mapes. Collected and edited by T. Wright. [*Camden Soc.*] 1841.

MÄTZNER. Altfranzösischer Lieder. Von E. Mätzner. 1853.

MEYER. Mélanges de Poésie Anglo-Normande. Par P. Meyer. [In *Romania*, iv. 170, 376.] 1875.

MEYER. Recueil d'Anciens Textes Bas-Latins, Provençaux, et Français. Par P. Meyer. 1874–1877.

MINOT. The Poems of Laurence Minot. Edited by Joseph Hall. 1897.

MITCHELL. A compendious Book of Godly and Spiritual Songs ; commonly known as 'The Gude and Godlie Ballatis.' Edited by A. F. Mitchell. *Scottish Text Society*, 1897.

MONE. Hymni Latini Medii Aevi. Edidit F. J. Mone. Three vols. 1853–5.

MORRIS. Early English Alliterative Poems. Edited by R. Morris. [*E.E.T.S.* O.S. i.] 1864.

MORRIS, *O.E.M.* An Old English Miscellany. Edited by R. Morris. *E.E.T.S.*, 1872. [Texts from Jesus College, Oxford, I. 29, Cotton Calig. A. ix, Egerton 613, *etc.*]

MORRIS—SKEAT. Specimens of Early English. A New and Revised edition. By R. Morris and W. W. Skeat. 1872.

Music, Cantelenas, Songs, etc., from an early XVth Century Manuscript. [Edited by L. S. Mayer.] Privately printed, 1906. [Texts from the Howard de Walden MS.]

NAGEL. Annalen der englischen Hofmusik. Von W. Nagel. [*Beitrag zur Monatshefte für Musik-Geschichte*, Band XXVI.] 1894–5.

O.H.M. The Oxford History of Music. Edited by W. H. Hadow, 6 vols. First two vols. are Parts I (1901) and II (1905) of *The Polyphonic Period*, by H. Ellis Wooldridge.

ORLEANS, CHARLES DUKE OF. Poems written in English by Charles Duke of Orleans during his Captivity in England after the Battle of Agincourt. Edited by G. W. Taylor. *Roxburghe Club*, 1827. [Text from Harl. 682.]

See also *Champollion-Figeac* and *D'Héricault*.

PARIS, G. Chansons du XVe Siècle. Par Gaston Paris. *Société des Anciens Textes Français*, 1875. [Texts from B.N. fr. 12744.]

PARIS, G. Les Origines de la Poésie Lyrique en France. Par Gaston Paris. [Review of *Jeanroy* (q.v.) in *Journal des Savants* (1891), 674, 729; (1892), 155, 407.]

PARIS, P. Chansonniers. Par P. Paris. [In *Hist. Litt.* xxiii. 512.] 1856.

PARIS, P. Le Romancero françois. Histoire de quelques trouvères et choix de leurs chansons. Par P. Paris. 1833.

Percy Society. Early English Poetry, Ballads, and Popular Literature of the Middle Ages. Edited from Original Manuscripts and Scarce Publications.

PERRY. Religious Pieces in prose and verse, edited from Robert Thornton's MS. (cir. 1440) in the Lincoln Cathedral Library, by G. G. Perry. *E.E.T.S.*, 1867; revised edition, 1889.

P.M.M.S. Plainsong and Mediaeval Music Society.

POLLARD. Fifteenth Century Prose and Verse. Edited by A. W. Pollard. 1903.

RAYNAUD. Bibliographie des Chansonniers Français des xiiie et xive Siècles. Par G. Raynaud. 1884.

RAYNAUD. Rondeaux et Autres Poésies du XVe Siècle. Par G. Raynaud. *Société des Anciens Textes Français*, 1889. [Texts from B.N. fr. 9223.]

RAYNAUD—LAVOIX. Recueil de Motets français des xiie et xiiie Siècles. Par G. Raynaud et H. Lavoix. 1882–4.

REL. ANT. Reliquiae Antiquae. Scraps from Ancient Manuscripts, illustrating chiefly Early English Literature and the English Language. By T. Wright and J. O. Halliwell. Two vols., 1841, 1843.

RIMBAULT. A Little Book of Songs and Ballads, gathered from Ancient Musick Books, MS. and Printed. By E. F. Rimbault. 1851.

RIMBAULT, *Ancient Vocal Music*. The Ancient Vocal Music of England: a Collection of Specimens, Referred to in a Series of Lectures, and Adapted to Modern Use, by E. F. Rimbault. In 24 parts. [1847.]

RITSON (1790). Ancient Songs, from the time of King Henry the Third to the Revolution. [By Joseph Ritson.] 1790.

Advertisement to 1829 edition says that this edition was printed in 1787, dated 1790, and published 1792.

RITSON (1829). Ancient Songs and Ballads, from the reign of King Henry the Second to the Revolution. Collected by Joseph Ritson. Two vols., 1829.

See s.v. Hazlitt-Ritson.

ROLLE. Yorkshire Writers. Richard Rolle of Hampole, an English Father of the Church, and his Followers. Edited by C. Horstman. Two vols. 1895–6. [*Library of Early English Writers.*]

Romania. Romania: Recueil trimestriel consacré à l'Étude des Langues et des Littératures romanes. Thirty-four vols. 1872–1905. [In progress.]

RYMAN. Die Gedichte des Franziskaners Jakob Ryman. Von J. Zupitza. [In *Archiv*, lxxxix. 167.] 1892.

SANDYS. Christmas Carols, Ancient and Modern, etc. By William Sandys. 1833.

SANDYS. Christmastide: its History, Festivities, and Carols. By W. Sandys. n.d.

SCHELER. Trouvères belges du xiie au xive Siècle. Par A. Scheler. 1876. Nouvelle série, 1879.

SCHIPPER. Englische Metrik in historischer und systematischer Entwickelung dargestellt, von J. Schipper. Three vols. 1882–8–9.

SCHLUTER. Über die Sprache und Metrik . . . des MS. Harl. 2253. Von A. Schluter. [In *Archiv*, lxxi. 153, 357.]

SCHMELLER. Carmina Burana: lateinische und deutsche Lieder und Gedichte einer Handschift des xiii. Jahrhunderts aus Benedictbeuern. Herausgegeben von J. A. Schmeller. Third edition. 1894.

SHOREHAM. The Poems of William of Shoreham. Edited by M. Kenneth. Part i. [*E.E.T.S.* E.S. lxxxvi.] 1902.

SIDGWICK. Popular Ballads of the Olden Time. Selected and Edited by Frank Sidgwick. Three vols. 1903–4–6. [In progress.]

SKEAT. Chaucerian and Other Pieces. Edited by W. W. Skeat. 1897.

Supplementary vol. vii of *Chaucer* (q.v.).

SKELTON. The Poetical Works of John Skelton. With Notes, etc., by A. Dyce. Two vols., 1843.

SMITH. A Common-place Book of the Fifteenth Century. Edited by Lucy Toulmin Smith. 1886. [Text from 'The Boke of Brome' MS. at Brome Hall, Suffolk.]

STAFFORD SMITH. Musica Antiqua. Selection of Music . . . from the . . . twelfth to the . . . eighteenth century . . . By John Stafford Smith. Two vols., [1812].

STAFFORD SMITH, *Collection of English Songs*. A Collection of English Songs, in Score for Three or Four Voices, Composed about the Year 1500, Taken from MSS. of the Same Age, Revised and Digested by John Stafford Smith. [1779.]

STENGEL. Codicem manu scriptum Digby 86, ed. Edmund Max Stengel. 1871.

SYLVESTER. A Garland of Christmas Carols. By Joshua Sylvester. 1861.

THURAU. Der Refrain in der französischen Chanson. Von Gustav Thurau. [*Litterarhistorische Forschungen*, xxiii.] 1901.

VARNHAGEN. Die Kleinere Gedichte der Vernon-und-Simeon-Handschrift. Von Hermann Varnhagen. [In *Anglia*, vii. 280.]

VARNHAGEN. Zu Mittelenglischen Gedichten. Von Hermann Varnhagen. [In *Anglia*, ii. 225 ; iii. 59, 275, 415, 533 ; iv. 180.]

WACKERNAGEL. Altfranzösische Lieder und Leiche. Von W. Wackernagel. 1846.

WOOLDRIDGE. Early English Harmony from the 10th to the 15th Century. With facsimiles from MSS. By H. E. Wooldridge. *P.M.M.S.*, two vols., 1897.

WOOLDRIDGE—CHAPPELL. Old English Popular Music. By William Chappell. Revised by H. Ellis Wooldridge. Two vols., 1893.

WRIGHT, *Carols* (1836). Songs and Carols, Printed from a Manuscript in the Sloane Collection in the British Museum. Preface signed Thomas Wright. (Pickering), 1836. [Text, twenty pieces only, from Sloane 2593.]

WRIGHT, *N.B.M.* The Nutbrowne Maid. From the earliest Edition of Arnold's Chronicle. Preface by Thomas Wright. (Pickering), 1836.

WRIGHT, *Owl and Nightingale*. The Owl and the Nightingale : An early English Poem attributed to Nicholas de Guildford, with some shorter poems from the same manuscript. Edited by Thomas Wright. *Percy Society*, 1843. [Texts from Cott. Calig. A. ix.]

WRIGHT, *P.S.* Songs and Carols, now first printed, from a Manuscript of the Fifteenth Century, edited by T. Wright. *Percy Society*, 1847. [Texts from Eng. Poet. e.1, then in Wright's possession.]

WRIGHT, *S.C.C.* Specimens of Old Christmas Carols. Edited by T. Wright. *Percy Society*, 1841. [Texts from Sloane 2593, Harl. 2252, 5396, etc.]

WRIGHT, *S.L.P.* Specimens of Lyric Poetry, composed in England in the reign of Edward the First. Edited by Thomas Wright. *Percy Society*, 1842. [Texts from Harl. 2253.]

WRIGHT, *W.C.* Songs and Carols from a Manuscript in the British Museum of the Fifteenth Century. Edited by Thomas Wright. *Warton Club*, 1856. [Texts from Sloane 2593.]

WÜLCKER. Altenglisches Lesebuch. Von R. P. Wülcker. 1874, 1879.

WÜLFING. Der Dichter John Audelay und sein Werk. Von J. E. Wülfing. [In *Anglia*, xviii. 175.] 1896.

NOTES

NOTE ON SPELLING

The spelling of the manuscripts has been preserved in poems earlier than the fifteenth century, except that *v* is substituted for consonantal *u*, *th* for þ, *y* or *gh* for ȝ, I for *y* (pronoun), and *is* for *ys*. Occasionally, also, variant spellings within the same poem have been unified. The spelling of fifteenth century poems has been more freely modified, in order to make it more uniform and easier for a modern reader. The following are the more important changes, in addition to those noted above, which have been made where they bring about an approximation to modern usage; *i*, *e*, or *th*, as the case may be, for *y* or *vice versâ; sh* or *sch* for *x; -eth* for *-et* or *-it*. Final long vowels have been doubled (e.g. *see* for *se*, *too* for *to*). Final *l* and *s* have also been doubled (e.g. *all* for *al*, *grass* for *gras*). A final *e* has been added to a long vowel followed by a consonant (e.g. *quene* for *quen*, *there* for *ther*). Sixteenth century poems, except those in Balliol MS. 354, which are treated for this purpose as belonging to the fifteenth century, are put into modern spelling throughout.

I

Rawl. G. 22. Printed *E.B.M.* ii. 5 (facsimile, i. plate III).

1. The initial M is left blank in the MS.

7. The whole line is torn and blurred. The reading is that suggested in *E.B.M.*

II

Harl. 978. First printed in Burney, *History of Music* (1776–89) ii. 407, and frequently since. Wooldridge, *O.H.M.* i. 326, reproduces the musical notation, showing certain alterations in the original composition, and gives a modern transcription; cf. Coussemaker, *L'Art Harmonique aux xii*e *et xiii*e *Siècles* (1865), p. xlvi; Ellis, ii. 419; Grove, iii. 765 (art. by W. S. Rockstro).

The body of the song (ll. 3–14 of our text) comes first in the manuscript and is followed by this interesting direction as to the manner of performance, 'Hanc rotam cantare possunt quatuor socii. A paucioribus autem quam a tribus vel saltem duobus non debet dici praeter eos qui dicunt pedem. Canitur autem sic: Tacentibus ceteris, unus inchoat cum his qui tenent pedem; et cum venerit ad primam notam post crucem inchoat alius, et sic de ceteris. Singuli vero repausent ad pausationes scriptas et non alibi, spatio unius longae notae.' The *crux* follows our l. 3; the *pausationes* are shown by vertical lines after ll. 4, 6, 7, 9, 11, 14. Then follow ll. 1, 2, marked as a *Pes*, i.e. 'foot' or 'burden'. Against l. 1 is written, 'Hoc repetit unus quociens opus est, faciens pausacionem in fine'; against l. 2, 'Hoc dicit alius, pausans in medio et non in fine, sed immediate repetens principium'. The composition, then, is a *Rota* or Rondel, a form of mediaeval descant or harmonised part-music, in which all the parts are sung to the same words. Professor Wooldridge says of it, 'This amazing production, the sole example probably of its species . . . exhibits the leading qualities of this kind of music, ingenuity and beauty, in a degree still difficult to realise as possible to a thirteenth century composer'. The musical sense of the term Rondel is to be distinguished from the literary sense in which it is applied to a particular kind of refrain-poem developed from the popular dance-songs or *rondets de carole* (cf. note on No. X). The literary form and the arrangement of the burden in

'Sumer is icumen in' are not those of any type of dance-song, but at the most an adaptation for the purposes of a learned musician of the theme of a popular *reverdie* or song of greeting to the spring, such as elsewhere inspired dance-songs. Whether the air is also an adaptation of a popular melody we cannot say; but such borrowings were not unusual in descant. Mr. Joseph Wright assigns the language to 'thirteenth century Wessex; Berkshire or Wiltshire'. Another evidence of the learned character of the piece is to be found in these alternative Latin words which accompany it in the manuscript:—

'Perspice christicola,
Quae dignatio!
Caelicus agricola
Pro vitis vitio
Filio
Non parcens exposuit
Mortis exitio;
Qui captivos semivivos
A supplicio
Vitae donat,
Et secum coronat
In caeli solio.'

There are no Latin words for the *Pes*.

III

Douce 139. Printed Stafford Smith, i. 11; *E.B.M.* ii. 10 (facsimile, i. plate VI); cf. *O.H.M.* ii. 100.

The words are set as a two-part song, and according to Prof. Wooldridge the composition 'expresses a musical thought' and 'is remarkable throughout for the freedom of its treatment, and for the evidence that it displays of the writer's complete mastery of the limited resources of his time'.

IV

Harl. 2253. Printed Böddeker, 147; Wright, *S.L.P.*, 27; Ritson (1790), 24; (1829), i. 56; *etc.*

The dialect is Southern.

V

Harl. 2253. Printed Böddeker, 164; Wright, *S.L.P.*, 43; Ritson (1790), 31; (1829), i. 63; *etc.*

The poem has been translated into the Southern dialect, but was probably originally written in that of the N.E. Midlands.

It is a love-song, but has the setting of a *reverdie* or salute to the spring. The opening lines are closely parallel to those of a contemporary *estrif, The Thrush and the Nightingale* (Digby 86, printed *Rel. Ant.* i. 241, and Hazlitt, Early Popular Poetry, i. 50; and Auchinleck MS., printed D. Laing, *A Penni-worth of Witte, etc.* (Abbotsford Club, 1857), 45, and H. Varnhagen in *Anglia*, iv. 207):—

'Somer is comen with love to toune
With blostmė and with bridės roune;
The note of hasel springeth;
The dewės darkneth in the dale
For longing of the nighttegale;
This fowelės murie singeth.'

A religious adaptation of the *reverdie* theme in the 13th century Egerton 613 (printed *Rel. Ant.* i. 100; Morris, *O.E.M.*, 197; Wülcker, i. 44) begins:—

'Somer is comen and winter gon;
This day biginnis to longe;
And this foulės everichon
Ioye hem wit songe.'

19. *thisė*: MS. reads 'this'.
22. *doht*: MS. 'doh'.

VI

Harl. 2253. Printed Böddeker, 174; Wright, *S.L.P.*, 92; Ritson (1790), 30; (1829), i. 62; *etc.*

12. Prof. Ker refers us to a story, more than a century earlier, in Giraldus Cambrensis, *Gemma Ecclesiastica*, i. 43 (R.S. ii. 119):—

'Exemplum de sacerdote, qui in Anglia Wigorniae finibus his nostris diebus interiectam quandam cantilenae particulam, ad quam saepius redire consueverant, quam refectoriam seu refractoriam [*refrain*] vocant, ex reliquiis cogitationum, et quoniam ex abundantia cordis os loqui solet, quia tota id nocte in choreis circiter ecclesiam ductis audierat, mane ad missam sacerdotalibus indutus, et ad aram stans insignitus, pro salutatione ad populum, scilicet *Dominus vobiscum*, eandem Anglica lingua coram omnibus alta voce modulando pronuntiavit in hunc modum, *Swete lamman dhin are*. Cuius haec dicti mens esse potest, *Dulcis amica, tuam poscit amator opem*. Huius autem eventus occasione episcopus loci illius, Willelmus scilicet de Norhale [*1184–90*], sub anathematis interminatione publice per synodos et capitula prohiberi fecit, ne cantilena illa, propter memoriae refricationem, quae ad mentem facinus revocare potest, de caetero per episcopatum suum caneretur.'

40. Ritson conjectures: 'Els to al that ys on grounde.'

VII

Harl. 2253. Printed Böddeker, 172; Wright, *S.L.P.*, 90.

34. *Const*: MS. 'cost'.

VIII

Camb. Gg. iv. 27. Ellis, ii. 463, says that this poem and the next, together with a third from the same MS., were printed for private circulation by Henry Bradshaw on 11 July, 1864; but we have failed to find a copy.

A similar poem in alternate French and English lines is in the fifteenth century Douce MS. 95, f. 6.

4. *treyé* = trié, proven.

22. *ha! tret*; so Prof. Brandin for 'hattȝ'.

25. *par* here and later is written 'pur'.

28. *treser*: MS. 'creser'. *tres* intensifies *servir*.

46. *claunchant*, an A.-N. form of '*clinquant*', tinkling.

IX

Camb. Gg. iv. 27. See note on VIII.

4. *Saltz*: so MS. Perhaps 'salutz'.

7. *pry* omitted in MS.

10. *fay*: MS. 'say'.

44. *strive*: MS. 'strue'.

X

Chaucer, i. 359, from *The Parlement of Foules*, 680–692.

The lines are a 'roundel' sung by certain birds to Nature; and Chaucer says 'The note, I trowe, ymakėd was in Fraunce'. The French *rondel* (later *rondeau*) of the 13th–15th centuries was a development of the popular dance-song (*rondet*, *rondet de carole*), and therefore consisted of two elements, a varying text sung by the leader of the dance and an unvarying *refrain* sung by the chorus. It is probable that in the primitive *rondet* of the folk these simply alternated; later they were connected by rhyme and combined into a more or less complicated stanza. There are many varieties of the developed *rondel*, but in each the stanza consists of three parts; (a) the complete refrain, (b) one line or more of text, followed by one line or more of the *refrain*, (c) two lines or more of text, followed by the complete *refrain*. The commonest variety is an eight-line one, sometimes called a *triolet*, of which the following, by Adan de le Hale (Raynaud, ii. 108) may serve as an example.

'*Hareu ! li maus d' amer*
M' ochist !
Il me fait desirrer,
Hareu ! li maus d' amer !
Par un douch resgarder
Me prist.
Hareu ! li maus d' amer
M' ochist !'

The rondel, as our Chaucer examples (Nos. X, XIII) show, may be of one or more stanzas. Chaucer uses a thirteen-line variety. A fourteen-line variety is represented by No. XVII. The literary sense of the term rondel must be distinguished from the musical sense (cf. note to No. II), although the two may, as in some of Adan de le Hale's songs, be combined.

XI

Chaucer, iii. 83, from *The Legend of Good Women* (text B), 249–269. Text A gives the refrain as

'Alceste is here, that al that may desteyne.'

This poem and Nos. XII, XIV, XVI, XCV, XCVI, XCVII, CXVI and CXVII are *balades*. The *balade*, like the *rondel*, is a development of the French dance-*chanson* with its *refrain*. It consists of three stanzas, varying as regards the number of the lines, but arranged on a limited number of rhymes, which are the same for each stanza. The last line of each stanza is the *refrain*. Sometimes, as in Nos. XVI, XCV, XCVII, CXVI and CXVII, a final section, corresponding in arrangement to the latter part of a stanza, is added. This is technically known as an *envoy*.

XII

Chaucer, i. 389. First printed by W. W. Skeat from Rawl. Poet. 163 in *Athenaeum*, 4 April, 1891.

One might be tempted to find in the word 'Tregentil' at the foot of the text a poetical by-name adopted by Chaucer; but Madan, iii. 318, finds in it only the name of a scribe.

XIII

Chaucer, i. 387; from Pepys MS. 2006, the index to which gives the poem the title *Merciles Beaute*.

XIV

Chaucer, i. 409; assigned to him, like No. XIII, by conjecture; cf. Skeat, *The Chaucer Canon*, 61–2. The refrain is taken from Machault, 'En lieu de bleu, Damė, vous vestez vert'.

XV

Skeat, 448, no. XXV; cf. *The Chaucer Canon*, 122. The dialect is East Anglian. The poem represents a variety of the *virelai*, a form of *rime couée*, in which the tail-rhyme of one stanza becomes the principal rhyme of the next.

XVI

Harl. 682. Printed in *Charles Duke of Orleans*, 121.

The *balade* is a translation from that by Charles of Orleans beginning 'J'ai fait l'obseque de ma Dame' (ed. Champollion-Figeac, 127; ed. d'Héricault, i. 88). Modern scholars are disposed to regard the English poems in Harl. 682 as being translations, partly from the French of Charles of Orleans, partly from other French originals not now known, made by a fifteenth century writer other than Charles himself; cf. G. Bullrich, *Über C. d' O. und die ihm zugeschriebene englische Übersetzung seiner Gedichte* (1893); C. Münster, *Die Lautverhältnisse in der mittelenglischen Übersetzung der Gedichte des Herzogs K. von O.* (1894). R. L. Stevenson's *Familiar Studies of Men and Books* contains a delightful sketch of Charles of Orleans and his sojourn as a prisoner in England from 1415 (Agincourt) to 1440. Champollion-Figeac, 265, and Bullrich, 13, print as his some English poems from sources other than Harl. 682, which may be genuine.

XVII

Harl. 682. Printed in *Charles Duke of Orleans*, 174.

No French original for this roundel, by Charles of Orleans or any other writer, is known.

11. *to* not in MS.

XVIII

Ashm. 191; *Camb. Ff.* i. 6. Printed from the former in *E.B.M.* ii. 66 (facsimile, i. plate XXX); and the latter in *Rel. Ant.* i. 25. We take verses 1, 2, 5 from the Ashm. MS., and 3, 4, 6 from the Camb. MS. In the latter the poem is ascribed to 'A. Godwhen'.

XIX

Our text has been made by collation of (i) print in R. Arnold's *Customs of London* (sig. N 6), commonly known as 'Arnold's Chronicle', printed about 1502 at Antwerp (second edition, about 1521), and (ii) manuscript in Ball. 354. The only other text is in the Percy Folio, Addl. MS. 27,879 (c. 1650), printed by Hales and Furnivall in *Bishop Percy's Folio Manuscript* (1868) iii. 174, together with the Balliol text, there printed for the first time, though noted by Chappell, 50.

'The Nutbrown Maid' has had an interesting literary history. First printed about 1502 as above, it was in circulation as a penny chapbook in 1520. Wright, in his preface to Pickering's black-letter print of the poem (1836), says 'I am told that in a manuscript of University College, Oxford, there is a list of books on sale at a stall in that city in 1520, among which is the "Not-Broon Mayd", price one penny'. A MS. exactly corresponding to the above description is at Corpus Christi College, Oxford (MS. 131); the list of books therein was edited by F. Madan for the Oxford Historical Society, in their *Collectanea*, First Series (1885), Part III, 'Day-book of John Dorne, Bookseller in Oxford, A.D. 1520'. The poem is there numbered as 294, 'I notbrone mayde,' price one penny.

A religious parody, 'The New Notborune Mayd', was printed by John Skot, 'dwellynge in Foster Lane within saynt Leonardes perysshe'; and is reprinted in Hazlitt, *Early Popular Poetry*, iii. 1.

In 1558–9 the printer John King was fined two shillings and sixpence 'for that he Ded prynte the nutbrowne mayde without lycense' (Arber, *Stationers' Registers*, i. 93). The poem is mentioned in *Laneham's Letter* (1575) as being among Captain Cox's collection (ed. Furnivall, Ballad Society, 1871, pp. lxxvi, 30).

In the seventeenth century, Samuel Pepys had the poem

copied out in black-letter, and this copy is now in his Collection, i. 7. The Pepysian Library contains an imperfect copy of the 1502 Arnold, perfected in MS. from the 1521 edition.

Pepys's copy was printed in a literary monthly periodical, *The Muses Mercury*, for June 1707, with an editorial preface explaining 'how we came by this Rarity'. The date is four years after Pepys's death and sixteen years before the removal of his Library to Cambridge.

In 1718 the poem was paraphrased to the taste of the eighteenth century by Matthew Prior under the title of *Henry and Emma*. Prior was certainly acquainted with the original, as he writes, 11 April 1718, to Humphrey Wanley, mentioning the 'Customs of London' as containing the poem (Harl. MS. 3780, referred to by T. Wright as 3777, but Wanley's letters have since been rearranged).

In 1760 Capell included the poem in his *Prolusions*, part I, printing from Thomas Hearne's copy of the 1521 Arnold. Thence it was taken by Percy for his *Reliques* (1765, etc.), and once for all established in popular favour. Hazlitt printed it in *Early Popular Poetry* (1866), ii. 271. Douce in 1811 reprinted the whole of Arnold's Chronicle, and in his 'Advertisement', xi, suggests a German origin for the poem.

A parallel to the principal situation may be found in the thirteenth century romance *Jourdains de Blaivies* (ed. Hoffmann), 2100, where Oriabix begs to go with Jourdains on a quest, though it were as his *escuiers* or his *prouvendiere*.

See further notes in T. Corser's *Collectanea Anglo-Poetica*, i. 54, and by E. F. Rimbault in *Notes and Queries*, 3rd Series, vi. 495.

In the Balliol MS. 'Puella' is written first against l. 40, and 'Squyre' against l. 52.

8. *favour*: so MS. and 1521. ed. The first ed. reads 'fouour'.

28. *the*; so MS. and 1521; 'they', 1502.

97. *to take*: so MS. and 1521; 1502 omits 'to'.

166. So all texts. Furnivall inserts 'men' before 'many'.

260. This is an early direct reference to the famous romance; see Mead's edition (1904), xxx.

XX

Skelton, i. 398; Flügel, *N.L.*, 48.

Margery Wentworth, 'perhaps the second daughter of Sir Richard Wentworth, afterwards married to Sir Christopher Glemham of Glemham in Suffolk'.—Dyce.

1. Dyce quotes Gerard's *Herball* (1633), 664:—'Marierome is called . . . in English, Sweet Marierome, Fine Marierome, and Marierome gentle; of the best sort Marjerane.'

XXI

Skelton, i. 400; Flügel, *N.L.*, 49.

XXII

Skelton, i. 401; Flügel, *N.L.*, 49.

4. Cf. Eng. Poet. e. 1, Wright *P.S.*, 68:—

> 'And swans be swyfter than haukes of the tower.'

XXIII

Addl. 31922. Printed *Anglia*, xii. 237; Flügel, *N.L.*, 135; facsimile in Briggs, *Musical Notation*, plate XX.

6. *hath*; so in MS.

As a composer, Henry VIII is severely criticised in *O.H.M.*, ii. 322; 'Absence of talent and of musical individuality can alone account for [his songs'] extreme dullness.' On the 'Holly and Ivy' theme, see note to No. CXXXVIII.

XXIV

Addl. 31922. Printed *Anglia*, xii. 241; Flügel, *N.L.*, 135.

20. *we*; MS. 'me'.

13. Cf. Skelton, i. 83, *Boke of Phyllyp Sparowe*, l. 1050,

> 'She is the vyolet,
> The daysy delectable.'

XXV

Addl. 31922. Printed *Anglia*, xii. 239; Flügel, *N.L.*, 135.

A good account of William Cornish, Gentleman of the Chapel Royal and Master of the Children, is given by Mr. W. B. Squire in the *D.N.B.*

The burden sounds like a fragment of popular song, with a characteristic English greenwood motive, somewhat incongruously fitted by Cornish to his allegorical poem of love. But the name Amyas is not uncommon in Tudor records, and, as it happens, occurs more than once in connection with woodcraft. On Sept. 20, 1485, Thomas Amyas received a grant of the Keepership of Woods and Warrens of the Lordship of Kirtlington. Probably he resigned this almost immediately for a better post, as William Compton obtained a similar grant dated from Jan. 14, 1486, and on Jan. 18, 1486, Thomas Amyas was appointed Porter of Hertford Castle. There was also one John Amyas, who became Yeoman of the Crown on Oct. 3, 1485, and in 1487 was acting as Yeoman of the Doors of the King's Chamber. He was still Yeoman at the accession of Henry VIII, but on Feb. 14, 1520, was made Serjeant at Arms, and subsequently got a joint grant of this post with his son Thomas in survivorship. To it was attached an annuity of 12d. a day charged on Wigmore lands, and therefore this John and Thomas may fairly be identified with the John and Thomas Amyas who on Oct. 5, 1517, had been appointed Keepers of the Chase of Moktre in the Lordship of Wigmore. They still held this office in 1526 and John was still of the royal household in 1527. A Thomas Amyas was Yeoman of the Chamber to the Princess Mary in 1525. On Aug. 12, 1524, a pardon was granted to William, Thomas, and Peter Ameas of Lentwardyn, alias of Moketre (W. Campbell, *Materials for a History of the Reign of Henry VII*, i. 244, 254, 272, 403, 550; ii. 80, 141, 179, 222, 294, 388, 559; J. S. Brewer, *Letters and Papers of the Reign of Henry VIII*, ii. 876, 1172; iii. 1262, 2161; iv. 273, 710, 867, 873, 1158, 1332, 3051).

XXVI

Addl. 31922 and *Royal Appx.* 58. Printed *Anglia*, xii. 235, 260; Flügel, *N.L.*, 134.

12. Royal MS., 'always'.
15. *thee*; Addl. MS., '*se*'.
18. Royal MS., 'young men'.
19. Addl. MS., 'true for to be'.
20. Royal MS.,

    'Promise I made that know no man shal'.

21. Addl. MS., 'while I live'.
24. Addl. MS.,

    'Hap what will hap, fall what shall';

and Royal MS.,

'Hap what shall hap will befall'.

XXVII

Addl. 31922. Printed *Anglia*, xii. 236; Flügel, *N.L.*, 135.

17. Flügel prints 'and so I trew' in both places.
38. *le bel*; MS. 'labell'.

XXVIII

Addl. 31922. Printed *Anglia*, xii. 255.

The poem appears in the MS. in many not very intelligible repetitions; we have re-arranged it so as to eliminate these.

Nos. XXVIII and XXIX represent late examples of that commonest form of the twelfth century *chanson d'aventure*, which, from its invariable theme of an amorous encounter between a *chevalier* and a shepherdess, received the name of *pastourelle*. 'Hey, troly, loly, lo!' is properly a refrain, although not here so used, and belongs to the class of nonsense or onomatopœic refrains, of which there are other examples in these poems. (See Nos. XXXIII, XXXVI, LV, LXIV, LXVI, LXVII, LXXIII, XCI, CXXI, CXXXI, CXLIV, CXLVII, CXLIX.) These have various origins; some, such as the 'Terly, terlow' of No. LXVI, represent the sounds of musical instruments accompanying a song (the *dorenlot* of the *pastourelles*); others, such as perhaps 'Troly, loly, lo' itself, those of the human voice, jodelling or otherwise singing meaningless notes on the musical scale. See Paris, *Origines*, 731, 738; G. Thurau, *Der Refrain in der französischen Chanson (passim)*.

XXIX

Rawl. C. 813. Printed *Archiv*, lxxxvii. 433, by J. Zupitza, who calls it 'Under the Greenwood Tree'.

26. *sire*; MS. reads 'fader'.

20. *trepitt*; Zupitza quotes 'trippet, *sb.* a quarter of a pound', from Yorkshire Words in *Reprinted Glossaries* (17), English Dialect Society.

XXX

Addl. 31922. Printed *Anglia*, xii. 248.

XXXI

Royal Appx. 58. Printed *Anglia*, xii. 260; Flügel, *N.L.*, 138. Earlier prints in Ritson, (1790), lv; (1829), i. lxxvi; Stafford Smith, i. 31; and Chappell, 57, all with tune. Also Wooldridge-Chappell, i. 37.

No other version of tune or words is known; but Wooldridge, *loc. cit.*, and *O.H.M.*, ii. 325, points out another tune of the same name in Addl. MSS. 17802–5, where it appears as the subject of three Masses, by John Taverner, Christopher Tye, and John Shephard, who flourished about 1530–1540. Other MSS. containing these Masses are at Christ Church, Oxford, and in the Bodleian (Bodl. MSS. Mus. e. 1–5, *etc.*).

Several poems afford parallels to the words; 'Blou northerne wynd' in Harl. 2253, printed Böddeker, 168, the burden of which ten Brink supposes to be of popular origin (*Gesch. d. Eng. Lit.*, i. 381, 421); the ballad *The Unquiet Grave* (Child, ii. 234, No. 78):—

> 'The wind doth blow to-day, my love,
> And a few small drops of rain';

the Scottish popular song *Waly, waly, gin Love be Bonny*;—

> 'Martinmas wind, when wilt thou blaw,
> And shake the green leaves off the tree?'

and perhaps the canon:—

> 'Oaken leaues in the merry wood so wilde,
> When will you grow green a?
> Fayrest maid, and thou be with child,
> Lullaby maist thou sing a.'

(No. 6 in Ravenscroft's *Pammelia*, 1609.)

XXXII

Royal Appx. 58. Printed *Anglia*, xii. 263; Flügel, *N.L.*, 139; Rimbault, 57; Briggs, *Songs and Madrigals*, Songs p. 8, with modern transcription.

The song which Moros, the fool in W. Wager's *The Longer thou livest, the more Fool thou Art* (*Shakespeare-Jahrbuch*, xxxvi. 38), learnt of his dame, when she taught him mustardseed to grind, has the stanza—

'Litle pretty nightingale,
Among the braunches greene,
Geve us of your Christmasse ale,
In the honour of saint Steven.'

This, says *Wrath*, is—

'A song much like thauthor of the same,
It hangeth together like fethers in the winde.'

Doubtless it was made up of fragments of current ditties.

On the relation of the nightingale to mediæval amorous poetry, see the Essay, p. 270.

10. *to* omitted in MS.

14. *closèd*, encompassed. Cf. LXXX, 17.

XXXIII

Royal Appx. 58. Printed *Anglia*, xii. 264; Flügel, *N.L.*, 139; Rimbault, 53; Collier, *Extracts from the Registers of the Stationers' Company*, i. 193.

Other poems beginning in the same way are found in Ravenscroft's *Deuteromelia* (1609), printed by Rimbault, 55, and with music by Chappell, 92 (see Wooldridge-Chappell, i. 46); and in *Bassus*, printed *Anglia*, xii. 597.

This was amongst Captain Cox's 'ballets and songs' (*Laneham's Letter*, ed. Furnivall, cxxxi. 30). Moros (cf. note to No. XXXII) sings two lines, as the 'fote' of a song, which resemble the opening of the *Deuteromelia* version. Chappell, *loc. cit.*, says that this poem is mentioned in the Life of Sir Peter Carew as one of the Freemen's Songs which Sir Peter used to sing with Henry VIII (cf. *Archaeologia*, xxviii. 113).

6. MS. 'My thought on hure lay'.

20. *hey ho!* omitted in MS.

23–4. Collier and Rimbault read :—

> 'So fayre be seld on few
> Hath floryshe ylke adew.'

MS. reads 'ylke aden'.

XXXIV

Addl. 5465. Printed *Archiv*, cvi. 58; Briggs, *Songs and Madrigals*, Madr., 27. Earlier prints with music in Stafford Smith, *Collection of English Songs*, No. IV; and Rimbault, *Ancient Vocal Music*, part 11.

A certain Sir Thomas Philips or ap Philip was appointed Sheriff of Pembrokeshire in 1516 (Brewer, i. 541; ii. 766) and a Thomas Phillippis, B.A., received a chantry at Woodstock on Jan. 9, 1518 (Brewer, ii. 1218). He is probably the poet, as 'Sir' is often, in the case of a priest, the equivalent of the Cambridge *Dominus*, which indicates a B.A. A Robert Phelipps appears as a Gentleman of the Chapel in a household list of the reign of Edward VI (Rimbault, *Old Cheque-Book of the Chapel Royal*, x).

There is evidently an historical allusion in this poem, but the suggestion of a connection with the Yorkist plots of 1460 in the note, signed J. T. M. in Briggs, *Songs and Madrigals*, p. xvi, puts it too early. The references to 'the red or the white rose', 'the rose both red and white', the 'roses three', and the 'prince' would fit best with the birth of Prince Arthur, completing the union of York and Lancaster in his parents, in 1486; but in Addl. 31922 (*Anglia*, xii. 247) is a song which ends—

> 'Vive la Katerine et noble Henry!
> Vive le prince le infant rosary!'

and the 'rosary' here must be a son of Henry VIII who was born on Jan. 1, 1511, and died on Feb. 22, 1511 (Froude, i. 119).

19. Lines similar to this appear as burdens of traditional ballads :—

'Jennifer gentle and Rosemaree'

in a variant of *Riddles Wisely Expounded* (Child, i. 4) in Davies Gilbert's *Christmas Carols* (1823), 65; and

'Gentle Jenny cried rosemaree';

see Child, v. 304. Cf. note on XX, 1.

XXXV

Addl. 5465. Printed *Archiv*, cvi. 55, where Fehr prints it as two songs. Earlier print (of first verse only) in Hawkins, iii. 30.

10. MS. 'be constrained'.

XXXVI

Addl. 5465. Printed Flügel, *N.L.*, 144.

A similar poem in *Bassus* (*Anglia*, xii. 592) begins :—

'Who shall have my fayr lady,
Who but I, who but I, who?
Who shall have my fayr lady,
Who hath more ryght therto?'

Also in Stafford Smith, *Collection of English Songs*, no. VIII. Rimbault, *Ancient Vocal Music*, part 10, prints 'Who shall *court* my fair ladye' with music, heading it 'Dr. Fayrfax, 1480', and noting that it is 'from an ancient set of MS. Part Books of the time of Henry VII in the Editor's Library'.

XXXVII

Harl. 2252. Printed *Rel. Ant.*, i. 255, and Flügel, *N.L.*, 140, where it is printed with what is apparently another poem beginning :—

'Some do intend their youth for to spend.'

XXXVIII

Harl. 2252. Printed Flügel, *N.L.*, 140. Ritson (1790), 98, first printed it, noting that it is 'left unfinished by the copyist', and adding from the MS., after our last verse:—

'For whoo wyll seke
A mynyon eke
In ynglond or in fraunce . . .'

Ritson (1829), ii. 10, as before, but omitting the unfinished verse.

XXXIX

Hawkins, iii. 25; Rimbault, 47, from the same MS.; Flügel, *N.L.*, 144, from Rimbault.

Rimbault notes 'the music by which it is accompanied is the production of a composer named Thomas Fardyng, who appears to have been a gentleman of the Royal Chapel in the year 1511'. Five songs in Addl. 31922 are ascribed to Fardyng. He is mentioned as having a charge on the Countess of Richmond's estate in 1509, and on July 8, 1511, received an annuity of ten marks charged on Northants lands for his services to her. On May 9, 1513, he surrendered a corrody in Ramsay monastery. He remained a Gentleman of the Chapel until his death between Nov., 1520, and Feb., 1521 (Brewer, i. 33, 268, 571; iii. 245, 396, 479).

20. *meed*; Rimbault and Flügel print 'neede'; Hawkins 'mede'.

XL

Harl. 7578. Printed *Archiv*, cvii. 61. We have only printed a short extract from the poem, which is a long one.

XLI

Harl. 7578. Printed *Archiv*, cvii. 57.

12. *conceit*; the MS. gives 'consait', mis-read as 'consail' = counsel by Fehr, *ut supra*.

XLII

Hawkins, iii. 29; Ritson (1790), 113, from Hawkins, and again (1829), ii. 21, rearranged, as in Hazlitt-Ritson, 164.

4. The second *so* supplied by us.

17. *piggesnie*; cf. Chaucer, *The Milleres Tale*, 82.

XLIII

Hawkins, iii. 25.

XLIV

Hawkins, iii. 29.

XLV

T.C.C., *B.* 14. 39. We have not found this poem or any variant of it in print elsewhere. See notes on the following poem. The Latin words are written in red.

The dialect is Southern.

2. James, i. 440, in giving the opening of the poem, prints 'mater saluatoris', perhaps misled by a hole in the vellum at this point.

XLVI

Egerton 613. Printed Morris, *O.E.M.*, 194. In the MS. the stanzas are written in four lines each; the second stanza is written fourth, but marked in the margin to be inserted after the first.

Another version, hitherto overlooked, is in T.C.C., B. 14. 39, on the same page as our XLV above, and immediately following it. It is not noted by James, who probably took it to be part of the foregoing poem, which is in the same metre. There is no space left between the two poems; but the facts that the second occurs elsewhere by itself, and that it begins in the Trinity MS. with a two-line red initial letter, may justify the separation. Curiously, the Trinity version gives our fourth stanza as its second; and since it has not been printed, the following collation may be given.

1. For ou . . . . (*sic*).
5. I crie the grace of the.
10. In care . . .
12. To alle . . .
14. Bi hold tou him wid milde . . .
17. Bidde we moten come to . . .
19. Al the world it wes furlorn.
20. Thoru Eva . . .
21. To forn that ihu was iborn.
22. Ex te . . .
23. Thorou aue e wende awai.
24. The thester niht ant com ye . . .
28. . . . best of . . .
32. . . . berest that . . .
33. Heie quen in parais.
35. Moder milde ant maidan ec.
37. Vuel thou wost . . .
39. He nul . . .
41. So god ant so mild . . .
42. He bringet us alle into is blis.
44. He havet idut the foule put.

A third poem, in Ashm. 1393, printed *E.B.M.*, ii. 65 (facsimile, i. plate XXVIII), consists of the first four lines of each stanza of this poem, with two additional quatrains. It begins :—

'*Enixa est puerpera.*
A lady that was so feyre and bright',

and the two other verses are :—

'Hou swete he is, hou meke he is
Nullus memoravit.
In hevyn he is, and hevyn blis
Nobis preparavit.

Of alle wymmen thu berist the price,
Mater graciosa.
Graunte us allė paradyce,
Virgo gloriosa!'

The antithesis in the third stanza between *Eva* and *Ave*

is a beloved one. Thus in the Latin *Missus Gabriel de Coelis* (Daniel, v. 129) :—

> 'Et ex Eva formans Ave,
> Evae verso nomine';

and in the *Dame des Cius* of the thirteenth century Guillaume le Vinier (*Hist. Litt.*, xxiii. 596) :—

> 'Mout nous troubla
> Cele que Diex forma,
> Nom ot Eva,
> Par li estiens dampné.
> Par la bonté
> La Virgene od saintée
> Diex ot pité,
> La lettre retorna,
> Avant mist *A*,
> Et au daerrain *ve*,
> Pour *Eva* dist *Ave*,
> Par quoi somes sauvé.'

See also the lines quoted from the *Ave Maris Stella* in the note to No. LVI.

XLVII

T.C.C., *B.* 14. 39; not printed hitherto. The dialect is Southern. Other versions are in MSS. Cotton Calig. A. ix ('tempore circiter R. Hen. III exaratus') and Jesus Coll. Oxford, I. 29 (a deficient version), both printed by Morris, *O.E.M.*, 158–9; the Cotton version also printed by Wright, *Owl and the Nightingale*, 65. The relations between these three MSS. demand further investigation.

XLVIII

Harl. 2253. Printed Böddeker, 213; Wright, *S.L.P.*, 87. The text is a Southern translation of a Midland poem.

On the adaptation of the secular *chanson d'aventure* to the purposes of a religious theme, see the Essay (p. 286).

58. *me*; MS. 'us'.

XLIX

Harl. 2253. Printed Böddeker, 220; Wright, *S.L.P.*, 97; Wülcker, i. 49. The text is a Southern translation of a West Midland poem.

L

Sloane 2593. Printed Wright, *W.C.*, 32; *Archiv*, cix. 51; Wülcker, ii. 7. See Sidgwick, ii. 123.

Written in eight lines in the MS., with stops to show breaks. In 7–8 the division is marked after 'wretyn'.

LI

Sloane 2593. Printed Wright, *W.C.*, 16, and *Carols* (1836), No. V.

Other versions in Eng. Poet. e. 1, printed by Wright, *P.S.*, 21; and Balliol 354, printed in *Anglia*, xxvi. 232, by Flügel, *W.L.*, 62, *N.L.*, 116, and by Pollard, 85.

Cf. also Seld. B. 26, 'Of a rose synge we', printed in *E.B.M.*, ii. 108 (facsimile, i. plate L).

30. *schild*; MS. 'schyd'.

LII

T.C.C., O. 3. 58. Printed Fuller Maitland, 26–7 and 54–5.

The first three *caudae* are taken from St. Bernard's Nativity hymn, the *Laetabundus exultet fidelis chorus* (Daniel, ii. 61), but the poem is not a translation of the *Laetabundus*. Daniel quotes a drinking-song, in which all the *caudae* of the *Laetabundus* are similarly used. It begins :—

'Or hi parra,
La cerveyse nos chauntera,
Alleluia !
Qui que aukes en beyt,
Si tel seyt com estre doit,
Res miranda.'

LIII

T.C.C., *O*. 3. 58. Printed Fuller Maitland, 6–7 and 34–5. Other versions in Sloane 2593, printed Wright, *W.C.*, 88 ; Balliol 354, printed in *Anglia*, xxvi. 238 ; Seld. B. 26, printed *E.B.M.*, ii. 119 (facsimile, i. plate LVIII).

The *Alma redemptoris mater* is a well-known Advent antiphon (Daniel, ii. 318), but the poem is not a translation of it.

LIV

Sloane 2593. Printed *Archiv*, cix. 50 ; Wright, *W.C.*, 30 ; Bullen, 4 ; and often since.

Jacques de Cambrai, a thirteenth century *trouvère* (Hist. Litt., xxiii. 631) has the following lines :—

> 'Ensi com sor la verdure
> Descent rosée des ciels,
> Vint en vos cors, Virge pure,
> De paradis vos dous Fiels.'

1. MS. 'I syng a of a mayden'.

LV

Sloane 2593. Printed *Archiv*, cix. 48 ; Wright, *W.C.*, 23.

7. Fehr, in *Archiv* as above, prints :—

> 'Mary is so fayr of face and fote.'

The words 'of face', however, are deleted in the MS. and 'fote' is Fehr's error for 'sote'.

LVI

Sloane 2593. Printed *Archiv*, cix. 66 ; Wright, *W.C.*, 77.

The four Latin lines are the first stanza of a well-known Annunciation hymn of unknown authorship, but sometimes assigned to Venantius Fortunatus (Daniel, i. 204). The second stanza is

'Sumens illud Ave
Gabrielis ore
Funda nos in pace
Mutans nomen Evae.'

The rest of the hymn is less closely resembled by the English poem. Dutch and German versions of it also exist (Mone, ii. 216; Kehrein, *Kirchenlieder*, 49).

LVII

Douce 302; not printed hitherto. Another version in Balliol 354, printed *Anglia*, xxvi. 230; Flügel, *W.L.*, 60, and *N.L.*, 115. The dialect is that of Shropshire.

24. MS. apparently reads 'And his his blosum to bede'. We emend by the Ball. MS.

27. Reading doubtful.

34. *golde*; Ball. MS. 'molde'.

LVIII

Advoc. Lib. 19. 3. 1. Printed *Englische Studien*, xiv. 401.

A variant is in the Howard de Walden MS., No. 10.

LIX

Seld. B. 26. Printed *E.B.M.*, ii. 122 (facsimile, i. plate LX).

5, etc. 'Nowel' is added at the end of each verse.

11. *wonne* is wanting in the MS.

LX

Balliol 354. Printed *Anglia*, xxvi. 254; Flügel, *W.L.*, 76.

Another version in T.C.C., O. 3. 58; printed Fuller Maitland, 8–9 and 36–7.

LXI

Eng. Poet. e. 1. Printed Wright, *P.S.*, 39.

5. *fulfilt*; MS. 'spilt', doubtless copied from the line above.

LXII

Harl. 5396. Printed Wright, *S.C.C.*, 33.

Another version, one verse longer, from Camb. Ii. iv. 11, is printed *Rel. Ant.*, i. 203.

12. *Fro*; MS. 'For'.

LXIII

Eng. Poet. e. 1. Printed Wright, *P.S.*, 19.

Other versions are in the Howard de Walden MS., and Addl. 5666 (with music), printed Hazlitt-Ritson, introduction, xlviii; referred to by Ritson, the MS. being then in his possession, (1790), xl; (1829), i. lvi.

1. The first stanza is probably a burden, though not printed as such by Wright.

26. *hanged*; MS. 'hang'.

35. *whether*; MS. 'wher'.

LXIV

Eng. Poet. e. 1. Printed Wright, *P.S.*, 12.

Other versions in Advoc. Lib. 19. 3. 1, printed *Rel. Ant.*, ii. 76, by D[avid] L[aing]; Balliol 354, printed *Anglia*, xxvi. 250, Flügel, *N.L.*, 120; and Royal Appx. 58, printed *Anglia*, xii. 270, Flügel, *N.L.*, 119.

1. Again Wright does not print the first stanza as burden.

6. Wright prints 'to hyr chyld sayd', following Bodl. MS. ('hayd' in 8); Balliol MS., 'thus gan she say'; our reading from Advoc. Lib. MS.

15. Wright prints 'I bekydde am kyng'; in the Bodl. MS. 'am' is written in modern ink over the

original, which is apparently 'sir'. The Advoc. Lib. MS. reads,

'I am kend for heven kyng',

the Balliol MS.,

'I am knowen as hevyn kyng'.

Bekid; from *kithe*, to proclaim; see Murray, *N.E.D.*, under *kid*, p.pa.

47. *sette*; MS. 'set'.

LXV

England and Pollard, xiii. 710, from the play known as the *Secunda Pastorum.* A similar salutation is in the *Prima Pastorum* (xii. 458). Mr. Pollard assigns the composition of the latest stratum of the Townley Plays, to which both Shepherd's Plays belong, to about 1410, and the extant text to about 1460.

LXVI

Text combined from Balliol 354, printed *Anglia*, xxvi. 237, and Flügel, *W.L.*, 66; and Eng. Poet. e. 1, printed Wright, *P.S.*, 95. Two stanzas of another version were appended, as the Shepherds' song, apparently by Thomas Mawdycke, on May 13, 1591, to the MS. of the *Two Coventry Corpus Christi Plays*, ed. Hardin Craig (E.E.T.S., 1902), 32.

1. Parallels for the burden may be seen in *Grange's Garden*, at the end of John Grange's *The Golden Aphroditis* (1577), sig. Q 4:—

'Then Alleluya they crie,
with downe, downa, downe, downe,
Terlyterlowe, terlyterlowe,
pype downe, downa, downe, downe.'

and in a canon in Ravenscroft's *Pammelia* (1609),

'Tere liter lo, terli terlo,
Terli ter li ter lo', etc.

See also note to No. XXVIII.

LXVII

Balliol 354. Printed *Anglia*, xxvi. 243; Flügel, *W.L.*, 70, and *N.L.*, 117; Pollard, 87.

22. This stanza is placed seventh in the MS., *b* and *a* being written in the margin against stanzas 6 and 7.

47. *skirt* and *scripe* interchanged in MS.

LXVIII

Harl. 5396. Printed Wright, *S.C.C.*, 32; Sandys, 2.

1–2. Wright prints the refrain in one line as

'Christo paremus canticam, excelsis gloria'.

But our reading is certainly that of the MS.

4. Wright prints 'song ther', which is certainly wrong. The MS. may be read as 'songen' or 'song eur' = sang ever.

8, 9, 11–13, and 15–17. The first word or two in each of these lines is torn away in the MS. In 11, Wright prints

'As yn scripturas we fynde',

but the MS. is clearly

'. . . scriptur as we finde'.

Sandys prints, marking the omissions.

15. A foot is missing in this line.

LXIX

Sloane 2593. Printed *Archiv*, cvii. 49; Wright, *W.C.*, 94.

LXX

Ashm. 1393. Printed *E.B.M.*, ii. 65 (facsimile, i. plate XXVIII). Cf. Balliol 354, printed *Anglia*, xxvi. 268.

13. *game*; so *E.B.M.* MS. 'grame'.

17. A sequence (*sequentia*) is, strictly speaking, a non-metrical text interpolated for musical purposes in the traditional liturgy. Out of precisely such an interpolation

grew the Epiphany liturgical play, the *Officium Stellae*; cf. Chambers, *The Mediæval Stage*, ii. 8, 45.

LXXI

Lansdowne 379; not printed hitherto. The MS. spells 'trwe', 'renwe', etc.

18. *in folde*; not in MS., supplied by us.

LXXII

Advoc. Lib. 19. 3. 1. Printed *Englische Studien* (by K. Breul), xiv. 402.

Another version in Harl. 275, f. 146 *b*, printed in *Notes and Queries*, Ser. 2, ix. 439, begins:—

'Joy we alle now yn this feste
For verbum caro factum est'

and then proceeds as in our lyric.

Some of the Latin lines are from hymns. Thus *Pastor creator omnium* is from the Nativity hymn *A solis ortus cardine* of Sedulius (Daniel, i. 143); *Veni redemptor gentium* is the beginning of the Advent hymn of St. Ambrose (Daniel, i. 12), in which also is the line *Non ex virili semine*; but the precise phrase *Sine virili semine* is in both the Nativity hymns *Resonet in laudibus* (Daniel, i. 327) and *Puer natus in Bethlehem* (Daniel, i. 334).

31. *hight*; MS. 'heghe'.

33. *king full right*; 'ist von einer späteren hand zugesetst'.—Breul.

The last two verses in the Harl. MS. are as follows:—

'For he was kyng of kynges ay;
Primus rex aurum optulit;
For he was god and lord verray;
Secundus rex thus pertulit.

For he was man; the thyrde kynge
Incensum pulcrum tradidit;
He us alle to his blys brynge,
Qui mori cruce voluit.'

LXXIII

Eng. Poet. e. 1. Printed Wright, *P.S.*, 82.
17. *hath*; MS. 'have'.

LXXIV

T.C.C., O. 3. 58. Printed Fuller Maitland, 12–13 and 40–41.

Other versions in Eng. Poet. e. 1, printed Wright, *P.S.*, 52; Balliol 354, printed *Anglia*, xxvi. 239. Cf. also Seld. B. 26, printed *E.B.M.*, ii. 104 (facsimile, i. plate XLV), five stanzas, each beginning with two or three words of Latin.

Of the Latin lines, *A solis ortus cardine* is the beginning of Nativity hymns both by St. Ambrose (Daniel, i. 21) and by Sedulius (Daniel, i. 143), *Hostis Herodes impie* is from the Epiphany hymn of Sedulius (Daniel, i. 147), *O lux beata Trinitas* from the evening hymn of St. Ambrose (Daniel, i. 36), and *Exultet celum laudibus* from a hymn used on the feast-days of Apostles (Daniel, i. 247).

11. A common simile; an early instance is in Bodl. MS. Tanner 169*, f. 175, in the *Compassio Mariae*, c. 1270:—

'For so gleam glidis thurt the glas,
Of thi bodi born he was.'

LXXV

Balliol 354. Printed *Anglia*, xxvi. 260; and Flügel, *W.L.*, 77.

LXXVI

Eng. Poet. e. 1. Printed Wright, *P.S.*, 42.

A poem with the same refrain in Balliol 354, printed *Anglia*, xxvi. 190.

LXXVII

Text combined from Sloane 2593, printed Wright, *W.C.*, 48; and Eng. Poet. e. 1, printed Wright, *P.S.*, 50.

LXXVIII

Balliol 354. Printed *Anglia*, xxvi. 262.

Another version in Kele's *Carolles* (Bliss, 51).

16. *compass* from Kele; Balliol MS. reads 'overpass'.

13. *Shere Thursday* is Maundy Thursday, the day before Good Friday.

28. Cf. Eng. Poet. e. 1, Wright, *P.S.*, 72:—

> 'With dredfull othes, the wych hym lothes,
> Thei cryd, *crucifige*.'

43. *Lungeus* = Longinus or Longimus, the name given in the *Acta Pilati* (ed. Tischendorf, B. text, ch. xi.) to the soldier who pierced the side of Christ on the cross. He is a regular figure in the miracle-plays; cf. Chambers, *Mediæval Stage*, ii. 75, 323. Cf. *Rel. Ant.*, i. 126, 'A charme for the tethe-werke':—

> 'I conjoure the, laythely beste, with that ilke spere,
> That Longyous in his hand gane bere.'

LXXIX

T.C.C., O. 9. 38. Printed Furnivall, *H.V.*, 126. He says 'written mostly as prose'.

LXXX

Eng. Poet. e. 1. Printed Wright, *P.S.*, 38.

Another version in Sloane 2593, printed Wright, *W.C.*, 65.

13. The Sloane MS. reads:—

> 'But hyid here faste to that hylle.'

16. *hanged* from the Sloane MS.

17. The Sloane MS. reads, 'wrethin in a brere'.

23. Emended from Sloane MS.

The fifth stanza in the Sloane MS. is:—

> 'Thin swete body that in me rest,
> Thin comely mowth that I have kest,
> Now on rode is mad thi nest;
> Leve chyld, quat is me best?'

LXXXI

Balliol 354. Printed *Anglia*, xxvi. 175; Flügel, *N.L.*, 142.

No other early version known, but a traditional version with a different burden was recovered in the middle of last century, and contributed from North Staffordshire to *Notes and Queries* (1862), Third Series, ii. 103, by a correspondent signing himself ε.τ.κ. This and the Balliol text were printed and compared by F. Sidgwick in the same publication in 1905, Tenth Series, iv. 181. The following is the traditional version :—

1. 'Over yonder's a park, which is newly begun,
All bells in Paradise I heard them a-ring;
Which is silver on the outside, and gold within.
And I love sweet Jesus above all things.

2. And in that park there stands a hall,
Which is covered all over with purple and pall.

3. And in that hall there stands a bed,
Which is hung all round with silk curtains so red.

4. And in that bed there lies a knight,
Whose wounds they do bleed by day and by night.

5. At that bed side there lies a stone,
Which is our blessed Virgin Mary then kneeling on.

6. At that bed's foot there lies a hound,
Which is licking the blood as it daily runs down.

7. At that bed's head there grows a thorn,
Which was never so blossomed since Christ was born.'

LXXXII

Balliol 354. Printed *Anglia*, xxvi. 259.

LXXXIII

Balliol 354. Printed *Anglia*, xxvi. 191.

Another version, three verses longer, in Eng. Poet. e. 1, printed Wright, *P.S.*, 57, and by Flügel in *Anglia*, *loc. cit.*

A long poem with the same refrain is in the Porkington MS.; it is also used by Dunbar in the *Lament for the Makaris Quhen He Was Seik*; cf. No. LXXXII.

LXXXIV

Lambeth 853; extracted from 'Part II' as printed by Furnivall, *P.R.L.*, 150, omitting ll. 25–32 and 41–64 as there numbered. Furnivall also prints a parallel version, from Camb. Hh. iv. 12, of 'Part II' only. 'Part I' is of eight stanzas in the Lambeth MS.; it begins—

> 'In a tabernacle of a tour,
> As y stood musynge on the moone,
> A crownèd queene, moost of honour,
> Me thoughte y sigh sittinge in trone.'

There is another text of this in Douce MS. 78 (= Bodl. 21652) ascribed by Madan, iv. 513, to Lydgate, without authority; this has not been printed.

Another version, hitherto unnoticed, and not seen by us, is in MS. Anglais 41 (formerly Supplément français 819) in the Bibliothèque Nationale at Paris, catalogued by Gaston Raynaud, *Catalogue des Manuscrits Anglais de la Bibliothèque Nationale* (1884), 16, as 'Stances anglaises avec le refrain latin Quia amore langueo'.

Cf. Richard Rolle, *The Form of Perfect Living* (ed. C. Horstman, i. 29):—

> 'Amore langueo. Thir twa wordes er wryten in the boke of lufe, that es kalled the sang of lufe, or the sang of sanges. For he that mykel lufes, hym lyst oft syng of his luf, for ioy that he or scho hase whan thai thynk on that that thai lufe, namely if their louer be trew & lufand. And this es the Inglisch of thies twa wordes; "I languysch for lufe".'

LXXXV

Douce 381. Printed *E.B.M.*, ii. 51 (facsimile, i. plate XX).

3. *drie*; MS. 'dryve'.

LXXXVI

Bassus, sig. C 2. Printed *Anglia*, xii. 591.

LXXXVII

Addl. 5465. Printed *Archiv*, cvi. 60; Briggs, *Madrigals*, no. 5.

LXXXVIII

Bassus, sig. A 2. Printed *Anglia*, xii. 589; Flügel, *N.L.*, 114.

11. Perhaps a reference to the famous tune and ballad 'Fortune my foe'; see Chappell, 162.

LXXXIX

Bassus, sig. I 1. Printed *Anglia*, xii. 595; Flügel, *N.L.*, 114.

XC

Digby 86. Printed Horstman-Furnivall, ii. 761. The dialect is Southern.

A second version in the Auchinleck MS. (printed in *A Penni worth of Witte*, (etc.), ed. D. Laing for the Abbotsford Club (1857), 119; and *Anglia*, iii. 291, by H. Varnhagen) consists of six stanzas corresponding to our 1, 2, 3, 5, 6, 7, with a final stanza:—

'Jesu Crist ous above,
Thou grant ous for thi moder love,
At our lives ende,
When we han rightes of the prest,
And the deth be at our brest,
The soule mot to heven wende.
Amen.'

A third begins on l. 121 of a longer poem, *Lustneth alle a lutel throwe*, in Harl. 2253 (printed Böddeker, 225).

XCI

Harl. 913. Printed Heuser, 174; also in *Rel. Ant.*, ii. 177. The dialect is Anglo-Irish. A fragment of a translation in Latin follows in the MS.

In Harl. 7358 is a poem of which each verse begins:—

'Lollay, lollay, thu lytel chyld,
Wy wepys thou so sore?'

printed Heuser, 211.

25. *it* not in MS.

37. A variant of this verse is noted by Heuser in Camb. Oo. vii. 32, where there is a drawing of Fortune's wheel; see *Catalogue*, iv. 543. A single page in MS. 317 of Ghent University Library bears eight short scraps, Latin, French, and English, in a fourteenth century hand, printed by H. Logeman in *Archiv*, lxxxvii, 431–2, among which is:—

'La dame de fortune estraungement fest sun pas
A tous hom ele est commune de tourner haut en bas
Sa vy nest pas une diversement fest sun pas
Quy creyst a fortune sowent dirra allas.'

followed by an English translation:—

'The levedy dame fortune scho ys both frend and fo
Ye riche sco makes pore and pore ryche als so
Scho tournes wo intyl wele and wele intyl wo
Noman trou dam fortune for algates yt thar be so.'

38. *fo*; Heuser reads MS. as 'vo' and suggests 'ro'.

XCII

Harl. 2253. Printed Böddeker, 195; Wright, *S.L.P.*, 60. Also in Ritson (1790), 33; (1829), i. 65; Hazlitt-Ritson, 56; Wülcker, i. 107.

11. *greveth*; so Böddeker; the MS. reads 'graueth'.

6–7. Cf. Harl. 913, printed Heuser, 124:—

'Her it is and her nit nis,
Al so farith the world is blis.'

XCIII

Harl. 7322. Printed Furnivall, *P.R.L.*, 227.

4. *blomen*; MS. reads 'blowen'.

XCIV

Thornton MS. Printed Perry, *Religious Pieces, E.E.T.S.* (1867), 95 (without Latin); and as pseudo-Rolle by Horstman, i. 373.

We have noted twelve versions of this poem, all differing considerably:—(i) Harl. 913, printed Heuser, 176; *Rel. Ant.*, ii. 216; and Furnivall, *E.E.P.*, 150; seven English stanzas alternated with Latin translation. (ii) The present version from the Thornton MS., noted by Halliwell in *The Thornton Romances* (Camden Soc., 1844), introduction, xxxvi, where he refers to six other MSS. containing the poem, as follow (iii–viii). (iii) the Porkington MS.; printed Halliwell, *E.E.M.*, 39, fourteen stanzas. (iv) Selden supra 53. (v) Rawl. C. 307. (vi) Rawl. Poet. 32. (vii) Lambeth 853; printed Furnivall, *H:V.*, 88; twelve stanzas. (viii) A roll in the possession of T. Bateman. To these we can now add:—(ix) Camb. Ii. iv. 9, printed by Heuser, 213, twenty-seven verses, mostly of four lines each; (x) Balliol 354, printed *Anglia*, xxvi. 216, sixteen stanzas; (xi) T.C.C., R. 3. 21, f. 33 *b*, believed to be unprinted, seven stanzas with *Memorare novissima* at the end; and (xii) in J. G. Nichols' *Ancient Allegorical, Historical, and Legendary Paintings* (1838), copied from a since-destroyed mural inscription beneath a fresco of the death of Becket on the walls of the Guild Chapel, Stratford-on-Avon (plate xvi). Guest, *History of English Rhythms* (ed. Skeat, 1882), 515, says a corrupt copy of one verse was discovered by Sir Walter Scott on a tombstone at Melrose.

XCV

Chaucer, i. 390.

The Envoy is only found in one MS. (Addl. 10340).

XCVI

Chaucer, i. 392.

XCVII

Chaucer, i. 394.

Harl. 7333 records that Chaucer sent this poem to King Richard II at Windsor Castle.

XCVIII

Eng. Poet. e. 1. Printed Wright, *P.S.*, 8.

7. MS. reads 'Sythyn yt is we wele we do'.

12. MS. reads 'That ye wyll do'.

XCIX

Eng. Poet. e. 1. Printed Wright, *P.S.*, 9.

19, 20. In Balliol 354 (*Anglia*, xxvi. 277) is a poem entitled *Fraus Fraude*, which begins:—

> 'Whan netilles in wynter bere Rosis rede,
> And thornys bere figges naturally,
> And bromes bere appylles in euery mede,
> . . . . .
> Than put in a woman yor trust and confidens.'

A longer version in Eng. Poet. e. 1 (Wright, *P.S.*, 66).

27. *be* inserted by us.

C

Sloane 2593. Printed *Archiv*, cix. 44; Wright, *W.C.*, 10.

CI

Sloane 2593. Printed *Archiv*, cix. 42; Wright, *W.C.*, 5.

1. A long metrical prayer in Addl. 5901, f. 329*b*, begins in the same way.

23. *hoppe*; MS. reads 'hope'.

37. *moneyere* suggested by Prof. W. P. Ker for MS. 'monewere'.

CII

Sloane 2593. Printed Wright, *W.C.*, 24; *Rel. Ant.*, ii. 166.

CIII

Sloane 2593. Printed *Archiv*, cix. 46; Wright, *W.C.*, 20.

1. *durke*; MS. reads 'drukke'.
6. *clothèd*; MS. reads 'clothis'.
1. For 'durke and dare', cf. *Cursor Mundi*, l. 25432.

CIV

Sloane 2593. Printed *Archiv*, cix. 47; Wright, *W.C.*, 22.

Other poems to the refrain of 'Service is no heritage' are in Rawl. Poet. 36, f. 2; Advoc. Lib. 19. 3. 1; and Ashm. 48:—

'The servynge man that takythe wage,
Lett hyme not spende, but kepe for age;
For servys ys none erytage;
Therfor take hede.'

The phrase is quoted as a proverb in *All's Well that Ends Well*, I. iii. 26.

CV

Sloane 2593. Printed *Archiv*, cix. 45; Wright, *W.C.*, 15.

Cf. Eng. Poet. e. 1, printed Wright, *P.S.*, 44.

7. *thou* not in MS.

CVI

Sloane 2593. Printed Wright, *W.C.*, 19; also in *Rel. Ant.*, ii. 165.

24. So MS. Perhaps 'He must him seken besily'; but 25–6 are also corrupt, and conjecture seems idle.

CVII

Seld. B. 26. Printed *E.B.M.*, ii. 161 (facsimile, i. plate XC).

Another version in T.C.C., O. 3. 58, printed Fuller Maitland, 18–19 and 46–7.

7. Cf. a proverb of Hendyng, 'Under boske shal men weder abide', in *Rel. Ant.*, i. 113.

CVIII

Sloane 2593. Printed Wright, *W.C.*, 86; also in *Rel. Ant.*, ii. 166.

17–18. Cf. the *Merchant of Venice*, V. i. 90:—

> 'How far that little candle throws his beams!
> So shines a good deed in a naughty world.'

CIX

Sloane 2593. Printed Wright, *W.C.*, 87; also in *Rel. Ant.*, ii. 167.

4. Gerarde gives 'Satin-flower, called also Penny-flower' as the English name of *Viola lunaris* [? = *Botrychium lunaria*, Moonwort], and says that it is called 'Sattin' in Norfolk. G. Henslowe, *Medical Works of the Fourteenth Century* gives 'Penigras' and 'Penyword' as equivalents of *Hydrocotyle vulgaris*, and 'Penigras' also as an equivalent of *Cotyledon umbilicus*.

16. A popular proverb, found amongst the proverbs of Hendyng (*Rel. Ant.*, i. 112):—

> 'Tonge breketh bon,
> Ant nad hire selve non.'

Also in T.C.C., O. 2. 45, f. 351:—

> 'Tunge bregt bon thegh heo nabbe hire silfe non.
> Ossa terit lingua careat licet ossibus illa.'

The MS. reads 'Thow the self have none', 'tungės' being our insertion.

CX

Eng. Poet. e. 1. Printed Wright, *P.S.*, 23.

23–6. A similar stanza appears in a poem in Harl. 4294, printed *Rel. Ant.*, i. 252 :—

'When thou goo to the nale,
Synge as a nyghtyngale ;
Beware to whom thou telle thy tale.
Whatsoever ye thynk avyse ye wele.'

21. *had-I-wist* ; cf. Balliol 354, printed *Anglia*, xxvi. 266 :—

'And ever beware of had I wyste.'

Also poem no. 5 in R. Edwardes' *Paradice of Dainty Devises* (1596) is 'Beware of had I wist'.

CXI

Eng. Poet. e. 1. Printed Wright, *P.S.*, 28.

Another version in Balliol 354, printed *Anglia*, xxvi. 267.

9. Balliol MS. :—

'Ever the birde sat syngyng still.'

25. *showed* ; MS. reads 'show . . .', the last letters being illegible.

CXII

Balliol 354. Printed *Anglia*, xxvi. 168.

Longer versions in Lambeth 853, printed Furnivall, *H.V.*, 91, fifteen stanzas ; and T.C.C., O. 9. 38, f. 22, unprinted, eleven stanzas.

For the refrain-word, cf. Eng. Poet. e. 1, Wright, *P.S.*, 57.

6. *sone* ; not in MSS.
12. *all* ; not in Balliol MS. ; supplied from Trinity MS.
17. *haled* ; Trinity MS. 'knelyd'.
30. *maketh* ; so Trinity MS. ; Balliol MS. 'makyd'.
31. *sorte* ; so Trinity MS. ; Balliol MS. 'thought'.

CXIII

Harl. 4294. Printed *Rel. Ant.*, i. 275.
11. *a*; not in MS.

CXIV

Harl. 7358. Printed Wright, *W.C.*, 106 (in Notes). Another version in Sloane 2593, printed Wright, *W.C.*, 11, and *Carols* (1836), no. III.

CXV

Addl. 26737, f. 107 *b*. Here printed for the first time. Other versions (i) in Hawkins, iii. 31, reprinted by Ritson (1790), 120; (1829), ii. 12; Hazlitt-Ritson, 156. (ii) Rimbault, 65, from a MS. then in his possession. This MS. may be Addl. 15117 (as printed in Wooldridge-Chappell, i. 111); Chappell, 238, says 'the first stanza of words with tune is in a MS. of the latter part of Henry [VIII]'s reign, formerly in the possession of Stafford Smith, now that of Dr. Rimbault', and Addl. 15117 answers to this description. But Rimbault prints more than one stanza.

The poem is referred to by Pistol in 2 *Henry IV*, II. iv. 211:—

> 'Then death rock me asleep, abridge my doleful days.'

CXVI

Chaucer, i. 405.

Skeat points out that Henry IV was received as King by the Parliament on 30 September, 1399, and that an additional grant of 40 marks yearly was made to Chaucer on 3 October of the same year. This dates the poem almost to a day.

CXVII

Chaucer, i. 398.

23. *Fryse*; Skeat notes that in 1396 some Englishmen were present in an expedition against Friesland, and that Froissart says that the Frieslanders would not ransom prisoners taken by their enemies; consequently they could not exchange prisoners, and eventually put their prisoners to death.

CXVIII

Sloane 2593. Printed Wright, *W.C.*, 70; and *Carols* (1836), no. XII.

1. MS. omits *none*; supplied by Wright.

CXIX

Eng. Poet. e. 1. Printed Wright, *P.S.*, 26.

16. Probably in dialect.

20. Apparently a popular saying; a poem with the refrain,

'How judicare come in crede',

is in Lambeth MS. 491, printed *Archiv*, lxxxvi. 387. Cf. also *An Old English Song* printed from Arundel 292 in *Rel. Ant.*, i. 291:—

'Now wot i qwou *judicare* was set in the crede'.

CXX

Eng. Poet. e. 1. Printed Wright, *P.S.*, 43.

CXXI

Eng. Poet. e. 1. Printed Wright, *P.S.*, 27.

3. *nis*; MS. reads 'is'.

CXXII

Hawkins, iii. 37; reprinted by Ritson (1790), 112; (1829), ii. 20; Hazlitt-Ritson, 164.

CXXIII

Addl. 31922. Printed *Anglia*, xii. 230; Flügel, *N.L.*, 146; Briggs, *Madrigals*, no. 6 (the words wrong).

Another version in Addl. 5665, 'The Kynges Balade'; printed Stafford Smith, i. 44; Rimbault, 37. With music also in Chappell, 56, and Wooldridge-Chappell, i. 42, where Wooldridge says it occurs in Royal Appx. 58, but the words do not.

The poem is mentioned in *The Complaynt of Scotland* (1548); and was quoted by Latimer in his second sermon to Edward VI (see Wooldridge, i. 44).

12. Both MSS. read thus.

19. Addl. 5665 reads 'But pass the day'.

CXXIV

Text combined from Balliol 354, printed *Anglia*, xxvi. 276; Lambeth 306, printed *Rel. Ant.*, i. 248; and Eng. Poet. e. 1, printed Wright, *P.S.*, 89.

A similar poem, to be sung as a catch, is in *Merry Drollery* (1670), reprinted in Jamieson's *Ballads*, ii. 316.

5. *Chad*; St. Chad's day is March 2, the 1st being that of St. David, with whom St. Chad is usually associated, especially in folk-rhymes.

18. Cf. Harl. 2253, Böddeker, 177:—'When that he is dronke ase a dreynt mous.'

30. MS. 'accripe'; but see Chaucer, *Rom. of the Rose*, 541:—

> 'Hir flesh [as] tendre as is a chike.'

34. Cf. Harl. 7371, *Rel. Ant.*, i. 269 and ii. 41:—

> 'Northampton, full of love,
> Beneath the girdel, and not above.'

39. *mouth*; MS. 'moke'.

CXXV

Seld. B. 26. Printed *E.B.M.*, ii. 179 (facsimile, i. plate XCVII).

9. *other*; MS. reads 'outhe' or 'outher'.

11. *manner*; *E.B.M.* reads 'man'.

CXXVI

Text combined from Balliol 354, printed *Anglia*, xxvi. 284; and the Porkington MS., printed Halliwell, *E.E.M.*, 6.

3. Balliol, 'of all my payne'.

5. Porkington, 'ye wylle hit here'.

8 and throughout, *may*, Porkington; 'can', Balliol.

12. Porkington :—

> 'And alle my lowſ, swyt, hit ys fer yow.'

15. Porkington, 'that'; Balliol, 'but'.

18. Balliol reads :—

> 'In myn observaunce in dyversiteis.'

19. Porkington, 'now the tyme . . .'

22. Porkington, 'that this morne . . .'

25–7. Balliol :—

> 'In the mornyng whan I shall rise,
> me lyst right well for to dyne,
> But comonly I drynk non ale ywis.'

44. Porkington, 'Glowys . . .'

46. *not*; both MSS. 'as'; the correction made by Flügel.

49. Flügel prints :—

> 'My dublet is narower than it was.'

52. Porkington :—

> 'In yche a spas and stede by a spone.'

62. *coy*; Balliol, 'quaynt'; Porkington, 'cayey'.

55. *can*; MSS. 'cam', *i.e.* I can mourn for the time it takes to go a mile. For *one mileway* cf. *The Boke of St. Albans, Of Fysshynge wyth an Angle*:—'Lete it boylle halfe a myle way', and cf. note on CXLIV, 9

CXXVII

Sloane 2593. Printed Wright, *W.C.*, 100; and *Carols* (1836), no. XX.

6. *Knew*; Wright misprints 'Know'.

16. *sel*; Wright misprints 'sal'.

For the whole poem cf. a passage in *A lutel Soth Sermun* from MSS. Cott. Calig. A. ix and Jesus Coll. Oxford 29, printed Wright, *Owl and Nightingale*, 80, and Morris, *O.E.M.*, 186–7, ll. 51–64:—

'Thes persones ich wene
ne beoth heo noght for-bore.
Ne theos prude yungemen
that luvieth Malekin
And theos prude maidenes
that luvieth Ianekin
At chirche and at cheping
hwanne heo togadere come
Heo runeth togaderes
and speketh of derne luve
Hwenne heo to chirche cometh
to the haliday
Everuch wile his leof iseon
ther yef he may,' *etc.*

Jankin, the jolly clerk of Oxenford, was the fifth husband of the Wife of Bath; cf. her *Prologue*, 525, sqq.

CXXVIII

Eng. Poet. e. 1. Printed Wright, *P.S.*, 63; *E.B.M.*, ii. 183 (facsimile, i. plate C); Chappell, 42. All these give the words as attached to a tune, which, however, seems properly to belong to another poem (Wright, *P.S.*, 79), beginning:—

'Tydyngis trew ther be cum new
Sent from the trynyte'.

At the foot of the music is written 'Thys is the tewyn for the song foloyng; yf so be that ye wyll haue a nother tewyn, it may be at yowre plesur, for I haue set alle the songe'.

Another version in Harl. 541, printed Ritson (1790), xxxiv; (1829), i. xlix; Hazlitt-Ritson, xliii.

16. *nothing*; MS. reads 'noyng'.

CXXIX

Eng. Poet. e. 1. Printed Wright, *P.S.*, 81.

CXXX

Seld. B. 26. Printed *E.B.M.*, ii. 177 (facsimile, i. plate XCVI). This is a three-part song, the words in each part differing slightly; we have selected our version from the three parts.

4. *avale*; lower, degrade.

4. *stake*; an ale-stake is an alehouse sign; cf. Chaucer, *Cant. Tales*, *Prologue*, 667, and Skeat's note.

6–8. Cf. *Rel. Ant.*, i. 83, in a burlesque sermon, 'Drynke thu to me, and y to the, and halde the coppe in are'.

CXXXI

Balliol 354. Printed *Anglia*, xxvi. 282.

Curious parallels to this song are afforded by several folk-rhymes, wassail-songs, and others; cf. Ravenscroft's *Deuteromelia* (1609), no. 17, Freemen's Song for four voices, an early version of the 'cumulative' drinking-song still traditionally popular, with the refrain,

> 'Sing gentle butler *balla moy*';

reprinted in Rimbault, 120; also *Drinking* in Ravenscroft's *Briefe Discourse* (1614), 10, a four-part song with refrain,

> 'But still me thinks one tooth is drie'.

For a version of the folk-song, see *The Athenaeum*, 2 January, 1847, page 18, in an article on Worcestershire folk-lore :—

'Roll, roll,
Gentle butler, fill the bowl', *etc.*

2. Cf. in a poem in Hazlitt-Ritson, 161 :—

'Bevux bien, par tutte la company'.

5. *bellamy* = *bel ami*. Cf. England and Pollard, 300, in *The Deliverance of Souls*, 229 :—

'how ! thou belamy, abyde.'

Also in a poem both in Balliol 354, printed *Anglia*, xxvi. 135, and Bodl. Eng. Poet. e. 1, printed Wright, *P.S.*, 53, occurs the line,

'Ffill the cuppe wel, belamye'.

See also the quotation from *Deuteromelia* above. A remarkable corruption of the word by 'popular etymology' is shown by the fact that the burden of the 'cumulative' song is now sung :—

'We'll drink to the barley-mow.'

24. For the pun on Water and Walter, cf. 2 *Henry VI*, IV. i. 35.

CXXXII

Cott. Vesp. A. xxv. Printed Lemcke's Jahrbuch, ii. 85, by Böddeker; *Rel. Ant.*, i. 324; Flügel, *N.L.*, 148.

5. Flügel reads 'yowr swete harte'.

CXXXIII

Dyce 45. Printed by Dyce, Skelton, i. introduction, vii; reprinted from there by Bullen, *Lyrics from Elizabethan Dramatists* (1891), 288 (notes), and Gayley, *Representative English Comedies*, i. 259.

The better-known, but inferior, version from *Gammer Gurton's Needle* has been often reprinted; Hawkins, iii. 21; Gayley, *op. cit.*, i. 216; Manly, *Specimens of the Pre-Shaksperean Drama*, ii. 107; *etc.*

23–4. Even so Falstaff consumed but 'one half-pennyworth of bread to this intolerable deal of sack' (1 *Henry IV*, II. iv. 591).

CXXXIV

Sloane 2593. Printed Wright, *W.C.*, 93; *S.L.P.*, 4; Ritson (1790), 81; (1829), i. 140; Hazlitt-Ritson, 120. Another version amongst John Awdlay's poems in Douce 302 is printed by W. Sandys, *Christmastide*, 218.

CXXXV

Seld. B. 26. Printed *E.B.M.*, ii. 107 (facsimile, i. plate XLVII).

1–6. In the burden and first verse the MS. reads 'Go day'.

CXXXVI

Balliol 354. Printed *Anglia*, xxvi. 241; Flügel, *W.L.*, 69; *N.L.*, 123; Pollard, 86.

13. *stokkes.* The Lord of Misrule at Christmas kept stocks, like the Earl of Gloucester in *King Lear* or any other lord, and exercised his festival jurisdiction by condemning to them offenders against the amenities of the revel; cf. three examples in Chambers, *Mediæval Stage*, i. 406, 408, 410, including a lord at court in 1551 who had 'pillory, gibbet, hedding block, stokkes, little ease'.

CXXXVII

Balliol 354. Printed *Anglia*, xxvi. 257; Flügel, *W.L.*, 77; *N.L.*, 123; Pollard, 92.

This is the best version of several; (i) in the Porkington

MS., printed *Rel. Ant.*, ii. 30, where it appears to have been confused with another poem. (ii) Wynkyn de Worde's *Carolles*, reprinted *Anglia*, xii. 587; Flügel, *N.L.*, 123; Ritson (1790), 125; (1829), ii. 14; Hazlitt-Ritson, 158. (iii) Addl. 5665, printed Ritson (1790), 127; (1829), ii. 16; Hazlitt-Ritson, 160; Flügel, *N.L*,, 124.

A distinct poem on the slaying of the boar is in Eng. Poet. e. 1 (Wright, *P.S.*, 25).

CXXXVIII

Eng. Poet. e. 1. Printed Wright, *P.S.*, 85.

'Veni coronaberis' is the refrain of a poem in Lambeth 853, printed Furnivall, *H.V.*, 1. Husk, *Carols*, 85, prints another Holly and Ivy carol from a broadside of c. 1710, beginning :—

> 'The holly and the ivy
> Now are both well grown.
> Of all the trees that are in the wood
> The holly bears the crown.'

Cf. also Henry the Eighth's song (No. XXIII). The disputes between holly and ivy recall the *débats* or *estrifs* which are common enough in mediæval literature, Latin, French, and English (cf. Chambers, *The Mediæval Stage*, i. 79). A writer in *The Gentleman's Magazine* (1779), 137, describes a Shrovetide custom in East Kent, in which the girls of a village burnt a 'Holly Boy' stolen from the boys, and the boys burnt an Ivy-Girl stolen from the girls. These rites were performed in different parts of the village. With this may be put a quotation in Brand, *Popular Antiquities* (ed. Ellis, 1841, i. 268) from M. Stevenson, *The Twelve Months* (1661), 4, 'Great is the contention of holly and ivy, whether master or dame wears the breeches'; and the significance of the fact that in No. CXLI Holly has 'mery men' and Ivy has 'jentill women' becomes apparent. Segregation or opposition of the sexes is not uncommon in festival custom, and may be traced to a very primitive stratum of religious observance (*Mediæval Stage*, i. 105).

CXXXIX

Eng. Poet. e. 1. Printed Wright, *P.S.*, 44.
6 and 9. *we*; MS. reads 'thei'.

CXL

Eng. Poet. e. 1. Printed Wright, *P.S.*, 84.
10. *lepe*; cf. note to CXXXVI, 13.

CXLI

Balliol 354. Printed *Anglia*, xxvi. 279; Flügel, *W.L.*, 83.
14. *sloe*; the MS. reads 'sho'.

CXLII

Seld. B. 26. Printed *E.B.M.*, ii. 132 (facsimile, i. plate LXIX).

A poem of 96 lines in Lansdowne 762 has for refrain

'I praye to God, spede wele the plough'.

It is printed with *Pierce the Ploughman's Crede* by W. W. Skeat, E.E.T.S., 1867. In *Henslowe's Diary* (ed. Greg, i. 16) it is recorded that a play called 'god spead the plowe' was acted 27 December, 1593, and 5 January, 1593–4. On 1 March, 1601, John Harrison entered 'A booke called God spede the ploughe' on the *Stationers' Register* (Arber, iii. 180). For a poem in praise of wheat, see Sloane 2593, Wright, *W.C.*, 38.

3–6 are repeated under the music in the MS.

CXLIII

Sloane 2593. Printed Wright, *W.C.*, 84, and *Carols* (1836), no. XVII.

15. *chape*; cf. *All's Well that Ends Well*, IV. iii. 164.

CXLIV

Wynkyn de Worde, *Christmasse Carolles*; reprinted *Anglia*, xii. 587; Flügel, *N.L.*, 151.

Another version in Balliol 354, printed *Anglia*, xxvi. 194, together with the other.

9. Cf. *The Squyr of Lowe Degre* (ed. Mead, C text, 489–91):—

> 'He had not ryden but a whyle,
> Not the mountenaunce of a myle,
> Or he was ware of a vyllage.'

See note on CXXVI, 55.

CXLV

Addl. 31922. Printed *Anglia*, xii. 245; Flügel, *N.L.*, 151.

CXLVI

Addl. 5665. Printed Flügel, *N.L.*, 151. Earlier prints in Stafford Smith, i. 28; *Rel. Ant.*, ii. 199; Rimbault, 59.

A poem in Addl. 31922, printed *Anglia*, xii. 244, and Wooldridge-Chappell, i. 50, begins in the same way, but is wantonly meant; it has music by D. Cooper.

Moros in Wager's *The Longer thou livest, the more Fool thou Art* (*Shakespeare-Jahrbuch*, xxxvi. 18) named amongst his songs—

> 'There dwelleth a jolly ſoster here by west'.

CXLVII

Addl. 5465. Printed Flügel, *N.L.*, 147; Briggs, *Songs and Madrigals*, Madr. 1. Earlier prints in Hawkins (with music), iii. 9–16; Rimbault, 31.

We omit the last verse.

Rimbault quotes Hawkins's remark that this poem 'is supposed to be a satire on those drunken Flemings who came into England with the princess Anne of Cleves, upon her marriage with Henry VIII', but suggests that it belongs to a much earlier period, and may be the work of Skelton, as in the *Interlude of Magnyfycence*, 'Courtly Abusyon' exclaims

'Rutty bully, joly rutterkyn, heyda!'

Dyce's Skelton, i. 249; see his note thereon.

CXLVIII

Sloane 2593. Printed Wright, *W.C.*, 31, and *Carols* (1836), no. VI.

Cf. the description of Chaunteclere in Chaucer, *The Nonne Preestes Tale*, 39 ff.

CXLIX

Balliol 354. Printed *Anglia*, xxvi. 197.

4. The MS. reads 'Sawyste thow not . . .' in the first stanza only.

Cf. a song, no. 16, in Ravenscroft's *Melismata* (1609):—

'And seest thou my Cow to day Fowler.'

CL

Balliol 354. Printed *Anglia*, xxvi. 278; three lines to each verse. See Sidgwick, iii. 211–6.

25. *had* omitted in MS.

40. *He*; MS. reads '&'.

CLI

Kele's *Carolles*. Printed Bliss, 53.

Another version of the burden and first verse in Ravenscroft's *Pammelia* (1609), no. 31, copied by Hawkins into Addl. MS. 5336.

CLII

Howard de Walden MS. Printed in *Music, Cantelenas, Songs, etc.*, no. 12.

A two-part song, the tenor consisting of 'Benedicamus Domino. Alleluia Alleluia-a'. It may have been sung as a grace at a Winchester civic feast.

4. *see*: MS. 'sue'.

INDEX OF FIRST LINES

[*The first lines of the refrains are shown in italic, those of the poems in roman type, without regard to the types used in the text.*]